Flyin' West

and other plays

Flyin' West

and other plays

Pearl Cleage

Theatre Communications Group

Flyin' West and Other Plays is published by Theatre Communications Group, Inc., 520 Eighth Ave., New York, NY 10018–4156.

This publication is made possible in part with public funds from the New York State Council on the Arts, a State Agency.

TCG books are exclusively distributed to the book trade by Consortium Book Sales and Distribution, 1045 Westgate Dr., St. Paul, MN 55114.

Due to space constraints, credits for cited material continue on page 340.

ISBN-13 978-1-55936-168-2

LIBRARY OF CONGRESS CATALOGING-IN-PUBLICATION DATA
Cleage, Pearl.
Flyin' west and other plays / by Pearl Cleage.—1st ed.
p. cm.
Contents: Flyin' west—Blues for an Alabama sky—Bourbon at the border—
Late bus to Mecca—Chain.
ISBN 1-55936-168-9 (pbk. : alk. paper)
1. Afro-Americans—Drama. I. Title.
PS3553.L389A6   1999
812'.54–dc21   99-18987
CIP

Book and cover design by Lisa Govan
Cover painting by Francis Livingston, used by permission of <u>AT&T: OnStage</u>®

First Edition, September 1999
Third Printing, March 2014

For my husband, Zaron W. Burnett, Jr.,
from whom I continue to steal my best lines
and with whom I share my best moments.

For my daughter, Deignan Cleage Lomax,
the light of my life, whose love inspires and sustains me.

For Owen Dodson, Ted Shine,
Paul Carter Harrison, Carlton and Barbara Molette,
and Richard Wesley for being playwrights
and teachers.

And for Kenny Leon–
working with you has been
the pleasure of my day.

———————

Contents

Preface

Don't start me to talkin'
I'll tell everything I know.

—Sonny Boy Williamson
"DON'T START ME TALKIN'"

The danger in asking a writer to introduce her own work is, of course, that she will yield to the overwhelming temptation to explain; to try once and for all to answer the question: *What's your play about?*

This is rarely a good idea. The plays were written to stand alone, save a few pithy notes in the program. They are rarely helped by well-intentioned comments from the playwright. If the joke doesn't work at the top of Act II, all the explaining in the world won't save the moment.

That said, I will confess only that I truly love writing plays. As a child of the Black Arts Movement *and* the Woodstock Generation, I still believe that theatre has a ritual power to call forth the spirits, illuminate the darkness and *speak the truth to the people.*

If these plays don't manage to do that, the weakness is mine. If they do, I also claim the magic.

Pearl Cleage
Atlanta, Georgia
January 1999

Flyin' West

Production History

Flyin' West was originally commissioned and produced by The Alliance Theatre Company in Atlanta, Georgia (Kenny Leon, Artistic Director; Edith H. Love, Managing Director), in association with AT&T: *OnStage®* in November 1992. It was directed by Kenny Leon; the set design was by Dex Edwards, the lighting design was by P. Hamilton Shinn; the costume design was by Jeff Cone and the musical composition was by Dwight Andrews. The cast was as follows:

SOPHIE WASHINGTON	Sharlene Ross
MISS LEAH	Carol Mitchell-Leon
FANNIE DOVE	Elizabeth Van Dyke
WIL PARRISH	Donald Griffin
MINNIE DOVE CHARLES	Kimberly Hawthorne
FRANK CHARLES	Peter Jay Fernandez

Characters

SOPHIE WASHINGTON, a black woman, born into slavery, 36

MISS LEAH, a black woman, born into slavery, 73

FANNIE DOVE, a black woman, 32

WIL PARRISH, a black man, born into slavery, 40

MINNIE DOVE CHARLES, a black woman, 21

FRANK CHARLES, a very light-skinned black man,
born into slavery, 36

Time

Fall 1898

Place

Outside the all-black town of Nicodemus, Kansas

Setting

The play takes place in and around the house shared by Sophie, Fannie and, more recently, Miss Leah. The women are wheat farmers, and the house sits in the midst of the vastness of the Kansas prairie. Activity takes place mainly in the house's kitchen-dining-living room, which has a table, chairs, a small desk and a wood-burning stove. In the back and upstairs are other bedrooms, one of which will also be the scene of the action during the play. Other activities take place in the area outside the front door, including wood gathering and chopping and the hanging of clothes to dry. There is also a brief arrival scene at the nearby train station, which need only be suggested.

Act One

SCENE ONE: a fall evening

SCENE TWO: two days later; early afternoon

SCENE THREE: the same day; evening

SCENE FOUR: the next morning

SCENE FIVE: late that night

Act Two

SCENE ONE: early the next morning

SCENE TWO: the next Sunday; early morning

SCENE THREE: Sunday afternoon

SCENE FOUR: Sunday evening

SCENE FIVE: Monday morning

SCENE SIX: Seven months later; April 1899

Playwright's Note

The Homestead Act of 1860 offered three hundred and twenty acres of "free" land, stolen from the dwindling populations of Native Americans, to U.S. citizens who were willing to settle the Western states. Although many settlers lived in traditional family groups, by 1890 a quarter of a million unmarried or widowed women were running their own farms and ranches. The farmwork was hard and constant, but many of these women were able to survive due to their own physical stamina and determination and the help of their neighbors.

Large groups of African-American homesteaders left the South following the Civil War to settle all-black towns. The so-called "Exodus of 1879" saw twenty to forty thousand African-American men, women and children—"Exodusters"—reach Kansas under the guidance of a charismatic leader, Benjamin "Pap" Singleton, who escaped from slavery and claimed later: "I am the whole cause of the Kansas migration!"

Crusading black journalist Ida B. Wells's call to her readers to leave Memphis, Tennessee, after an 1892 lynching and riot, was heeded by over seven thousand black residents of the city, who packed up as many of their belongings as they could carry and headed West in search of a life free from racist violence. Unfortunately, their dreams were shattered, as many Western states enacted Jim Crow laws as cruel as any in the Old Confederacy; these laws effectively destroyed most of the black settlements by the early 1900s.

This is a story of some of the black people who went West.

Act One

_____

Scene One

A fall evening. Sophie enters rapidly. Her heavy coat is unbuttoned, and her scarf flies out around her neck. It is chilly, but the cold has exhilarated her. She has just returned from a trip into town. She has a large bag of flour slung over her shoulder and a canvas shoulder bag full of groceries. She is carrying a shotgun, which she places by the door. She slings the bag of flour carelessly on the table and, coat still on, puts the other bag on a chair. She fumbles through her pockets; she withdraws a letter, which she holds for a moment thoughtfully, then sticks it in the growing pile on the overflowing desk. She fumbles through her pockets again and withdraws some long strips of black licorice. She takes a bite, sighs, chews appreciatively. She pulls a chair over to the window, opens the window wide and sits down, propping her booted feet up on the windowsill. She looks out the window with great contentment, takes another bite of licorice and chews slowly, completely satisfied with the candy's sweetness, the chill in the air and the privacy of the moment.

7

Miss Leah enters haltingly. She walks unsteadily but has no cane to steady herself, so she holds onto the furniture as she walks slowly into the room. She is looking for something, and her manner is exasperated. Sophie does not notice her. Miss Leah looks at Sophie, immediately notices the open window and her irritation increases.

MISS LEAH: Well, ain't you somethin'!

SOPHIE: I didn't know you were up, Miss Leah. Want a piece? *(Sophie gets up and closes the window, then stokes the fire)*

MISS LEAH: I hate licorice.

(Miss Leah stumbles a little. Sophie moves to steady her and is stopped by a "don't you dare" look from Miss Leah.)

SOPHIE: You miss your cane?

MISS LEAH: I don't need no cane! I told you that before. You can lay it next to my bed or prop it against my chair like it walked out there on its own. It still ain't gonna make me no never mind. I don't want no cane and I don't need no cane.

SOPHIE: Suit yourself. *(Takes another bite of licorice as she hangs her coat)*

(Miss Leah's shawl is hanging there in plain view. Sophie starts to reach for it, stops, decides to ignore it and begins putting things away. Miss Leah finally speaks with cold dignity.)

MISS LEAH: I am looking for my shawl, if you must know.

SOPHIE: It's right . . .

MISS LEAH: Don't tell me! If you start tellin' me, you'll just keep at it till I won't be able to remember a darn thing on my own.

SOPHIE: I'll make some coffee.

MISS LEAH: I don't know why. Can't nobody drink that stuff but you.

SOPHIE: It'll warm you up.

MISS LEAH: It'll kill me.

SOPHIE: Well, then, you haven't got much time to put your affairs in order.

MISS LEAH: My affairs are already in order, thank you. *(Pulls a chair as far from the window as possible and sits with effort)* It's too cold for first October. *(Shivering)* Where's my shawl? Don't tell me!

SOPHIE: I bought you some tobacco.

MISS LEAH: What kind?

SOPHIE: The kind you like.

MISS LEAH *(Pleased in spite of herself)*: Well, thank you, Sister Sophie. Maybe a good pipe can cut the taste of that mess you cookin' up in Fan's good coffeepot.

(Miss Leah proceeds to "make a pipe" while Sophie makes coffee.)

What are we celebrating?

SOPHIE: We are celebrating my ability not to let these Nicodemus Negroes worry me, no matter how hard they try.

MISS LEAH: Then we ought to be drinking corn whiskey. *(She lights the pipe and draws on it contentedly)* Are you still worrying about the vote?

SOPHIE: I just told you. I'm celebrating an end to worrying. *(A beat)* I rode in by way of the south ridge this morning. Smells like snow up there already.

MISS LEAH: What were you doing way over there?

SOPHIE: Just looking . . .

MISS LEAH: Ain't you got enough land to worry about?

SOPHIE: I'll have enough when I can step outside my door and spin around with my eyes closed and wherever I stop, as far as I can see, there'll be nothing but land that belongs to me and my sisters.

MISS LEAH: Well, I'll try not to let the smoke from my chimney drift out over your sky.

SOPHIE: That's very neighborly of you. Now drink some of this.

MISS LEAH *(Drinks and grimaces)*: Every other wagon pull in here nowadays got a bunch of colored women on it call themselves homesteadin' and can't even make a decent cup of coffee, much less bring a crop in! When I got here, it wadn't nobody to do nothin' for me but me . . .

MISS LEAH AND SOPHIE: . . . and I did everything there was to be done and then some . . .

MISS LEAH: That's right! Because I was not prepared to put up with a whole lotta mouth. Colored men always tryin' to tell you how to do somethin' even if you been doin' it longer than they been peein' standin' up. *(A beat)* They got that in common with you.

SOPHIE: I don't pee standing up.

MISS LEAH: You would if you could! *(Sips coffee and grimaces again)*

SOPHIE: Put some milk in it, Miss Leah.

MISS LEAH: When I want milk, I drink milk. When I want coffee, I want Fan's coffee!

SOPHIE: Suit yourself. *(A beat)* People were asking about Baker at the land office.

MISS LEAH: What people?

SOPHIE: White people. Asked me if I had heard anything from him.

MISS LEAH: Ain't no white folks looking to settle in no Nicodemus, Kansas.

SOPHIE: It's some of the best land around here. You said it yourself.

MISS LEAH: Ain't nothin' good to no white folks once a bunch of colored folks get set up on it!

SOPHIE: There's already a new family over by the Gaddy's and a widower with four sons between here and the Jordan place. They've probably been looking at your place, too.

MISS LEAH: Who said so?

SOPHIE: Nobody said anything. I just mean since you've been staying with us for a while.

MISS LEAH: Well, I ain't no wet-behind-the-ears homesteader. I own my land. Free and clear. My name the only name on the deed to it. Anybody lookin' at my land is countin' they chickens. I made twenty winters on that land and I intend to make twenty more.

(While Miss Leah fusses, Sophie quietly goes and gets her shawl and gently drops it around her shoulders.)

SOPHIE: And then what?

MISS LEAH: Then maybe I'll let you have it.

SOPHIE: You gonna make me wait until I'm old as you are to get my hands on your orchard?

MISS LEAH: That'll be time enough. If I tell you you can have it any sooner, my life won't be worth two cents!

SOPHIE: You don't really think I'd murder you for your land, do you?

(Miss Leah looks at Sophie for a beat before drawing deeply on her pipe.)

MISS LEAH: I like Baker. And Miz Baker sweet as she can be. They just tryin' to stay in the city long enough for her to get her strength back and build that baby up a little.

SOPHIE: She'll never make it out here and you know it.

MISS LEAH: Losing three babies in three years take it out of you, girl!

SOPHIE: They wouldn't have made it through the first winter if Wil Parrish hadn't been here to help them.

MISS LEAH: You had a lot of help your first coupla winters, if I remember it right.

SOPHIE: And I'm grateful for it.

MISS LEAH: Some of us were here when you got here. Don't forget it!

SOPHIE: All I'm trying to say is the Bakers have been gone almost two years and he hasn't even filed an extension. It's against the rules.

MISS LEAH: Against whose rules? Don't nobody but colored folks know they been gone that long no way. Them white folks never come out here to even check and see if we're dead or alive. You know that good as the next person. *(A beat)* Sometimes I suspect you think you the only one love this land, Sister, but you not.

SOPHIE: What are you getting at?

MISS LEAH: Just the way you were speechifyin' and carryin' on in town meetin' last week like you the only one got a opinion that matter.

SOPHIE: Why didn't the others speak up if they had so much to say?

MISS LEAH: Can't get a word in edgewise with you goin' on and on about who ain't doin' this and that like they spose to.

SOPHIE: But you know I'm right!

MISS LEAH: Bein' right ain't always the only thing you got to think about. The thing you gotta remember about colored folks is all the stuff they don't say when they want to, they just gonna say it double-time later. That's why you gonna lose that vote if you ain't careful.

SOPHIE: It doesn't make sense. A lot of the colored settlements have already passed rules saying nobody can sell to outsiders unless everybody agrees.

MISS LEAH: Ain't nobody gonna give you the right to tell them when and how to sell their land. No point in ownin' it if you can't do what you want to with it.

SOPHIE: But half of them will sell to the speculators! You know they will!

MISS LEAH: Then that's what they gonna have to do.

SOPHIE: We could have so much here if these colored folks would just step lively. We could own this whole prairie. Nothing but colored folks farms and colored folks wheat fields and colored folks cattle everywhere you look. Nothing but colored folks! But they can't see it. They look at Nicodemus and all they can see is a bunch of scuffling people trying to get ready for the winter instead of something free and fine and all our own. Most of them don't even know what we're doing here!

MISS LEAH: That's 'cause some of them come 'cause they ain't never had nothin' that belonged to 'em. Some of them come 'cause they can't stand the smell of the city. Some of them just tired of evil white folks. Some of 'em killed somebody or wanted to. All everybody got in common is they plunked down twelve dollars for a piece of good land and now they tryin' to live on it long enough to claim it.

SOPHIE: Everybody isn't even doing that.

MISS LEAH: Everybody doin' the best they can, Sister Sophie.

SOPHIE: And what happens when that isn't good enough?

MISS LEAH: Then they have to drink your coffee!

(Sophie laughs as Wil and Fannie enter outside. We can still see the activity in the house, but we no longer hear it. Miss Leah smokes her pipe and Sophie works on her ledgers at the messy desk. Sophie pushes Fannie's papers aside carelessly, completely focused on her work.

Wil is dressed in work clothes. Fannie is dressed in boots, long skirt and shawl, and carries a basket of flowers. They are strolling companionably and chatting with the ease of old and trusted friends.)

WIL: I guess I'd have to say the weather more than anything. I miss that Mexican sunshine. Makes everything warm. You know how cold these creeks are when you want to take a swim? Well, I like to swim, bein' from Florida and all, so I close my eyes and jump in real quick! But that water would nigh 'bout kill a Mexican. They don't know nothin' 'bout no cold. They even eat their food hot!

(Fannie, laughing, stops to pick a flower to add to her already overflowing basket.)

FANNIE: Look! *(Holds the flower up for Wil's inspection)* That'll be the last of these until spring.

WIL: I imagine it will be. I ate a Mexican hot pepper one time. It looked just like a Louisiana hot pepper, but when I bit into it, it nigh 'bout lifted the top of my head off. Them Mexicans were laughing so hard they couldn't even bring me no water. I like to died!

FANNIE: You really miss it, don't you?

WIL: Miss Fannie, sometimes I surely do. But I know Baker needs somebody to keep an eye on things for him until he gets back. And now I got Miss Leah's place to look in on too.

FANNIE: Do you think they'll be back this spring?

WIL: He swears they will.

FANNIE: Sophie doesn't think they're strong enough for this life.

WIL: Sometimes people are a lot stronger than you can tell by just lookin' at 'em.

FANNIE: Did he say anything about the baby?

WIL: Said he's fat and healthy and looks just like him, poor little thing!

FANNIE *(Laughing)*: Shame on you! *(A beat)* Has Miss Leah said anything to you about going home?

WIL: No. Not lately.

FANNIE: Good! We're trying to convince her to stay the winter with us.

WIL: She's not tryin' to go back to her place alone, is she?

FANNIE: She really wants to, but she's just gotten so frail. Sophie says it was just a matter of time before she fell and broke something.

(A beat.)

WIL: You know what else I like? I mean about Mexico?

FANNIE: What?

WIL: I like Mexicans.

FANNIE: Well, that works out nice, I guess.

WIL: Everybody livin' in Mexico don't like Mexicans, Miss Fannie. They separate out the people from the stuff they do like and go on about their business like they ain't even there.

FANNIE: I never met any Mexicans.

WIL: Nicest people you ever wanna see. Friendly, but know how to keep to they self, too. Didn't no Mexicans ever say nothin' out of the way to me as long as I was livin' down there. They a lot like them Seminoles I grew up around in Florida. When I run away, them Indians took me in and raised me up like I was one of their own. They most all gone now. Ain't got enough land left to spit on, if you'll forgive me sayin' it that way.

FANNIE: Do you think you'll go back? To Mexico, I mean.

WIL: I used to think so but I spent seven years down there. As long as I spent on anybody's plantation, so I guess I'm back even. *(A beat)* I might even be a little bit ahead.

(Wil hands Fannie a flower that has fallen out of her basket.)

FANNIE *(Embarrassed)*: My mother loved flowers. Roses were her favorites. My father used to say, "Colored women ain't got no time to be foolin' with no roses," and my mother would say, as long as colored men had time to worry about how colored women spent their time, she guessed she had time enough to grow some roses.

WIL: I like sunflowers. They got sunflowers in Mexico big as a plate.

FANNIE: Sophie likes sunflowers, too, but they're too big to put inside the house. They belong outside. *(A beat)* It's lonely out here without flowers. Sophie laughed the first time everything I planted around the house came into bloom. She said I had planted so many flowers there wasn't any room for the beans and tomatoes.

WIL: That's where your sister's wrong. There's room for everything to grow out here. If there ain't nothin' else out here, there's plenty of room.

(They stand together, looking at the beauty of the sunset. Wil turns after a moment and looks at Fannie, quietly removing his hat and holding it nervously in his hands.)

FANNIE: You think it's going to a long winter, Wil?

WIL: They're all long winters, Miss Fannie. This one will be about the same.

FANNIE: Sophie found her laugh out here. I don't remember ever hearing her laugh the whole time we were in Memphis. But everything in Kansas was funny to her. Sometimes when we first got here, she'd laugh so hard she'd start crying, but she didn't care. One time, she was laughing so hard I was afraid she was going to have a stroke. She scared me to death. When she calmed down, I asked her, well, why didn't you ever laugh like that in Memphis? And she said her laugh was too free to come out in a place where a colored woman's life wasn't worth two cents on the dollar. What kind of fool would find that funny, she asked me. She was right, too. Sophie's always right.

(While Fannie speaks, Wil reaches out very slowly and almost puts his arm around her waist. She does not see him, and he stops before touching her, suddenly terrified she would not appreciate the gesture. She picks up the flowers, then hesitates.)

We're friends, aren't we?

WIL: Yes, Miss Fannie. I would say we are.

FANNIE: Then I wish you'd just call me Fannie. You don't have to call me Miss Fannie.

WIL *(Embarrassed)*: I didn't mean to offend you, Miss . . . I just sort of like to call you that because it reminds me that a colored women is a precious jewel deserving of my respect, my love and my protection.

FANNIE *(Taken aback and delighted)*: Why, Wil! What a sweet thing to say!

WIL: My mother taught it to me. She used to make me say it at night like other folks said prayers. There were some other things she said, too, but I can't remember them anymore. When I first run off after they sold her, I tried to close my eyes and remember her voice sayin' 'em, but all them new Indian words was lookin' for a place in my head, too. So I lost 'em all but that one I just told you. She used to say if a colored man could just remember that one thing, life would be a whole lot easier on the colored woman.

FANNIE: Can I put it in the book?

WIL: With Miss Leah's stories?

FANNIE: It's not just Miss Leah's stories anymore, Wil. It's sort of about all of us.

WIL: I would call it an honor to be included.

FANNIE: Well, good! *(Suddenly embarrassed, she adjusts her shawl and prepares to go inside)*

WIL: Walkin' with you has been the pleasure of my day.

FANNIE: Would you like some coffee before you start back?

WIL: No, thanks. I want to catch the last of the light. Give my best to your sister.

FANNIE: I will.

WIL: And Miss Leah.

FANNIE: Yes, I will.

WIL: Tell her . . . Miss Leah . . . maybe I'll stop in . . . tomorrow?

FANNIE: We'll look for you.

WIL: Well, good evening then.

FANNIE: Good evening.

(Wil starts off. Miss Leah comes to the window and watches the parting.)

Wil . . .

(He turns back hopefully. Fannie walks to him and puts a flower in his buttonhole.)

Take this for company on your way back.

WIL: Why, thank you! I do thank you.

FANNIE: Good evening, Wil.

WIL: And to you . . . Miss Fannie.

(He tips his hat and walks off, adjusting the flower in his buttonhole. Fannie watches him until he is gone, then walks slowly to the house. Miss Leah returns to her seat and begins rocking. She hums "Amazing Grace." Sophie looks at her. Miss Leah continues humming loudly and rocking with a smug look on her face.)

SOPHIE: What is it?

MISS LEAH: I ain't said a word to you.

SOPHIE: You're humming at me!

MISS LEAH: I ain't hummin' at nobody. I am just hummin'.

(Fannie enters.)

FANNIE: I'm sorry to be so late!

MISS LEAH: Sophie made coffee.

SOPHIE: She's been humming at me ever since.

(Fannie kisses Sophie's cheek and pats Miss Leah.)

FANNIE: Everything is fine at your place, Miss Leah. *(She puts the flowers in a vase and puts it in the center of the table)*

MISS LEAH: Everythin's fine but me.

FANNIE: Aren't you feeling good?

MISS LEAH: I'm too old to feel good. How's Wil Parrish feelin'?

FANNIE: He's just fine, thank you.

SOPHIE: Did he walk back with you? Why didn't he come in?

FANNIE: He'll be by tomorrow.

SOPHIE: You should have invited Wil Parrish in for a cup of coffee.

FANNIE: I did. He wanted to catch the last light.

MISS LEAH: Well, that sure was a friendly flower you stuck in his buttonhole a few minutes ago! But it's none of my business. *(Starts humming again)*

FANNIE: I ran into him watering his horse near the creek and he walked back with me. That's all.

SOPHIE: Has he heard from Baker?

FANNIE: He had a letter last week. Mother and baby are both doing fine.

SOPHIE: There's some people interested in that land.

FANNIE: Who?

SOPHIE: Families. White families.

FANNIE: In Nicodemus?

MISS LEAH: Just what I said!

FANNIE: I don't believe it. All the settlements they've got, why would they want to file a claim over here with us?

SOPHIE: Why don't you ask some of those land speculators holed up at the boardinghouse?

(Fannie lays out food and they all begin to seat themselves. Sophie moves to help Miss Leah to the table; Miss Leah waves her away. She will only accept help from Fannie.)

FANNIE: Well, it's neither here nor there. They'll be back on that land themselves by spring.

SOPHIE: I hope so. I don't need a whole bunch of strange white folks living that close to me!

(They are all seated, and Fannie lights a candle in the center of the table. The three join hands)

FANNIE: Bless this food, oh Lord, we are about to receive for the nourishment of our bodies, through Jesus Christ our Lord, Amen.

MISS LEAH: Jesus wept!

SOPHIE: Amen!

FANNIE: Baker's a good man to take his wife back East to have her baby. I don't think she could have survived losing another one out there.

MISS LEAH: These young women wouldn't have lasted a minute before the war. Overseer make you squat right down beside the field and drop your baby out like an animal. All ten of my sons was born after sundown 'cause that was the only way to be sure I could lay down to have 'em.

FANNIE: How did your babies know it was nighttime?

MISS LEAH: I knew it! If I felt 'em trying' to come early, I'd hold 'em up in there and wouldn't let 'em. Bad enough bein' born a slave without that peckerwood overseer watchin' 'em take the first breath of life before their daddy done seen if they a boy or a girl child.

FANNIE: I think Miz Baker will be all right. I think she was just scared and lonesome for her mother. She can't be more than twenty.

MISS LEAH: I wasn't but fourteen when I had my first one! Got up the next morning and strapped him on my back and went back out to the field. Overseer didn't notice him till the day half over. "What you got there, nigger?" he say to me. "This here my son," I say. "I callin' him Samson like in the Bible, 'cause he gonna be strong!" Overseer laugh and say, "Good! Colonel Harrison always lookin' for strong niggera to pick his cotton." I want to tell him that not what I got in mind for my Samson, but I kept my mouth shut like I had some sense. I ain't never been no fool.

FANNIE: Wil said he didn't think there would be snow for another couple of weeks at least.

SOPHIE: If he's got that much time to chit-chat maybe I can get him to help me repair that stretch of fence out beyond the north pasture.

FANNIE: He already did.

SOPHIE: He did? When?

FANNIE: Yesterday. He told me to tell you not to worry about it.

MISS LEAH (Enjoying Sophie's surprise): Now that Wil Parrish is a good man and a good neighbor. You can't ask for better than that. Don't you think so, Fan?

FANNIE: Yes. I do think so.

SOPHIE: Are you sweet on Wil Parrish?

FANNIE: We're friends, Sister.

MISS LEAH: You could do a lot worse. And he likes you. I can tell it sure as you sittin' here. Look at her blush! We gonna have a weddin' come spring!

SOPHIE: I already lost one sister. Don't give Fan away, too!

MISS LEAH: Shoot, you ought to be glad. Once Fan gets out of the way, you might find somebody fool enough to take a look at you.

SOPHIE: Two things I'm sure of. I don't want no white folks tellin' me what to do all day, and no man tellin' me what to do all night.

MISS LEAH: I'll say amen to that!

FANNIE *(Clears up the dishes quickly)*: Do you want to work on your stories some tonight?

(Sophie takes out her shotgun and begins to clean and oil it. She breaks it down quickly and efficiently. She has done this a thousand times.)

MISS LEAH: I'm too tired.

FANNIE *(Coaxing)*: Let's just finish the one we were working on Sunday night.

MISS LEAH: I keep tellin' you these ain't writin' stories. These are tellin' stories.

FANNIE: Then tell them to me!

MISS LEAH: So you can write 'em!

FANNIE: So we can remember them.

MISS LEAH: Colored folks can't forget the plantation any more than they can forget their own names. If we forget that, we ain't got no history past last week.

SOPHIE: But you won't always be around to tell it.

MISS LEAH: Long enough, Sister Sophie. Long enough. *(Miss Leah gets up unsteadily)* Good night, Fan.

FANNIE: Good night, Miss Leah.

(Miss Leah looks at Sophie who speaks without looking up.)

SOPHIE: You're not going to be mad at me all winter, are you?

MISS LEAH: Good night, Sister Sophie!

SOPHIE: Good night, Miss Leah.

(Miss Leah exits.)

FANNIE: Why do you agitate her?

SOPHIE: She'll live longer if she's doing it to irritate me. *(A beat)* I need a new hoop for that back wheel and it won't be in by Friday. Do you think Wil Parrish has got plans for his wagon on Friday?

FANNIE: You can ask him. He's going to stop by tomorrow . . . to see Miss Leah.

SOPHIE: Good . . . I'm sure Miss Leah will be pleased to see him.

FANNIE: I wish you wouldn't work at my desk. Look at this mess! What's this?

SOPHIE: It's from Miss Lewiston.

FANNIE: She's still coming isn't she? *(Anxiously reading the letter)*

SOPHIE: She "regrets she will be unable to fulfill the position of instructor at the Nicodemus School and wishes us the best of luck in finding someone else to assume this important responsibility."

FANNIE: She's getting married.

SOPHIE: And her husband's scared of life on the frontier. What kind of colored men are they raising in the city these days anyway?

FANNIE: She didn't say he was scared.

SOPHIE: She said he was nervous about moving to a place where there were still gangs of wild Indians at large.

FANNIE: People are scared of different things.

SOPHIE: No, they're not. They're either scared or they're not.

FANNIE *(Folding up the letter; resigned to it)*: Do you ever regret it? Coming West like we did.

SOPHIE: I never regret anything.

FANNIE: I miss the conversation more than anything, I think.

SOPHIE: Don't Miss Leah and I keep you amused?

FANNIE: That wouldn't be the word I'd use. No! Of course you do. That's not what I mean . . . I mean, the literary societies and the Sunday socials and the forums. Mama and Daddy's house was always full of people talking at the top of their lungs about the best way to save the race. And then somebody would start thumping away on

Mama's old piano and begging her to sing something. I used to hide at the top of the steps and watch them until I'd fall asleep right there.

SOPHIE: Well, Minnie ought to be able to fill you in on the latest in that kind of life.

FANNIE: London, Sister. It may well be on another planet. I can't believe she'll really be here. It seems like she's been gone forever.

SOPHIE: Almost a year and a half.

FANNIE: Fifteen months, three weeks and five days.

SOPHIE: But who's counting?

FANNIE: I miss her so! If I try to talk her into staying longer, don't let me!

SOPHIE: Why?

FANNIE: You know how Frank feels about the frontier.

SOPHIE: How can I stop you?

FANNIE: Kick me under the table or something! At least she'll be here for her birthday. She said Frank thinks it will take a couple of weeks to get the will settled. I hope everything turns out all right. Frank is counting so much on this inheritance.

SOPHIE: Frank better figure out how to work for a living! I picked up the new deeds today. One for you, one for me and one for Baby Sister. That ought to make her feel grown.

FANNIE: She's not going to believe it.

SOPHIE: Why? I always told her she'd have her share officially when she got old enough.

FANNIE: Knowing you, I think she thought you meant about sixty-five! Sometimes I try to imagine what Baby Sister's life is like over there. How it feels. It must be exciting. Museums and theatres all over the place. She said Frank did a public recital from his book and there were fifty people there.

SOPHIE: How many colored people were there?

FANNIE: She didn't say.

SOPHIE: None! No! Two! Her and Frank. Who ever heard of a colored poet moving someplace where there aren't any colored people?

FANNIE: Where do you expect him to live? Nicodemus?

SOPHIE: Why not? I'm giving her the deed to one-third of the land we're standing on and she's married to a man who'd rather take a tour of Piccadilly Circus!

FANNIE: Some people are not raised for this kind of life.

SOPHIE: Did we raise Min for the life she's living halfway around the world?

FANNIE: Of course we did. We always exposed her to the finest things.

SOPHIE: But why do all those fine things have to be so far away from Negroes?

FANNIE: I think our baby sister is having so much fun out there in the world, coming back here is probably the last thing on her mind.

SOPHIE: Do you know how much land they could be buying with all that money they're running through living so high on the hog?

FANNIE: They've got plenty of time to buy land.

SOPHIE: All that money and the best he can think of to do with it is move to England and print up some books of bad poetry.

FANNIE: They weren't that bad.

SOPHIE: They were terrible! *Odes to Spring.* You couldn't even tell a Negro wrote them.

FANNIE: What's so bad about that? We don't have to see spring differently just because we're Negroes, do we?

SOPHIE: We have to see everything differently because we're Negroes, Fan. I think Frank is going to find that out when they finish with this business about his father's will.

FANNIE: Min says Frank has hired a lawyer. You don't think they'll cut him out of the will, do you?

SOPHIE: How many white gentlemen do you know who want to share their inheritance with a bastard?

FANNIE: That's not fair.

SOPHIE: He's the one who kept talking about his father this and his father that, and the man wouldn't even come to wedding!

FANNIE: Well, I just try to give him the benefit of the doubt. Mama said every colored man deserved at least that much from a colored woman.

SOPHIE: Suit yourself. All I know is, we're going to have a school by spring if I have to teach in it myself!

FANNIE: Poor children would be crazy before they had a chance to learn their ABCs!

SOPHIE: *(Suddenly)*: Sh-h-h-h-h!

(Sophie motions toward the candle, and Fannie blows it out immediately. Sophie gets her gun, clicks it quickly into place and loads two shells. She goes quickly to the window and peers out. Fannie stands motionless, watching her. Sophie breathes a sigh of relief.)

Deer! Three of them! Come look.

(Sophie sets down the gun and she and Fannie stand looking at the deer in the moonlight.)

I'll be nice to Frank. For Min's sake. Butter won't melt in my mouth.

FANNIE: Promise?

SOPHIE: I promise.

(They embrace warmly. Fannie relights the candle, and Sophie fixes the fire in the stove.)

Did you talk Miss Leah out of going to the station with us?

FANNIE: I think so.

SOPHIE: You did? How?

FANNIE: I told her you didn't think it was a good idea.

SOPHIE: No wonder she's mad at me!

FANNIE: She's always mad at you!

SOPHIE: Well, good. Maybe she'll live to be a hundred!

(They exit for bed.
Blackout.)

Scene Two

Two days later; early afternoon. Sophie, Fannie and Wil are at the train station to meet Minnie and Frank. We hear the blast of the train whistle as the lights come up on the platform. Sophie and Wil are waiting patiently. Fannie is very excited.

FANNIE: It's so hard to wait once you see it, isn't it? Why is it taking so long? It doesn't even look like it's moving very fast anymore, does it?

SOPHIE: They're right on time.

WIL: And that's real lucky for you. This train don't never run on time.

FANNIE: But it's on time today, isn't it? And that's what counts!

WIL: Yes, it is, Miss Fannie. That's what counts!

FANNIE: Is it still moving? Can you tell? I can't tell! I'm going to find the station manager. *(She exits)*

SOPHIE: Fan told me you took care of my fence.

WIL: Yes.

SOPHIE: That was very neighborly of you. I'm much obliged.

WIL: You're welcome.

SOPHIE: Would you like to have dinner with us this evening?

WIL: You don't have to . . .

SOPHIE: I want you to come. And I'm sure Fan would enjoy having you.

WIL: Well, thank you. It'd be my—

(Fannie enters excitedly.)

FANNIE: It's pulling in! Oh, Sophie, I'm so excited. Do you see them yet? Can you see them, Wil?

SOPHIE: I don't see any . . . there she is!

FANNIE: Where? Where? I still don't . . . Minnie! Min! Here! We're here!

(Minnie enters on the run. She is wearing a fur-trimmed coat and carrying a fur muff. Her hat dips fashionably low over her face.)

MINNIE: Fannie! Oh, Fannie!

(Minnie, Fannie and Sophie embrace.)

Oh, Sister! I missed you both so much!

FANNIE: Look at you in that outfit!

SOPHIE: How about that hat? Who are you hiding from?

MINNIE *(Tugging it lower)*: They're all the rage in London!

SOPHIE: Where are your bags?

MINNIE: Frank has them. He stopped to send a telegram. He was talking to a man he met on the train . . . a white man. Maybe I better . . .

WIL: I'll give him a hand.

MINNIE: Thank you . . . ?

FANNIE: Wil Parrish, meet my baby sister, Minnie.

WIL: Pleased to meet you.

MINNIE: Pleased to be met.

(Wil exits.)

FANNIE: We borrowed Wil's wagon to pick you up.

SOPHIE: And Wil came with it to make sure Miss Fannie got to town and back safely.

MINNIE: Is he your sweetheart? Is he?

FANNIE: Don't pay Sophie a bit of mind.

SOPHIE: He's coming to dinner tonight. You can ask him yourself.

FANNIE: You better not say a word!

(Frank enters and stands watching them. Frank is immaculately dressed in fine clothes from head to toe. Coat, hat, suit, gloves, shirt—everything of the finest quality and very tasteful. The sheer richness of the clothing is obvious in every piece.)

FRANK: Secrets already?

MINNIE: Darling!

(Minnie runs to Frank and takes his arm protectively. Frank allows himself to be led toward her sisters.)

FANNIE *(Warmly)*: Frank. It's lovely to have you both!

(Frank puts down the small bag he's carrying, takes off one soft leather glove and extends his hand. Fannie kisses his cheek instead.)

FRANK: It's good to see you, too.

FANNIE: I was so sorry to hear about your father.

FRANK: Thank you.

FANNIE: Well, I know it was a long trip, but you're here at last!

FRANK: Nothing would do but Minnie had to come and see her sisters, isn't that right, darling?

FANNIE: You don't mind sharing her with us once in a while, do you?

FRANK: Of course not. And I've got some other things to share with you as well.

FANNIE *(Teasing and happy)*: Just how many riches do you think a poor frontier woman can stand at one time?

FRANK: I thought you might enjoy having an autographed copy of Mr. Dunbar's latest volume. *(He hands her a small book of poetry)*

FANNIE: Autographed? I've been trying to get my hands on any copy for months!

MINNIE: Frank walked me all over New Orleans to find it.

FANNIE: How can I ever thank you?

FRANK: It's my pleasure. *(A beat)* Hello, Sophie.

SOPHIE *(Nods formally)*: Frank . . .

FRANK: We'll try not to overstay our welcome.

FANNIE: Stay as long as you like. You're family.

MINNIE: That's just what I told him. We're family! This isn't like coming for a visit. This is coming home.

FRANK: But we have a home, don't we, darling?

MINNIE: Yes, of course we do. We have a lovely home.

FANNIE: And you're going to tell me all about . . .

FRANK *(Interrupts her)*: And where is our home, Minnie?

MINNIE: Frank . . .

(He stares at her coldly.)

It's in London.

FRANK: So this is really a visit, just like I said, isn't it?

MINNIE *(Softly)*: Yes, Frank.

FRANK *(False heartiness)*: Of course it is! And it's going to be a great visit. I'm sure of it. Well, how long does it take to get from here to there, anyway? I could do with a hot bath.

FANNIE: Of course you could. Wil's probably got the wagon loaded. Come on! Come on! Miss Leah's at the house and I know she's pacing up and down at the window right now.

(Fannie hooks Minnie's arm and draws her away from Frank. Minnie looks back anxiously at Frank, who stares at her impassively. He turns to find Sophie looking at him.)

SOPHIE: Welcome to Nicodemus, Frank.

(Frank tips his hat, bows slightly and exits pulling on his gloves. He leaves his small suitcase behind. Sophie looks after him, looks at the bag, shifts the shotgun easily to the crook of her arm, picks up the bag and exits.
Blackout.)

Scene Three

The same day, evening. Fannie is taking out plates and laying out food. Miss Leah is tottering around impatiently, making it difficult for Fannie to accomplish her tasks without tripping over Miss Leah. As Miss Leah talks to Fannie, Minnie is standing at the mirror in the bedroom trying to convince herself that her bruised face isn't that noticeable. Frank is taking off his jacket and unbuttoning his shirt. He catches a glimpse of Minnie looking in the mirror. He goes to her, stands behind her. She moves her hand from her face. He turns her slowly to face him. He gently, tenderly, touches her bruised face. She flinches. He kisses her gently. She relaxes, and he kisses her more passionately. She breaks away playfully. She looks in the mirror with resignation, grabs up her hat and puts it back on. She takes one last look at Frank, who still watches her. She throws him a kiss and goes out. He lies down on the bed, takes out a book and begins to read.

MISS LEAH: I don't see why she has to help him get settled right this minute. He's a grown man. He can unpack a suitcase, can't he?

FANNIE: I'm sure he can. I think Min just wants to make him feel at home here.

MISS LEAH: Why wouldn't he feel at home here?

(Minnie enters quickly. She is nervous that the others will notice her bruise.)

FANNIE: Thank goodness. Miss Leah was about to send me back there to rescue you.

MINNIE: Did you miss me?

MISS LEAH: Lord, chile, I thought that man had tied you to the bedpost back there. Take off that hat, honey, and let me look at you.

FANNIE: Aren't the flowers wonderful? I've got all your favorites . . .

(As Minnie slowly removes her hat, Fannie sees the large bruise above Minnie's left eye.)

Minnie! My god!

MINNIE *(Laughing nervously)*: It doesn't look that bad, does it?

MISS LEAH: What happened to your face, chile?

MINNIE: It's so silly.

(They wait in silence.)

I bought a new dress for the trip . . . and I . . . I wanted to show it to Frank . . . and I . . . the train . . . I stumbled in the train compartment. You know how clumsy I am. I bumped my head so hard I saw stars! And this is what I've got to show for it. Frank made me promise to be more careful. He worries so about me.

(An awkward pause. They don't believe her.)

I told him I used to be much worse. Remember that time I almost fell off the roof? I would have killed myself if it hadn't been for Sophie.

FANNIE: Yes, I remember . . .

MINNIE: Don't look so worried. I'll be careful. It was just an accident.

FANNIE: All right, Baby Sister.

(Sophie enters with wood in her arms.)

MISS LEAH: Close that door!

SOPHIE: Let me get in it first. Your turn to chop tomorrow, Minnie. Being a world traveler doesn't excuse you from your chores! *(Sees the bruise on Minnie's face)* What happened to your face?

MINNIE: I took a tumble, that's all. It looks a lot worse than it is.

SOPHIE: A tumble?

FANNIE: Minnie was showing off for her handsome husband and lost her balance on the train.

MINNIE: I know it looks awful. Here! I'll put my beautiful hat back on to hide it!

FANNIE: No! Anything but that!

MINNIE: Then let's not talk about it anymore.

(Sophie looks at Minnie and Fannie and takes off her coat.)

SOPHIE: Suit yourself.

MISS LEAH: How does living in . . .

MINNIE: London, Miss Leah. It's in England.

MISS LEAH: How does it agree with you?

MINNIE: Well, it was kind of scary to me at first. So many people and colored just right in there with everybody else.

MISS LEAH: No Jim Crow?

MINNIE: None.

MISS LEAH: I can't imagine such a thing.

MINNIE: That's why you have to come visit me. So you can see for yourself.

MISS LEAH: I don't need to see nothin' else new. I done seen enough new to last me. I don't know why anybody wants to be all up next to a bunch of strange white folks anyway.

SOPHIE: Because somebody told them they weren't supposed to!

MINNIE: Oh, they're not so bad. Frank and I even have some white . . . friends.

MISS LEAH: Lord, deliver us! What is this chile talking about?

MINNIE: Frank says he doesn't see why he only has to be with Negroes since he has as much white blood in him as colored.

SOPHIE: Frank is talking crazy.

MINNIE: It's true. His father was . . .

SOPHIE: A slave owner! Just like mine.

MINNIE: Frank said his father wanted to marry his mother. They were . . . in love.

SOPHIE: Did he free her?

MINNIE: No . . .

SOPHIE: Then don't talk to me about love.

FANNIE *(Quickly)*: Let's have some supper before you two start fighting. Min, go tell Frank to come to the table.

(Minnie exits to the bedroom as Wil approaches outside with flowers. Frank has gotten dressed up for dinner. When Minnie opens the door, he turns to her and strikes a pose for her approval. She kisses him and they go out arm in arm.)

MISS LEAH: There's Wil Parrish at the door.

(Fannie opens the door as he raises his hand to knock)

FANNIE: You're just in time.

WIL: I stopped for . . . these are for you.

FANNIE: They're lovely.

MISS LEAH: Just what we need.

WIL: Evenin', Miss Leah. How're you feelin'?

MISS LEAH: I'd feel a whole lot better if people stopped lettin' that cold air in on me.

(Frank and Minnie enter.)

FRANK: I'm starved!

FANNIE: Good! Why don't you sit here next to Min? Wil, you sit here by . . . Sophie. Miss Leah . . .

WIL: You're the first colored poet I ever saw.

FRANK: How many white ones have you seen?

WIL: None that I can recall . . .

FRANK: Then that makes me the first poet you've ever seen, doesn't it?

MINNIE: Frank . . .

(They all settle into their places and join hands.)

FANNIE: Sister, will you bless the table?

SOPHIE: Thank you for this food we are about to receive and for the safe journey of our beloved sister. *(A beat)* And Frank. Amen.

ALL: Amen.

(During the following, the meal is served, consumed and cleared away.)

FANNIE: Did you have a good rest?

FRANK: Enough to hold me, I guess. *(To Sophie)* Min tells me you're a mulatto.

(Sophie is startled.)

Oh, excuse me! I didn't mean to be so personal. It's just that I'm a mulatto myself and I was interested to know if there are many of us this far West. You know you can't always tell by looking!

SOPHIE: There are just a few.

FRANK: I can understand why. This is a lot closer to the field than most of us ever want to get! *(Laughs)*

MINNIE *(Quickly, to Wil)*: This is my husband's first visit to the frontier.

WIL: How do you like it so far?

FRANK: So far, so good. But to tell the truth, I've always been more of a city person.

SOPHIE: And what kind of person is that?

FRANK: Oh, I think one who enjoys a little more . . . ease than is possible way out here. Although I must admit your home is lovely. This table wouldn't be out of place in the finest dining rooms.

FANNIE: Why thank you, Frank!

SOPHIE: Tomorrow we'll go back to eating around the campfire like we usually do.

MINNIE: Don't listen to Sister! Fan is famous for setting the prettiest table in Nicodemus.

FRANK: I admire the ability to adapt to trying circumstances without a lowering of standards. I wouldn't have expected to see such delicate china way out here.

FANNIE: These were my mother's things. Sophie stopped speaking to me for a week when I told her I wasn't leaving Memphis without them, but I was determined.

SOPHIE: I should have left you and them standing in the middle of Main Street. Whoever heard of carrying a set of plates . . .

MINNIE: Mama's china!

FANNIE: Mama's good china!

SOPHIE: A set of plates halfway across the country when we hardly had room for Min.

MINNIE: You weren't going to leave me in the middle of Main Street, too, were you?

FANNIE: She couldn't have left us. Who would she have had to boss around?

MINNIE: I'd like to go back to Memphis sometime. Just to visit. Wouldn't you?

SOPHIE: Not me! Colored folks' lives aren't worth two cents in that town.

FANNIE: But everybody says things have gotten a lot better.

FRANK: Well, that may be true in Memphis, but we were in New Orleans to see my lawyers just before we came here and it's still pretty much the same as it's always been, if you ask me. They had just had a lynching the week before we got there. *(Laughs)* Just my luck!

MINNIE: After they hung the poor man, they threw his body down in the street right in the middle of the colored section of town.

MISS LEAH: Don't any of those New Orleans Negroes know how to use a shotgun?

FRANK: He pretty much brought it on himself from what I heard down at the bank. He was involved in some—

SOPHIE *(Cuts him off)*: I don't care what he was involved in.

FRANK: Doesn't it matter?

SOPHIE: No. Whatever it was, he didn't deserve to die like that.

FRANK: Well, I stand corrected. And I do apologize for introducing such inappropriate dinner table conversation.

MISS LEAH: I don't know why those Negroes stay down there!

SOPHIE: Because they haven't got the gumption to try something new. The day our group left Memphis, there were at least two hundred other Negroes standing around, rolling their eyes and trying to tell us we didn't know what it was going to be like way out there in the wilderness. I kept trying to tell them it doesn't matter what it's like. Any place is better than here!

FRANK: Well, that's something we agree on!

WIL: I'll say amen to that, too! If I never set foot in the Confederacy again, it's too soon for me.

FANNIE: Oh, no! You two can't start thinking like Sister! One Sophie is enough.

MISS LEAH: Too many if you ask me.

MINNIE: Has her coffee gotten any better?

MISS LEAH: Worse! And her disposition neither. I don't know how I'm gonna make it through the winter with her.

MINNIE: She's not so bad. You just have to remember to put cotton in your ears.

FRANK: I wish I'd thought of that on the train. Min was so excited she was talking a mile a minute the whole way out here. Weren't you, darling? She hardly took a deep breath.

MINNIE: I wasn't that bad, was I?

FRANK: I didn't want to hurt your feelings, darling, but you must have told me the same stories ten times!

MINNIE: I didn't mean to—

SOPHIE *(Cuts her off)*: Which one was your favorite?

FRANK: Oh, I think probably the one about you coming to the door asking to do the laundry and then moving right in. I guess you knew a good thing when you saw one!

MINNIE: Frank!

FRANK: What is it, darling? That is the way the story goes, isn't it?

FANNIE: I don't know what a good thing we were. Mama and Daddy both gone with the fever. So many people dying there weren't enough left well to take care of the sick ones. I was only twelve and Min still a baby.

MINNIE: So when Sophie came asking about doing the laundry, Fan asked her when she could start and Sophie said, "I can start right now. I'm free as a bird!" And once she came, it was like she'd always been there.

FANNIE: I loved the way she said it. I was scared to death and here was this one talking about free as a bird.

WIL: Are you gonna put that in the book?

MINNIE: What book?

FANNIE: I'm writing a book about Nicodemus. I'm going to call it "The True History and Life Stories of Nicodemus, Kansas: A Negro Town."

MINNIE: That sounds wonderful. Now we'll have two writers in the family.

FANNIE: Oh, I'm not really a writer. I'm more of a collector.

MINNIE: You could have a whole book with just Miss Leah's stories!

FANNIE: Well, some people don't think their stories are important enough to put in a book.

MISS LEAH: I'm not studyin' you, Fannie May Dove.

MINNIE: Why? I don't remember a time we went to your house when I didn't come back with a story.

MISS LEAH: Everybody knows them stories I got. Colored folks ain't been free long enough to have forgot what it's like to be a slave.

MINNIE: But you didn't always talk about slavery. You talked about how blue the sky would be in the summertime and about how you and the other children would sneak off from prayer meeting to play because you didn't want to work all week and pray all Sunday.

MISS LEAH: And got beat for it just as regular as a clock.

MINNIE: You used to tell me about how all your babies had such fat little legs, remember?

MISS LEAH: And where are they now? All them babies. All them grandbabies? Gone! Every last one of 'em!

MINNIE: But you loved them, Miss Leah. Who's going to know how much you loved them?

FRANK: Min's got a story, don't you, darling?

MINNIE: I thought you'd heard enough of my stories on the train.

FRANK: But you haven't told our story, darling.

MINNIE: I don't think this is . . .

FANNIE: Please? It's such a lovely story. With a happy ending.

FRANK: Go ahead, now. Don't be silly.

MINNIE: I was at school . . .

FANNIE: The conservatory . . . go on!

MINNIE: It was . . . it was spring. The campus was lovely then. Flowers were everywhere. But all anybody kept talking about was the handsome stranger who was here visiting for a couple of weeks.

FANNIE: That was Frank, all the way from England!

SOPHIE: Fannie! Let her tell it, or you tell it!

FANNIE: Go on! Sorry!

MINNIE: Pretty soon, everybody but me had met him or at least seen him. And then one afternoon, I was out walking and I thought I was alone, so I started singing and Frank was out walking too and he heard me.

FRANK: I really scared her!

MINNIE: I hadn't heard him behind me.

FRANK: I was tracking her like a wild Indian!

(Wil looks up sharply, but lets it pass.)

MINNIE: And then he said . . .

FRANK: I had been away from England for almost a month and I hadn't heard a note of Puccini in all that time. So I told her she sang like an angel and invited her to have dinner with me.

MINNIE: And I said my sisters hadn't raised me to have dinner with a strange gentleman who I met on a walk in the woods.

SOPHIE: You shouldn't have been walking in the woods alone in the first place.

FANNIE: But then it wouldn't be a love story! Go on, Min.

MINNIE: So I walked away and left him standing there.

FANNIE: And the next day a friend of hers invited her to attend an evening of Negro poetry at the Chitauqua Literary Society . . .

MINNIE: And I looked behind the podium and there was Frank!

FRANK: I recognized her right away . . .

MINNIE: And he nodded to me like we were old friends.

FANNIE: And then he dedicated a poem to her.

MINNIE: "A Song" by Mr. Paul Laurence Dunbar.

FRANK:

Thou art the soul of a summer's day,

Thou are the breath of the rose.

But the summer is fled

And the rose is dead

Where are they gone, who knows, who knows?

MISS LEAH: A Negro wrote that?

FANNIE: And me and Sister dashed down to New Orleans in time enough for the wedding and to see them set sail back to England.

FRANK: We'd only known each other a few weeks, but I knew Minnie was the girl for me. And she still is.

(Frank kisses Minnie gently, and she blushes.)

FANNIE: Beautiful! Now you tell one, Sister!

SOPHIE: I don't want to bore Frank with stories he's heard before.

MINNIE: Tell about the ritual. Tell about the day we left Memphis and came West to be free women.

SOPHIE: Fan's the one always thinking up ceremonies. Let her tell it.

FANNIE: Not this one! This came straight from you!

SOPHIE: When we got ready to leave Memphis . . .

MINNIE: When you two got ready. I was too little to get a vote.

SOPHIE: Well, I knew it was the right thing to do. Memphis was full of crazy white men acting like when it came to colored people, they didn't have to be bound by law or common decency. Dragging people off in the middle of the night. Doing whatever they felt like doing. Colored women not safe in their own houses. Then I heard there were Negroes going West.

MISS LEAH: Been done gone!

SOPHIE: Then that crazy Pap Singleton came to the church looking for people to sign up to go to Kansas. That man had eyes like hot coals. He said he was like Moses leading the children of Israel out of bondage in Egypt.

FANNIE: Sister didn't even let the man finish talking before she ran down the aisle to sign up! I think Reverend Thomas thought she had finally gotten the spirit!

SOPHIE: Pap said there'd be all-colored towns, full of colored people only! That sounded more like heaven than anything else I'd heard in church.

MINNIE *(To Wil)*: Why does that make you smile?

WIL: That's what landed me in Nicodemus, too. Looking for some neighbors that looked like me.

FRANK: At home, we go for weeks and never see another colored face. A few Indians once in a while—the Eastern kind—but that's not really the same thing is it?

MISS LEAH: Don't you get lonesome for colored people?

FRANK: To tell you the truth, I've seen about all the Negroes I need to see in this life. *(Laughs)*

MINNIE *(Quickly)*: Finish about the ritual, Sister!

SOPHIE: Another time.

MINNIE: Please!

FRANK: Don't whine, darling. Maybe Sophie is tired of talking.

MISS LEAH: Well, if she is, or if she ain't, I'm tired of listenin'!

MINNIE: You're not leaving us already, are you?

MISS LEAH: Knowing how long-winded some of the people at this table can be, you all will probably be sittin' here when I get up tomorrow mornin'. *(She gets up unsteadily)*

MINNIE: Let me help you.

MISS LEAH: One thing a woman my age should have the good sense to do alone is go to bed. Good night.

MINNIE, WIL, FANNIE AND SOPHIE: Good night, Miss Leah.

(Fannie and Minnie begin clearing off the dishes. Wil unobtrusively helps them. Frank pours himself another glass of wine.)

FRANK: They don't make you do the woman's work around here too, do they, Parrish?

WIL: Makes it go quicker when everybody does a part.

FANNIE: I couldn't have said it better myself!

(Sophie puts on her coat.)

MINNIE: Where are you off to?

SOPHIE: To bring in a little more of that wood I spent all week chopping in your honor.

MINNIE: Then the least I can do is help you carry it!

FANNIE: I'll help, too!

(They throw on their shawls and almost rush out the door.)

FRANK: You know the night air doesn't agree with you, Minnie!

FANNIE: We'll keep her warm, I promise.

(Fannie pulls a shawl over Minnie's head and pulls her out the door. Moonlight illuminates the yard. Cut wood lays in a stack near the house.)

SOPHIE: What's he talking about? You're healthy as a horse.

MINNIE: He just worries about me sometimes, that's all. I haven't been so strong lately . . .

FANNIE: But you're home now. I've got a whole week to toughen you up again!

MINNIE: I'm counting on it. *(A beat)* Sister?

SOPHIE: Yes?

MINNIE: Don't mind what Frank said about you coming to the door looking to do the laundry.

SOPHIE: Didn't I come to your door?

MINNIE: Yes.

SOPHIE: And didn't you need somebody to do the laundry?

MINNIE: Yes, but, sometimes Frank says things in a way that . . . that doesn't sound like how I know he means them.

SOPHIE: I'm not ashamed of anything I've ever done and if I was, taking in laundry to make an honest living wouldn't be the thing I'd pick. *(A beat)* You don't have to apologize to me for your husband, Min. If he's good to you, he's good enough for me. Is he good to you, Min?

MINNIE: Yes, he's good to me.

SOPHIE: Then he's all right with me.

FANNIE: Well, since you two are getting along so well, let's do it before you start fussing again!

MINNIE: Do what?

FANNIE: The ritual. Let's do it now!

MINNIE: Oh, yes, please! Can we?

(Wil sits down at the table and can be seen sharpening a small knife on a stone. Frank takes out a cigar, prepares it, smokes. The women stand in a circle, holding hands.)

SOPHIE: Because we are free Negro women . . .

FANNIE AND MINNIE: Because we are free Negro women . . .

SOPHIE: Born of free Negro women . . .

FANNIE AND MINNIE: Born of free Negro women . . .

SOPHIE, FANNIE AND MINNIE: Back as far as time begins . . .

SOPHIE: We choose this day to leave a place where our lives, our honor and our very souls are not our own.

FANNIE: Say it, Sister!

SOPHIE: We choose this day to declare our lives to be our own and no one else's. And we promise to always remember

the day we left Memphis and went West together to be free
women as a sacred bond between us with all our trust.

FANNIE AND MINNIE: With all our trust . . .

SOPHIE: And all our strength . . .

FANNIE AND MINNIE: And all our strength . . .

*(As they continue, Frank walks over to the window,
smoking. He looks at the women holding hands in the
moonlight.)*

SOPHIE: And all our courage . . .

FANNIE AND MINNIE: And all our courage . . .

SOPHIE: And all our love.

FANNIE AND MINNIE: And all our love.

(A beat.)

SOPHIE: Welcome home, Baby Sister.

*(The three embrace, laughing happily. Frank still watches
from the window.
Blackout.)*

Scene Four

*The next morning. Miss Leah is sitting in a chair mending some-
thing. Minnie kisses the sleeping Frank in the bedroom and
goes quietly out, closing the door behind her. She is brushing
her hair. She looks much younger than she did with her fancy
hat and sophisticated hairdo.*

MINNIE: You're up early.

MISS LEAH: Habit, chile. I don't know how to sleep past sun up.

MINNIE: Where are Fan and Sister?

45

MISS LEAH: Fan's already up washing and Sophie's probably off somewhere driving some other poor soul crazy. Come sit by me, chile. I couldn't hardly get a word in at dinner last night.

MINNIE: You always hold your own.

MISS LEAH: If you don't hold it, who gone hold it? Let me look at you. *(A beat)* You look more like yourself this morning.

MINNIE: I'm going to braid my hair with ribbons like you used to do it, remember?

MISS LEAH: I remember.

(Minnie starts braiding her hair, then messes up a braid.)

But don't look like you do. Sit down here, girl, and let me fix that head.

(Minnie sits on the floor between Miss Leah's knees. Miss Leah begins to braid Minnie's hair.)

MINNIE: Don't you think Frank is fine looking?

MISS LEAH: He'll do.

MINNIE: I want all my babies to look just like him!

MISS LEAH: He ain't that pretty.

MINNIE: Do you think I'll be a good mother?

MISS LEAH: You better be. Fan gone be too old for many babies by the time her and Wil stop dancin' around each other, and Sophie's too mean for anybody to marry. So I'm countin' on you, Baby Sister. None of this makes any sense without the children.

MINNIE: It would be hard to have a child way out here.

MISS LEAH: There's a lot worse places than this to have a baby. I'd of given anything to a had my babies in my own little house on my own piece of land with James pacing outside and the midwife knowin' what to do to ease you through it. Is that too tight?

MINNIE: It's perfect!

(In the bedroom, Frank gets up and begins dressing in expensive city clothes. He takes great care with his cuff links and tie. He is especially pleased with his hair.)

MISS LEAH *(Continuing her braiding)*: I was only thirteen when I got my first one. They wanted me to start early 'cause I was big and strong. Soon as my womanhood came on me, they took me out in the barn and put James on me. He was older than me and big. He already had children by half the women on the place. My James . . . *(A beat)* But that first time, he was hurting me so bad and I was screamin' and carryin' on somethin' awful, and that old overseer just watchin' and laughin' to make sure James really doin' it. He watch us every night for a week and after the third one I hear James tryin' to whisper somethin' to me real quiet while he doin' it. I was so surprised I stopped cryin' for a minute and I hear James sayin', "Leah, Leah, Leah . . ." He just kept sayin' my name over and over. *(A beat)* At the end of the week, I had got my first son. Do you have another ribbon?

(Minnie hands her one from her pocket.)

Fan's gonna skin you about her ribbons, Missy!
MINNIE: Did you love James?
MISS LEAH: I always thought I would've if they'd a let me find him for myself. The way it was, we stayed together after the war 'cause we was closer to each other than to anybody that wadn't dead or sold off and because James said we had ten babies that they sold away from us. We ought to have ten more we could raise free. Done! *(Finishes the braiding)*
MINNIE: I love my hair in braids.

MISS LEAH: Braid it or shave it off, I say. All the rest takes too much fussin' with. Don't leave a woman no time to think.

MINNIE: Why won't you let Fannie write down your stories?

MISS LEAH: Everything can't be wrote down . No matter what Fannie tell you, some things gotta be said out loud to keep the life in 'em.

MINNIE: Do you think James would have liked Kansas?

MISS LEAH: I think he would of if he could have walked his mind this far from Tennessee. It takes some doin' to be able to see a place in your mind where you never been before.

MINNIE: Frank's been so many places. London. Paris. Rome. Sometimes it seems like he's been everywhere and seen everything.

MISS LEAH: Well, I know that ain't true.

MINNIE: Why?

MISS LEAH: 'Cause this is his first time in Nicodemus.

MINNIE: I kept hoping he would like it here. I miss it so much. I tried to describe it to him, and sometimes I'd read him Fannie's letters, but . . .

MISS LEAH: Well, some people truly are city people. They like all that noise and confusion. It gives them somethin' to hide behind. Can't do that out here. First winter teach you that. Out here, nothin' stands between you and your soul.

MINNIE: It's more than that for Frank. He doesn't just hate the South and the frontier. He hates the whole country.

MISS LEAH: Well, maybe the boy's got more sense than I thought he did.

MINNIE: He said the first time he went to Europe he begged his father to leave him behind when it was time to go back to New Orleans. But he was only fourteen so his father refused.

MISS LEAH: Fourteen can be a grown man if you let it.

MINNIE: But he said he knew right then that as soon as he could, he was going to get on a boat for England and never look back. And he did, too.

(A beat.)

MISS LEAH: Baby?

MINNIE: Yes?

MISS LEAH: Do you ever miss colored people?

MINNIE: I miss colored people so much sometime I don't know what to do!

MISS LEAH: Well, that's good to hear. I thought you might be getting as tired of Negroes as Frank seems to be.

MINNIE: Frank doesn't mean any harm. He just doesn't feel like we do about Negroes. He might miss a friend or two, but when I ask him if he doesn't ever just miss being in a big group of Negroes, knowing that we are all going to laugh at the same time and cry at the same time just because we're all there being colored, he just shakes his head. I don't think he's ever felt it, so he can't miss it.

MISS LEAH: How can a Negro get that grown and not know how it feels to be around his own people?

MINNIE: He isn't used to being treated like other colored people. He gets so angry when we have to get on the Jim Crow car. When we can't go in the restaurants. I think if Frank had to live here, he might go mad.

MISS LEAH: Well, Negroes are supposed to get mad, so that's a good sign.

MINNIE: Not get mad, Miss Leah. Go mad.

MISS LEAH: Six of one. Half a dozen of the other.

(Frank enters from the bedroom.)

FRANK: Good morning! Darling! I didn't hear you get up.

MINNIE *(Jumps up to hug him quickly)*: I didn't want to wake you.

FRANK: What have you done to your hair?

MINNIE: Miss Leah braided it for me like she used to. Do you like it?

FRANK: I've never seen you with your hair in plaits.

MINNIE: Yes you have. I was wearing braids when you met me.

FRANK *(Being charming for the benefit of Miss Leah)*: You looked like such a little country girl then. When I first took Minnie to London, I made sure to take her shopping before I introduced her to my friends. But I always knew she had potential. Anybody could see that. And that's why I married her. Because Minnie deserves the best. Doesn't she?

MISS LEAH: She is the best.

FRANK: Yes, she is! I'm going to step out for a smoke, if you two will excuse me.

MINNIE: I'll come, too. *(To Miss Leah)* Do you want me to make you some breakfast before we go out? My coffee isn't as bad as Sister's.

MISS LEAH: Fan left me a fresh pot. Go ahead, chile. I'll he fine. I've been up long enough to be lookin' for a nap soon.

(Frank and Minnie exit to the yard. Miss Leah looks after them for a beat and then returns to her sewing.)

FRANK *(Angrily)*: I want you to put your hair back the way it was.

MINNIE: I always wore my—

FRANK: You look like a damn picaninny! We haven't been here twenty-four hours and look at you.

MINNIE: I'm sorry—

FRANK: You're always sorry, aren't you? Of course you are, but if you weren't so busy being sorry, you'd know there are some interesting things going on in Nicodemus these days.

MINNIE: What do you mean?

FRANK: Nothing. I'm going to ride into town to check at the telegraph office and . . . take a look around.

MINNIE: Don't be too late, will you?

(Frank exits. Minnie sits down on the porch wearily and draws her knees to her chest, rocking back and forth. In the kitchen, Miss Leah is oblivious. Blackout.)

Scene Five

It is late that evening. Sophie, Fannie and Minnie are up. Fannie is sewing something. Sophie is pulling some papers from the desk. Some of these are rolled maps or plans; these are Sophie's plans for the development of the town. Minnie is standing at the window. Fannie takes off her glasses, rubs her eyes sleepily. Minnie goes over to the fire and stirs it up, puts another log on.

FANNIE: Well, I think I'm going to leave the rest to you night owls! Don't worry. Nicodemus isn't big enough for Frank to get into trouble, even if he's looking for it.

MINNIE: Good night.

FANNIE: I'll be up early.

MINNIE: Me, too.

(Minnie and Fannie embrace. Fannie takes her sewing and begins to exit, patting Sophie affectionately as she passes.)

FANNIE: Good night, Sister.

SOPHIE: Check on Miss Leah?

FANNIE: Always.

(Fannie exits. Sophie pours herself a cup of coffee.)

MINNIE: You don't have to wait up with me.

51

SOPHIE: I won't be sleeping much between now and the vote next week.

MINNIE: What are you doing?

SOPHIE: I'm writing my speech for Sunday. I'm going to single-handedly convince these Negroes they have the right to protect their land from speculators and save Nicodemus!

MINNIE: Save it from what?

SOPHIE: From being just one more place where colored people couldn't figure out how to be free.

MINNIE: Are politics so important?

(A beat.)

SOPHIE: Come look at this. *(She spreads the plans out on the table)* These are the plans for Nicodemus. Here's the store and the post office. In the same places, but bigger. And open every day, not just two days a week. And here's the blacksmith and the school . . .

MINNIE: Who did this?

SOPHIE: I did. We want the school open by spring but the teacher we hired just wrote to say she won't come because she's getting married and her fool husband . . . *(She stops herself abruptly, not wanting to seem critical of Frank)*

MINNIE: Doesn't like the frontier, huh?

SOPHIE: I guess not.

MINNIE: This is wonderful.

SOPHIE: Fan drew the buildings. I was just going to write down what was going where, but Fan said, how about all the people in Nicodemus who can't read? *(A beat)* So the school goes here. The church stays where it is, but bigger. We've got fifty now in the Baptist pews alone! Then the doctor and the dentist will be here together so folks won't have to get their nerve up but once to go inside since it's different offices, but the same building. And see right here?

MINNIE: Yes.

SOPHIE: That's Fan's newspaper office and book publishing company.

MINNIE: Look! She put a little face waving out the window!

SOPHIE: That's her. Fan put us all on it. Here I am at the feed store. And here's Wil at the blacksmith. Here you are at the train station. Miss Leah's on here some place . . .

MINNIE: She forgot to draw Frank.

SOPHIE: I guess she did.

MINNIE: You know I'd come back if I could, don't you?

SOPHIE: I think you would if you wanted to.

MINNIE: It's not that simple.

SOPHIE: Why isn't it?

MINNIE: Does anybody really know what they want? Do you?

SOPHIE: Of course I do! I want this town to be a place where a colored woman can be free to live her life like a human being. I want this town to be a place where a colored man can work as hard for himself as we used to work for white folks. I want a town where a colored child can go to anybody's door and be treated like they belong there.

MINNIE: When you start talking about this place, you make it sound like paradise for colored people.

SOPHIE: It's not paradise yet, but it can be beautiful. The century is going to change in two years. This can be a great time for colored people. We can really be free instead of spending our lives working for the same people that used to own us. How are we ever going to be free if we have to spend all of our time doing somebody else's laundry?

MINNIE: You used to do laundry.

SOPHIE: There's nothing wrong with doing laundry until you start thinking that's all you can do. That's why the vote is so important. We have to help each other stay strong. The rule doesn't say they can't sell their land. It says they can't sell it unless they are prepared to look the rest of us in the eye and say who they are selling it to and why. As long as they have to face each other, nobody will have nerve enough to sell to speculators, no matter what they're offering.

MINNIE: But it wouldn't matter as long as most of the people here are colored, would it?

SOPHIE: If we start selling to speculators, everything will change. We may as well move back to Memphis. And before I do that, I'll get Wil Parrish to teach me how to speak Spanish and move us all to Mexico! *(She starts gathering up her maps)*

MINNIE: Wait, before you put it away. I was thinking maybe you could show it to Frank. So he could see how nice everything is going to be.

SOPHIE: Mr. Frank Charles ain't no more interested in an all-colored town than the man in the moon.

MINNIE: Frank's not so bad, Sister.

SOPHIE: Suit yourself.

MINNIE: Why don't you like him?

SOPHIE: I don't have to like him.

MINNIE: I know. But why don't you?

SOPHIE: I think Frank hates being colored. I don't understand Negroes like that. They make me nervous.

MINNIE *(Stung)*: You make me nervous.

SOPHIE: I didn't used to.

MINNIE: No. I guess you didn't.

(Sophie picks up the gun, puts on her coat.)

SOPHIE: I'm going to check the horses.

(Sophie exits. Minnie goes over to stoke the fire, then hears a noise. Frank crosses the yard quickly and enters. Minnie turns, thinking it is Sophie. She freezes.)

FRANK: What are you still doing up? It's late. *(He staggers over to her, sits and drinks a long pull from a silver flask without taking his eyes off of her)*

MINNIE: I was waiting for you.

FRANK: Why? Haven't I had enough bad luck for a nigger?

MINNIE: Are you all right?

FRANK: Do I look like I'm all right?

MINNIE: Let me get you some coffee . . .

FRANK: You don't need to get me a damn thing. Just sit still! Can you just sit still for once?

MINNIE: Yes, Frank.

FRANK: You know what happened tonight, don't you? I don't even have to bother telling you anything about it, do I?

MINNIE: What is it? What happened?

FRANK: I was gambling. A gentleman's game of poker with some of my friends from the train. Ran into them in town. And you know what? I lost. I lost everything. What there was left of it.

MINNIE: You were gambling with white men?

FRANK: White gentlemen, Min. And I lost every dime. And I want to thank you for that. Things were going fine until one of them asked me about the nigger woman who kept following me around the train. I laughed it off, but my luck changed after that so I know they suspected something.

(He stands behind her, touching her shoulders lightly.)

But I should have known better than to depend on you for luck. You're too black to bring me any good luck. All you got to give is misery. Pure D misery and little black pickaninnies just like you.

(He rubs her arms, then stops, keeping his hands lightly on her shoulders. She moves away in fear.)

MINNIE: Frank, were you . . .
FRANK: Shut up!

(She looks around for help in a panic.)

But the game wasn't a total loss. I found out something interesting. Do you know what I found out?
MINNIE: No, Frank.
FRANK: Your sisters are sitting on a fortune. That white man on the train? He said speculators are paying top dollar for these farms around here.
MINNIE: Sister would never sell this land!
FRANK: Of course she wouldn't because she's just like all the other Negroes around here. She's content to live her life like a pack mule out in some backwater town. . . . I never should have let you talk me into bringing you out here. We damn well could have waited in New Orleans like I wanted to. Taking that damn train all the way across the damn prairie. You know what they call your precious town? "Niggerdemus!" Niggerdemus, Kansas. Don't you think that's funny, Min?
MINNIE: Were you passing?
FRANK: I was letting people draw their own conclusions.
MINNIE: Who did you tell them I was?
FRANK: I told you to shut up!

(Frank pushes Minnie roughly, and she stumbles and falls to the floor at the moment that Sophie enters from the porch. Fannie follows Sophie almost immediately, awakened by the noise.)

FANNIE: Minnie! My God!
SOPHIE: What do you think you're doing?
FRANK: I'm talking to my wife. This is none of your affair.

MINNIE: It's all right! It was an accident. I just slipped, didn't I, Frank? I just slipped.

SOPHIE: Get out.

FRANK: You're pretty high and mighty for a nigger woman, aren't you?

MINNIE: Shut up, Frank! He's drunk! Don't listen to him!

FRANK: What did you say?

(He starts to move toward Minnie in a threatening manner. Sophie raises the shotgun and cocks it.)

MINNIE: No, Sister! Don't! Please don't! I'm going to have a baby!

(All stop.
Blackout.)

Act Two

Scene One

It is early the next morning. Sophie is standing at the window with her gun at her side. Frank is skulking around in the yard, coatless and cold. Fannie is getting a tea kettle off the stove. Miss Leah is taking some herbs from small jars laid out before her and preparing them for the tea. Minnie is wrapped in a blanket, propped up in a chair. She looks fragile and frightened.

MINNIE: He doesn't even have his coat with him.

SOPHIE: Good! Maybe he'll freeze to death.

FANNIE: Don't say that. You'll just upset her again.

SOPHIE: Upset her? Don't you think she ought to be upset? Don't you think we all ought to be upset?

MISS LEAH: Let her drink this tea and catch her breath before you start fussin' again.

(Frank exits the yard. Miss Leah hands a cup to Minnie.)

Drink all of it. It'll help you hold onto that baby.

59

MINNIE: This is such a hard time for Frank . . .

SOPHIE: For Frank?

MINNIE: He's my husband!

FANNIE: Of course he is. Be still, now.

MINNIE: He's so afraid they will try to trick him out of his inheritance

SOPHIE: Of course they will!

FANNIE: Sister, please!

MINNIE: His brothers hate him.

SOPHIE: His brothers used to own him!

MINNIE: That's not his fault too, is it?

SOPHIE: No. It's his fault for thinking that means they owe him something and if he doesn't get it, he has the right to put his hands on you.

MINNIE: I love him.

SOPHIE: That's not love.

(A beat.)

MINNIE: How would you know?

(Sophie looks at Minnie, picks up the shotgun and goes to sit on the porch steps. Miss Leah looks at Minnie, then goes to get a pipe and prepares it slowly.)

FANNIE: You know, Sister only wants what is best for you.

MINNIE: I know.

FANNIE: Sometimes I think if I'd known you were going to stay so long, I'd of thought longer about letting you go.

MINNIE: Me too. *(A beat)* Everything has changed. Everything. When Frank and I went to London, it was like a fairy tale. I felt so free! I could do anything, go anywhere, buy anything. And Frank was always there to show me something I had never seen before or tell me something I'd been waiting to hear all my life . . . and I loved to look at him. But then he changed . . . He was mad all the time.

FANNIE: Mad at who?

MINNIE: At everybody. But mostly me, I guess.

MISS LEAH: Why was he mad at you?

MINNIE: I don't know why! I think he just started hating colored people. We'd be walking down the street and he'd say: "Look at those niggers. No wonder nobody wants to be around them." When his father died and his brothers stopped sending money, it just got worse and worse. It was almost like he couldn't stand to look at me . . .

FANNIE: Hush, now. It's all right. Me and Miss Leah will take care of you now. There's not a baby in the world that can come before Miss Leah says it's time to.

MINNIE: Sometimes I used to think it must be a dream and that I'd wake up one day and Frank would be the way he used to be.

MISS LEAH: Grown people don't change except to get more like what they already are.

FANNIE: Frank is going through a bad time, that's all, but he's still Frank. He's still that man that swept you off your feet. The man you want to be the father of your children, isn't he?

MINNIE: He scares me sometimes. He gets so angry.

FANNIE: You know who else had a terrible temper?

MINNIE: Who?

FANNIE: Daddy. You were too young to remember it, but he did. And Daddy was a good man, but he had that temper and sometimes it would get the better of him. Just like your Frank. Sometimes he used to . . . not all the time, but . . . one time they woke me up, fussing about something, and Mama didn't hear me call her, so I went to the top of the stairs where I could see them without them seeing me. I always sat there . . . Daddy was sitting by the fireplace and Mama was talking a mile a minute.

I could tell he didn't like what she was saying, and then he got up real fast and grabbed her arm and he just shook her and shook her . . . I was so scared I ran back to bed, but I could still hear everything . . . Sometimes we have to be stronger than they are, Baby Sister. We have to understand and be patient.

MINNIE: What did Mama do?

FANNIE: Mama always said she was biding her time until we could get these white folks off our backs so she could get colored men straightened out on a thing or two a little bit closer to home, but until then, she said she'd give him the benefit of the doubt.

MINNIE: I've been trying to do that, too.

FANNIE: You love Frank, don't you?

MINNIE: I used to love him so much . . .

FANNIE: You still love him. I can see it on your face. You two can work it out. I know you can. For better or for worse, remember?

MINNIE: I'll try. I'll really try.

(Frank enters the yard, and Minnie sees him from the window.)

Frank!

(Minnie rushes past Sophie on the porch and into Frank's arms. He embraces her and grins evilly at Sophie.
Blackout.)

Scene Two

The next Sunday, early morning. Fannie and Miss Leah are up and ready for church. Sophie is finishing breakfast at the table alone. Frank and Minnie are in their room getting ready to go to church.

FANNIE: How was everything?

SOPHIE: Fine. Thank you.

FANNIE: Is your speech ready?

SOPHIE: As ready as it's going to be. I'm not going to worry about it. I'll say what I have to say and then we'll see which way it goes.

FANNIE: It'll go your way. You've hardly been home at all this week, out convincing everybody.

MISS LEAH: That's not why she hasn't been around here this week. Is it?

SOPHIE: I don't know what you mean.

(Sophie clears up her plate while Miss Leah watches her.)

MISS LEAH: You are the most stubborn colored woman I've ever seen in my life.

SOPHIE: I'll take that as a compliment coming from you.

FANNIE: Please don't get her started! I want us to ride to church and back in peace.

SOPHIE: I can't tell her who to marry, but I won't sit at a table with a man who called me an uppity nigger woman in my own damn house!

FANNIE: She's forgiven him. Can't you?

SOPHIE: He doesn't want my forgiveness. And she doesn't need it. She hasn't done anything wrong.

FANNIE: He made a mistake. He's sorry. I know he is. You haven't spoken a word to either one of them in a week. London is so far away and she'll be gone soon. Don't let her go without a word.

MISS LEAH: Colored women ain't got enough sisters to be cutting each other off so easy, I'd say.

SOPHIE: I pointed a gun at the man's head and wanted to use it!

FANNIE: And he's prepared to sit at table with you!

MISS LEAH: Which shows he ain't as smart as he thinks he is!

(Suddenly, Sophie laughs.)

SOPHIE: All right, you win!

FANNIE: Thank goodness! Now we can celebrate this birthday right!

SOPHIE: Don't get carried away. I said I'd be here. I didn't say I'd talk.

FANNIE: You know how special this birthday is. For all of us. How can you give her the deed if you won't even talk to her?

SOPHIE: You give it to her. *(She puts the envelope with the deed in front of Fannie)*

FANNIE: I can't. Not without you. It has to be all three of us or it doesn't mean anything. "With all our trust. And all our strength. And all our courage. And all our love." Remember?

(Minnie and Frank enter ready for church. They both stop when they see Sophie is still there.)

MINNIE: Good morning.

SOPHIE: Happy Birthday, Min. *(She hands Minnie the envelope)* This is for you.

MINNIE: A present? This early in the day? Can I open it?

SOPHIE: Ask Fan.

FANNIE: Go ahead.

MINNIE *(Reading, but confused)*: But what does it mean?

FRANK: It's a deed.

SOPHIE: It's the deed to your part of this land. You're twenty-one now.

MISS LEAH: Every colored woman ought to have a piece of land she can claim as her own.

FRANK: Do you know how much that land is worth?

SOPHIE: We're interested in buying more land, not selling what we've got.

FRANK: Well, from what that white fella told me on the train, not everybody around here feels that way. I heard some of your neighbors are considering some pretty generous offers.

MISS LEAH: Speculators!

FRANK: They're offering five hundred dollars an acre.

MISS LEAH: I can't believe it.

FRANK: Doesn't that at least make you more open to the idea? You could be a very rich woman.

SOPHIE: And I'd be standing in the middle of Kansas without any place to call home. You can't grow wheat on an acre of money.

FRANK: There's plenty of other land around from what I could see. What's the difference?

SOPHIE: The difference is we own this land. Whether they like it or not, and anybody who tries to say different is going to find himself buried on it.

FRANK: You wouldn't really kill somebody over a piece of ground out in the middle of nowhere, would you?

SOPHIE: This land is the center of the world to me as long as we're standing on it.

FRANK: And how do you think the rest of the world feels about sharing their center with a town full of colored people?

SOPHIE: I have no idea.

MINNIE: None of that matters! Can't you see that none of that matters? This is the land that makes us free women, Frank. We can never sell it! Not ever!

(Wil enters and comes to the door and knocks. Fannie opens it for him.)

FANNIE: We thought you'd changed your mind about coming to church with us.

WIL: On the day of Miss Sophie's speech? Not me! I'm sorry I'm late, I stopped by the telegraph office yesterday and there was a wire for Frank. *(Searches his pockets for it)* It was too late to bring it over yesterday and this morning I forgot it, so I went back. I thought it was probably the news you been waitin' for.

FRANK: I knew it! Didn't I tell you? I knew it! I felt our ship pulling up to the dock. Come on, Parrish! Where is the damn thing?

WIL: Here it is.

(Will hands Frank a telegram. Frank rips it open and reads. His face hardens.)

FRANK: What the hell?

MINNIE: What is it?

(Frank drops the telegram on the table, walks to the bedroom and slams the door. Fannie picks up the telegram.)

Read it, Fan.

FANNIE *(Reading)*: "Paternity denied. Stop. All claims to money, property, land and other assets of Mr. John Charles, late of New Orleans, Louisiana, denied. No legal recourse available."

MINNIE: You all go on without me. I need to . . . Frank needs me here, I think.

FANNIE: All right, Baby Sister. Be strong.

MINNIE: Yes, I will.

(Fannie, Sophie, Wil and Miss Leah exit. Minnie goes into the bedroom to Frank, who is sitting on the bed drinking from a silver flask.)

I'm so sorry!

FRANK: Are you? Sorry for what? Marrying a bastard?

MINNIE: Don't say that!

FRANK: Do you know what this means? This means I've got nothing. Not a dime. Nothing.

MINNIE: You can sell your books.

FRANK: Don't be so stupid. *(Pacing)* They think they can make me an ordinary Negro. That's what they think. They think they're going to have a chance to treat me colored and keep me here where every ignorant white man who walks the street can make me step off to let him pass. They think they can pretend I'm nothing and—presto!—I'll be nothing.

MINNIE: You won't let them do that.

FRANK: Let them? They've done it! We don't even have passage back to London. We're stuck here being niggers. Common, ordinary, niggers!

MINNIE: It'll be all right. We don't have a lot of money, but we've got a place to live. Not forever, but just until we get on our feet. Just until the baby comes! We do have a place.

FRANK: What are you talking about?

MINNIE: We can stay here. On our own land. Until you have a chance to figure things out.

FRANK: Do you really think I could live here? Right here?

MINNIE: Sophie has plans. You'll see. It's going to be beautiful. A paradise for colored people.

FRANK: A paradise for colored people . . .

MINNIE: This is our land, Frank. Nobody can take it from us. You don't have to have your father's money. We have land!

FRANK: You're right. We have land . . . *(A beat)* I'm sorry I snapped at you, darling. It's just that when I think about all the things I want to give you, it drives me crazy.

MINNIE: I love you. That's all I need.

FRANK: But you deserve so much more, Min. You're so beautiful. *(He kisses her. Touches her stomach gently)* Did you explain to my son that his daddy has a bad temper sometimes?

MINNIE: Please try, Frank. Just try . . .

FRANK *(His mood changes abruptly)*: Don't you think I'm trying? I'm trying to be a good husband to you. And I want to be a good father. But you have to help me.

MINNIE: I need to be able to trust you again.

FRANK: You can, darling. You can trust me. I swear it. I know the last few months haven't been easy, but I'll make it up to you. Do you believe me?

MINNIE: Yes, Frank . . .

FRANK: It'll be just like it used to be. We'll find another place, just like the one we had before, right on the square. You liked that place, didn't you, darling?

MINNIE: It was lovely, but it costs too much money to live that way. To live abroad . . .

FRANK: Your share of this land is worth over fifty thousand dollars. Do you know what we can do with that kind of money in London? We'll have the best of everything and so will our baby.

MINNIE: Sophie would never sell this land to speculators. Not for a million dollars.

FRANK: It wouldn't be all of it. Just your fair share. The town is full of people looking to buy some of this land before your sister gets that damn rule passed. This is the chance we've been waiting for. A chance for me to get back on my feet. To show my brothers I don't need their money.

MINNIE: They're not your brothers. They don't even claim you!

FRANK: They don't have to claim me. I look just like them!

MINNIE: No, Frank. I can't ask Sister to split up this land.

FRANK: I'm your husband. Don't you ever tell me no! *(He reaches to grab her arm)*

MINNIE *(Moving quickly out of reach)*: Don't, Frank! I don't care what you do to me, but I won't let you hurt our baby!

(Frank grabs Minnie's arm and brings her up against him sharply.)

FRANK: Don't you ever threaten me as long as you live, do you understand me? Do you?

(She nods silently.)

I'll kill you right now, Min. I'll break your damn neck before your precious sisters can hear you holler. I'll kill everybody in this house, don't you understand that? You want to know who I told those white men you were, Min? You really want to know?

(She struggles, but he holds her.)

I told them you were a black whore I won in a card game.

(He laughs and presses his mouth to hers roughly. Blackout.)

Scene Three

That afternoon. Frank enters the main room, pulling on hat and gloves, clearly preparing to go out. Miss Leah and Fannie enter the yard.

FANNIE: I thought Sister's speech went well this morning, didn't you, Miss Leah?
MISS LEAH: Speechifyin' and carryin' on. She ought to run for president.

(They open the door as Frank arrives at it.)

FANNIE: Frank! You startled me.

FRANK: I'm sorry. I didn't hear you coming.

FANNIE: Are you going out?

FRANK: I won't be long. I have some business to attend to in town.

MISS LEAH: On Sunday afternoon?

FANNIE: I'm sorry about the will. I want you to know you always have a place here with us.

FRANK: Yes. Thank you. We'll figure out something.

FANNIE: Is Min going in with you?

FRANK: No, she's resting. She'll be out in a few minutes. I won't be long. *(He exits quickly)*

(Fannie and Miss Leah begin making coffee and starting the evening meal.)

FANNIE: I believe he is sorry about what happened, don't you?

MISS LEAH: A man that will hit a woman once will hit her again.

(Sophie enters and meets Frank in the yard.)

FRANK: How was church?

SOPHIE: You should have been there. *(She crosses to the porch)*

FRANK: You're going to have to stop being so high and mighty. It doesn't become you.

(She turns to him from the porch steps.)

SOPHIE: I'm sorry for your troubles, because they're Min's troubles, too. But I think you should get on where you're going now and I'll go on inside.

FRANK: Well, suit yourself, as you always say, but I think I've got some news you might find interesting.

(Frank reaches in his pocket; Sophie shifts the gun.)

Take it easy! I'm unarmed . . . as always! *(He pulls out the deed)* I just thought you'd like to know that we're officially neighbors now. For the moment, anyway.

SOPHIE: What are you talking about?

FRANK: My wife wants me to share in her good fortune, so she's added my name to her deed.

SOPHIE: I don't believe you.

FRANK: I'd let you see it up close, but that probably isn't such a good idea. Hot-tempered woman like you . . .

SOPHIE: Get off my land. You make me sick.

FRANK: I'll get off your land. I'll get so far off it the post office won't even be able to find me.

SOPHIE: That suits me fine.

FRANK: Well, maybe you'll like your new neighbors better. Ask Min about them. She met them on the train. Well, she didn't really meet them, I didn't introduce her, of course, but she saw us talking. White gentlemen. She'll remember them. She wants to tell you, but she's a little nervous about it.

SOPHIE: Tell me what?

FRANK: You can see why. You've raised her to think this place is practically holy ground. She didn't even want to talk about selling it at first, but she came around.

SOPHIE: Minnie would never sell this land. You're lying.

FRANK: Well, you let her tell you. I figured under the circumstances, I would spend the night in town. I'm sure I'll have our share sold before tomorrow. Hope the sale doesn't hurt your chances in the vote next week. *(Laughs)* You know you're getting off easy when you think about it, Sister Sophie. I could stick around here and take over your precious town if I wanted to. You ever see a group of colored people who didn't put the lightest one in charge?

(In the rear bedroom Minnie raises up slowly. She is obviously in great pain and has been badly beaten. She

almost cannot stand. She staggers out of the bedroom. As Frank exits laughing, Minnie stumbles into the room where Miss Leah and Fannie are working.)

MISS LEAH: Lord, chile!

FANNIE: Sister! Sister! Come quick!

(Sophie rushes into the house and runs to help. Blackout.)

Scene Four

Monday morning. Fannie and Wil are sitting on the porch. Wil has a shotgun.

WIL: I don't understand how a colored man can hit a colored woman, Miss Fannie. We been through too much together.

FANNIE: Maybe there's just too many memories between us.

WIL: I don't think you can have too many memories. I know I wouldn't take nothin' for none of mine.

FANNIE: Not even the bad ones?

WIL: Nope. The bad ones always make the good ones just that much sweeter. *(A beat)* Does that paper really mean Frank can sell to speculators?

FANNIE: Well, if Baby Sister really signed it.

WIL: I never met a colored man like Frank before. Seem like he don't care 'bout colored people no different from white folks. Miss Leah says it's because mulattos got a war in them. And sometimes it makes 'em stronger but sometimes it just makes 'em crazy. Makes 'em think they got a choice about if they gonna be colored or not.

FANNIE: Sister's a mulatto and she never seems to be confused.

WIL: Well, you're right there. *(A beat)* Miss Fannie, I want you to know . . . I can take care of it.

FANNIE: Take care of what?

WIL: I mean, he's a colored man and I'm a colored man. We can settle it that way. Man to man.

FANNIE: I couldn't ask you to hurt anybody.

WIL: You can ask me to kill somebody, Miss Fannie. If I can't protect you and your sisters from a Negro who has lost his mind, what kind of man does that make me?

FANNIE: Have you ever killed a man?

WIL: Not a colored man, but I guess they ain't that much different from any other kind of man when you get down to it.

(Miss Leah and Minnie are in the bedroom. Minnie is lying down. Miss Leah is holding Minnie's hand and talking directly to her.)

MISS LEAH: When they sold my first baby boy offa the place, I felt like I couldn't breathe for three days. After that, I could breathe a little better, but my breasts were so full of milk they'd soak the front of my dress. Overseer kept telling me he was gonna have to see if nigger milk was really chocolate like they said it was, so I had to stay away from him 'til my milk stopped runnin'. And one day I saw James and I told him they had sold the baby, but he already knew it. He had twenty been sold offa our place by that time. Never saw any of 'em. When he told me that, I decided he was gonna at least lay eyes on at least one of his babies came through me. So next time they put us together I told him that I was gonna be sure this time he got to see his chile before Colonel Harrison sold it. But I couldn't. Not that one or the one after or the one after the ones after that. James never saw their faces. Until we got free. Then he couldn't look at 'em long enough. That was a man who loved his children. Hug 'em and kiss 'em and take 'em everywhere he go.

I think when he saw the fever take all five of them,

one by one like that . . . racin' each other to heaven . . . it just broke him down. He'd waited so long to have his sons and now he was losing them all again. He was like a crazy man just before he died. So I buried him next to his children and I closed the door on that little piece of house we had and I started walkin' west. If I'd had wings, I'd a set out flyin' west. I needed to be some place big enough for all my sons and all my ghost grandbabies to roam around. Big enough for me to think about all that sweetness they had stole from me and James and just holler about it as loud as I want to holler.

MINNIE: I didn't want to sign it. I was just so scared. I didn't want him to hurt the baby. I can't make him stop . . . hitting me. I just . . . want him . . . to stop . . . hitting me.

MISS LEAH: They broke the chain, Baby Sister. But we have to build it back. And build it back strong so the next time nobody can break it. Not from the outside and not from the inside. We can't let nobody take our babies. We've given up all the babies we can afford to lose. *(A beat)* Do you understand what I'm sayin' to you?

MINNIE *(Whispers)*: Yes, ma'am.

MISS LEAH *(Kisses her and pulls a blanket over her)*: Good. Go to sleep now. That baby needs a nap!

(Miss Leah goes out to Wil and Fannie.)

FANNIE: Is she . . .

MISS LEAH: She's sleeping. She held onto that baby, too. I told you she was stronger than you think.

FANNIE: Thank God!

MISS LEAH: Where is Sister?

WIL: She wanted to be sure Frank was headed toward town and not back this way. She told me to bring you the things you wanted from the house for Miss Minnie.

*(He hands Miss Leah a small packet, which she takes
and opens carefully.)*

MISS LEAH: I hope she didn't forget anything.

WIL: She had it written down.

(Sophie enters quickly.)

SOPHIE: He's on his way in, but he's moving slow. Is everything there you need?

MISS LEAH: It's here. It's here . . .

SOPHIE: Min?

FANNIE: Sleeping. She's going to be okay.

SOPHIE *(Taking charge)*: All right, here's what we're going to
do. Wil, I need you to ride out and catch up with Frank.
Tell him Min sent you to tell him she loves him more
than anything and . . . everything is going to be okay.
Tell him she wants him to come here tomorrow afternoon because I'll be in town to try and stop the deal.
Tell him she wants to go with him to the land office so
they won't have any trouble no matter what I do.

WIL: What if he doesn't believe me? He might think it's a
trick.

SOPHIE: Tell him colored men have to stick together. He'll
believe you. Tell him . . . tell him . . . the message is from
Fan. That she's on their side now. That should make
him feel safe.

FANNIE: What are you going to do when he gets here?

(A beat.)

SOPHIE: You and Miss Leah go in the back with Min.

FANNIE: But what are you going to do?

SOPHIE: A colored man who will beat a colored woman doesn't
deserve to live.

FANNIE: Just like that?

SOPHIE: No. Just when he tries to kill my sister and her baby before it's even born yet!

FANNIE: Stop it! That's just what I was afraid of.

SOPHIE: What you were afraid of? Me?

FANNIE: Of what you might do.

SOPHIE: What I might do? Why aren't you afraid of what he is already doing?

FANNIE: He's her husband, Sister!

SOPHIE: If he wasn't her husband would you care what I did to him for beating her half to death?

FANNIE: That's different.

SOPHIE: You know as well as I do there are no laws that protect a woman from her husband. Josh beat Belle for years and we all knew it. And because the sheriff didn't do anything, none of us did anything either. It wasn't a crime until he killed her! I'm not going to let that happen to Min. I'm going to watch him prance across this yard and then I'm going to step out on my front porch and blow his brains out.

FANNIE: And then we'll be savages just like he is!

SOPHIE: No! Then we'll be doing what free people always have to do if they're going to stay free.

(A beat.)

FANNIE: Isn't there any other way, Sister?

SOPHIE: This morning, while I was standing in that church painting a picture of the future of this town, he beat her and did God knows what else to her in this house. Where she's always been safe. We can't let him do that, Fan. All the dreams we have for Nicodemus, all the churches and schools and libraries we can build don't mean a thing if a colored woman isn't safe in her own house.

(Fannie turns away.)

WIL *(Quickly)*: You don't have to do this. I already told Miss Fannie. All you have to do is say the word.

SOPHIE: What are you talking about?

WIL: I can take care of it. You can wait here with your sisters and I'll take care of everything.

SOPHIE: I appreciate the offer, but the day I need somebody else to defend my land and my family is the day *that* somebody's name will be on the deed. I need you to help me do what needs to be done. Not do it for me.

WIL: You can count on me.

SOPHIE: Good! Go on now. I don't want him to get too far ahead of you.

WIL: I'll catch him. *(He exits)*

MISS LEAH: I can't let you do this.

SOPHIE: I'm not asking you. This is something I have to do.

MISS LEAH: And why is that? Because he hit your baby sister or because he wants to sell your land to some white folks?

SOPHIE: Aren't those reasons good enough for you?

MISS LEAH: Where's the pie tin?

(Miss Leah gets up and starts laying out utensils and ingredients to make a pie. This activity goes on through-out the following dialogue.)

SOPHIE: What?

MISS LEAH: The pie tin.

FANNIE: It's in the cupboard. What are you doing?

MISS LEAH: We're going to make an apple pie.

SOPHIE: An apple pie?

MISS LEAH: In case you forgot, this is still the state of Kansas, a part of the United States of America. Men beat their wives every day of the week, includin' Sunday, and white folks cheat colored folks every time they get a mind to.

SOPHIE: I know all that.

MISS LEAH: Good. I remember when y'all first got here. Green as you could be. Even you, Sister Sophie, way back then. Your group was as raggedy as any we'd seen. All of y'all lookin' like somethin' the cat dragged in. And then here come Min, bouncin' off the back of your wagon, hair all over her head, big ol' eyes and just the sweetest lil' face I ever saw. Didn't even know enough to be scared. *(A beat)* Hand me the sugar.

FANNIE: Are you feeling all right?

MISS LEAH: Am I feelin' all right? If I was you, I'd be worried about folks talkin' 'bout shootin' somebody. That's who I'd be worryin' about. It's a messy business, shootin' folks. It ain't like killing a hog, you know. Sheriff has to come. White folks have to come. All that come with shootin' somebody. But folks die all kinds of ways. Sometimes they be goin' along just as nice as you please and they heart just give out. Just like that. Don't nobody know why. Things just happen. *(A beat)* One day a little bit before I left the plantation, Colonel Harrison bought him a new cook. Ella. She was a big, strong woman. She didn't make no trouble either. Just worked hard and kept to herself. Ella knew a lot about herbs. What to put in to make it taste good. Colonel Harrison just love the way she cook. He used to let her roam all over the plantation pickin' wild herbs to put in her soups and stews. And she wouldn't tell nobody what she use. Said it was secrets from Africa. White folks didn't need to know. Colonel Harrison just laugh. He was eatin' good and didn't care 'bout where it come from no way. But after a while, that overseer started messin' around her. Tryin' to get Colonel Harrison to let him have his way with her, but Colonel Harrison said no and told him to stay from around her. She belonged in the kitchen. But that ol' overseer still wanted her and everybody knew next time he had a chance, he was gonna get her.

So one day, Colonel Harrison went to town. Gonna be gone all day. So that overseer put some poor colored man in charge of our misery and walked on up to the house like he was the master now 'cause Colonel Harrison gone off for the day. And when he walk up on the back porch, he had one thing on his mind, but Ella had been up early too, and the first thing he saw before he even saw her was a fresh apple pie coolin' in the window. And it smelled so good, he almost forgot what he come for. And Ella opened the screen door and smile like he the person she wanna see most in this world and she ask him if he'd like a glass of cold milk and a piece of her hot apple pie. Of course he did! What man wouldn't? And he sat down there and she cut him a big ol' piece and she told him it was hot and to be careful not to burn hisself . . . And do you know what happened? Well, he didn't even get to finish that piece of pie Ella cut for him so pretty. Heart just stopped right in the middle of a great big bite. By the time the master got back, they had him laid out in the barn and Ella was long gone. *(A beat)* But she did do one last thing before she left.

FANNIE: And what was that?

MISS LEAH: She gave me her recipe for apple pie.

(Blackout.)

Scene Five

Monday morning. Miss Leah is in the back sitting with Minnie, who is lying down. Sophie and Wil are hiding outside. Fannie is alone in the kitchen; she checks the time and then goes to the oven and takes out a perfect pie.

Frank enters the yard furtively. Fannie sees him and watches him from the window. She takes off her apron and goes to the door. She opens it before he knocks. He steps back, startled.

FANNIE: Come in, Frank.

(Frank hesitates.)

Sister's gone to town. Please. Come in.

FRANK: Parrish said you were going to come into the land office with me. Are you ready?

FANNIE: It's all right. Sister isn't angry anymore. She wants to make you an offer.

FRANK: What kind of offer?

FANNIE: Please. Come inside so we can talk.

FRANK: I don't want any trouble.

FANNIE: We're prepared to make you an offer for your land.

FRANK: You can't afford what they're paying in town.

FANNIE: We're prepared to pay exactly what they're paying in town.

FRANK: You don't have that kind of money. Minnie said so.

FANNIE: Sister and I didn't involve Min in all the details of our household finances. I'll go into town with you now and we can make all the arrangements. Do you have the deed?

(Franks shows it and puts it back in his pocket.)

Good!

FRANK: That's fine by me. I don't care where the money comes from as long as it ends up in my pocket so I can get the hell out of this place! *(Extends his hand)* Can we seal the deal, Fannie? Just the two of us?

FANNIE: Done.

(They shake hands.)

FRANK: You know I'm sorry it had to go this far in the first place. I love Minnie . . . how is she?

FANNIE: She's asleep right now. Miss Leah's with her.

FRANK: Good, good.

FANNIE: She wanted me to wake her up as soon as you got here, but I told her to get a few more minutes rest and I'd give you a piece of homemade apple pie to keep you busy in the meantime.

FRANK: You're not angry with me? About Min, I mean. You know how aggravating she can be sometimes. She's such a child.

FANNIE: I understand. She has to understand that a wife's first allegiance is to her husband.

FRANK: Well, you're a very understanding person and I appreciate that, but I would just as soon we get on our way. I don't think your sister would be too happy to come home and find me sitting at her table eating up all her . . .

FANNIE *(Holding out a piece to him)*: . . . apple pie. My specialty. Sister won't be home for hours yet. Besides, now that we know we'll be able to keep the land in the family, Sister's not one to hold a grudge.

FRANK: I don't know about that. She didn't seem to mind swinging that shotgun my direction.

FANNIE: We've got to put all that behind us now. For Min's sake and for the sake of your baby. I know Sister's prepared to let bygones be bygones. In fact, when she saw me rolling out the crust for this pie, she told me to make sure you got a piece of it.

FRANK: She did? Well, it takes a better man than I am to refuse an invitation for a piece of your famous apple pie! *(He sits and begins to eat heartily)* Delicious! Well, you tell Sophie she's not going to have to worry about Frank Charles hanging around getting in her hair. Not me! *(Laughs, coughs a little)* Soon as I get everything signed and proper, good-bye Niggerdemus! Hello London!

They treat me like a human being over there. You wouldn't believe it. Half the people we know don't even know I'm colored. I told Min if she was just a couple of shades lighter, we could travel first-class all over the world. Nobody would suspect a thing. *(Laughs, coughs a little, loosens his tie)* Don't get me wrong. I don't outright pass. I just let people draw their own conclusions.

(Frank coughs harder as Fannie watches impassively.)

Can you get me a glass of water, please? I feel a little . . . strange.

FANNIE: No, Frank. I can't do that.

FRANK: Please! I . . . water . . . my throat's on fire! *(He suddenly realizes)* What have you done? My God, help me! Please help me!

(She watches him as he tries to stand, but can't. He looks at her in a panic, then slumps over dead. Fannie shudders slightly: it's over. She composes herself, goes to the door and waves a signal to Sophie and Wil, who come immediately. Wil checks the body to be sure Frank is dead. He nods to Sophie, and they begin gathering Frank's things to remove the body.

Minnie and Miss Leah, hearing the activity, enter from the back. Minnie moves slowly, both from her injuries and from her reluctance to see the result of their collective action. Minnie and Miss Leah see that Frank is dead. Miss Leah watches Minnie, who moves toward the body, then stops, looking at Frank with a mixture of regret and relief. She approaches the body slowly, her anger and fear battling her bittersweet memories of the love she once felt for Frank. She reaches out and touches him tentatively, realizing the enormity of what they have

done. She draws back, but reaches out again, almost involuntarily, to touch Frank's arm, his hand, his shoulder. She moves through a complex set of emotions, ending with her knowledge of the monster Frank had become. Her face now shows her resolve, and even her body seems to gain strength. She steels herself and reaches into Frank's pocket to withdraw the deed. She clutches the deed in her hand, then looks to Sophie, who stands watching her. Minnie takes a step toward Sophie and extends the deed to her, anticipating Sophie's demand for her to return the deed. Instead, Sophie closes Minnie's hand around the deed and gently pushes Minnie's hand back to her. Minnie, grateful and relieved and finally safe, clutches the deed to her chest with both hands.
    Blackout.)

Scene Six

Seven months later, April 1899. Miss Leah is sleeping in her chair at the table. A cradle is on the table and one of Miss Leah's hands touches it protectively. Minnie enters from the back, dressed for a dance in town. She stops and looks at Miss Leah and her baby. She does not go to them, but looks at them for a minute and then around the room, slowly. She walks past the sideboard, touching it absently. She walks to the door and stands looking out at the full moon. She absently touches the broach at her throat. Her hair is braided with ribbons and she wears bright clothes. She looks calm and healthy. She feels Miss Leah's eyes on her and turns. They share a look. Both smile slowly.

MINNIE: It's as bright as noon out there.

MISS LEAH: That's a good luck moon. It's gonna be a good day tomorrow.

MINNIE: Do you think so?

MISS LEAH: It's gonna be a good day every day.

MINNIE: How do I look?

MISS LEAH: You look beautiful, Baby Sister.

MINNIE: Is she sleeping? Look! Her eyes are wide open! Hello, darling!

MISS LEAH: She's thinkin'.

MINNIE *(Crooning to the baby)*: What can my sweet baby be thinking, huh? What are you thinking about?

MISS LEAH: Leave the chile in peace now! Everybody's got a right to their own thoughts.

MINNIE: Do you think she's warm enough?

MISS LEAH: You're gonna smother the child if you're not careful. It's spring! Time to let some air get to her.

MINNIE: I know. I even took my shawl off while I was hanging clothes out today.

MISS LEAH: You better stop that foolishness! This is still pneumonia weather!

MINNIE: You just said winter was over, Miss Leah.

MISS LEAH: Well, it'll be back before you know it.

(Fannie and Sophie enter from the back. Fannie is dressed up, and Sophie has on a severe, dark blue dress.)

FANNIE: How do we look? *(She twirls around happily)*

MINNIE: You look wonderful! Wil Parrish will be beside himself to have such a beautiful fiancée!

SOPHIE: If colored people paid as much attention to saving the race as they do to their dancing, we'd be free by now.

FANNIE: Oh, hush! It's been so peaceful around here since you pushed that vote on through and the speculators went home, it's time to do a little dancing!

MINNIE: You're too plain, Sister.

SOPHIE: Too plain! This is my best dress!

MINNIE: It needs . . . something. Here!

(She takes the broach from her own bodice, kisses it and pins it on Sophie.)

It's Mama's! Don't lose it!

SOPHIE: I'll guard it with my life!

(Wil enters the yard. He carries flowers.)

FANNIE: He's right on time! *(She opens the door happily)* Good evening, Wil.

WIL: And to you, Fannie. These are for you. Hello, Miss Leah. Everybody.

MISS LEAH: Please get these women out of here. They are drivin' my granddaughter crazy with all their chatterin'!

MINNIE: We're going! We're going! Are you sure she'll be okay? I can stay here with—

MISS LEAH: I'm not so old I can't handle one little baby! Go on and leave us some peace.

WIL: Baker and his Mrs. passed me on their way!

SOPHIE: They didn't have that bad baby with them, did they?

MISS LEAH: You know that girl don't go no place without carryin' that big-head boy with 'em.

FANNIE: He's not that bad!

SOPHIE: Bad enough! *(Fussing with the pin)* Go on! Go on! I'm coming.

MINNIE, FANNIE AND WIL: Good night.

(Minnie, Fannie and Wil exit.)

SOPHIE: Too plain! That girl will have me looking like a Christmas tree if I'm not careful.

MISS LEAH: You look fine.

SOPHIE: Thank you.

MISS LEAH: Now don't you go makin' any speeches tonight! This is a dance.

SOPHIE: I won't, Miss Leah. Not tonight.

MISS LEAH: Go on, now!

SOPHIE *(Putting the gun beside Miss Leah's chair)*: We won't be too late.

(Sophie exits to the yard. As Miss Leah speaks the following dialogue, Sophie walks into the middle of the yard and looks up at the full moon. She extends her arms and slowly turns around to encompass her land, her freedom, the moon, her life and the life of her sisters. She is completely at peace. Miss Leah reaches into the cradle and gently lifts the well-wrapped baby out and looks into her face.)

MISS LEAH: Yes, my granddaughter. We got plenty to talk about, me and you. I'm going to tell you about your mama and her mama and her gran'mama before that one. All those strong colored women makin' a way for little ol' you. Yes, they did! 'Cause they knew you were comin'. And wadn't nobody gonna keep you from us. Not my granddaughter! Yes, yes, yes! All those fine colored women, makin' a place for you. And I'm gonna tell you all about 'em. Yes, I sure am. I surely am . . .

(As Miss Leah rocks the baby, crooning softly to her, Sophie continues to spin slowly in the moonlight as the lights fade to black.)

END OF PLAY

Blues for an
Alabama Sky

Production History

Blues for an Alabama Sky was originally commissioned by The Alliance Theatre Company in Atlanta, Georgia (Kenny Leon, Artistic Director; Edith H. Love, Managing Director), where it premiered in July 1995, under the direction of Kenny Leon. The set design was by Rochelle Barker, lighting design was by Judy Zanotti, costumes were by Susan E. Mickey, sound was by Brian Kettler and musical composition was by Dwight Andrews. The production subsequently returned to Atlanta as part of the Culural Olympiad, in conjunction with the Olympic Games in the summer of 1996. The cast was as follows:

ANGEL ALLEN	Phylicia Rashad
GUY JACOBS	Mark C. Young
DELIA PATTERSON	Deidrie N. Henry
SAM THOMAS	Bill Nunn
LELAND CUNNINGHAM	Gary Yates

Characters

ANGEL ALLEN: a thirty-four-year-old black woman who looks five years younger, former back-up singer at the Cotton Club

GUY JACOBS: a thirtyish black man, costume designer at the Cotton Club

DELIA PATTERSON: a twenty-five-year-old black woman, social worker on staff at the Margaret Sanger family planning clinic

SAM THOMAS: a forty-year-old black doctor at Harlem Hospital

LELAND CUNNINGHAM: a twenty-eight-year-old black man from Alabama, a six-week resident of Harlem

Time and Place

It is the summer of 1930 in Harlem, New York.

The creative euphoria of the Harlem Renaissance has given way to the harsher realities of the Great Depression. Young Reverend Adam Clayton Powell, Jr. is feeding the hungry and preaching an activist gospel at Abyssinian Baptist Church. Black Nationalist visionary Marcus Garvey has been discredited and deported. Birth-control pioneer Margaret Sanger is opening a new family planning clinic on 126th Street, and the doctors at Harlem Hospital are scrambling to care for a population whose most deadly disease is poverty. But, far from Harlem, African-American expatriate extraordinaire, Josephine Baker sips champagne in her dressing room at the Folies Bergère and laughs like a free woman.

Setting

The setting is an apartment building in Harlem. Three of the characters occupy two apartments which are across the hall from each other. There is a lot of running between apartments and access to and fro should be so easy that at times it seems to be one large living space.

Guy's apartment is slightly larger than Delia's and should have a couch large enough for someone to lie down on. In one corner of the room is a sewing area. It has a sewing machine, a woman's dress form, a full-length mirror, pieces of fabric, sewing supplies and a crowded clothes rack. This corner is Guy's workspace and is off-limits to others. In contrast to the congenial clutter of the rest of the apartment, this space is efficiently organized. On the wall, there is a large photograph of Josephine Baker. She is smiling broadly. There is a door opening to the bedroom, which is unseen.

Delia's apartment is a small studio. There is a small table with two chairs and a tiny bookcase full to bursting with books and pamphlets. A door opens to a bedroom which is unseen.

Both apartments have small hot plates, but no kitchens.

There should also be a window facing the street from the larger apartment so that characters can talk out the window to people in the street area.

Act One

Act Two

Act One

Scene One

Sunday morning, 3 A.M. The street is quiet. Suddenly, there is the sound of two people half-dragging, half-carrying a third. Guy and Leland enter on each side of a loudly drunken Angel.

ANGEL: I can't believe it. I just can't believe it. I . . . can . . . not . . . believe . . . it. Can you believe it?
GUY *(Struggling to keep Angel on her feet)*: I can't believe it.
ANGEL: Me either! I can't believe it!

(She stumbles. Leland catches her.)

ANGEL: Damn!
GUY: Home at last! Thank God. And thank you, brother. I don't think we would have made it that last two blocks without you!
LELAND: Is she sick?
GUY *(Surprised at the question)*: She's drunk!

ANGEL *(Indignant)*: And so what? If you can't be drunk in Harlem, where the hell can you be drunk? Besides, we're celebrating, aren't we?

GUY: Of course we are, Angel. *(To Leland)* Thanks again, Ace. I think I can take it from here.

ANGEL: Tell him why we're celebrating. *(To Leland)* Did he tell you why we're celebrating?

LELAND: No, he . . .

ANGEL: And I didn't tell you, did I?

GUY: Don't answer. You'll just encourage her.

ANGEL: Did I?

LELAND: No, you . . .

ANGEL: So, tell him, Guy. He has a right to know. Don't you think you have the right to know?

LELAND: I don't want to . . .

ANGEL: Of course you do. Tell him.

GUY: And then will you come upstairs before you wake up the whole building?

ANGEL *(Drunkenly indignant)*: They need to wake up! Negroes sleeping their damn lives away. *(Screams)* Wake up!

GUY: Hush, girl! You gonna get us all evicted.

ANGEL: Then tell him.

GUY: Her gangster just dumped her. So she's celebrating.

ANGEL: He's not a gangster. He's a businessman and he didn't dump me. He got married! *(Her drunken indignation dissolves into helpless tears)* He got married!

GUY *(Soothingly, trying to steer her into the building)*: He's Italian, Sweetie. They always get married.

(Delia emerges from her bedroom in robe and slippers and comes outside to see what all the noise is about. Leland is still hovering awkwardly around the stoop. Angel is now weeping and clinging to Guy.)

DELIA: What happened? *(She takes Angel's other arm)*

GUY: Nick got married.

ANGEL *(Wailing)*: Don't keep saying it!

GUY: Sh-h-h! It's okay. Come on now. Here we go.

(As Delia, Guy and Angel go inside Guy's apartment, Leland stands looking after them. He turns to go and sees that Angel has dropped the chiffon scarf she had draped around her neck. His first impulse is to return it immediately, but then he stops, folds it carefully and puts it in his breast pocket, then exits.

Upstairs, Guy is making coffee on the hot plate. Delia is taking off Angel's shoes and jewelry, and is putting one of Guy's robes on her. Angel is drunk and miserable.)

ANGEL: He left me, Deal! He left me!

DELIA: He didn't deserve you.

ANGEL: But I loved him.

DELIA: Of course you did.

GUY: Hang on, Sweetie. Coffee coming up!

ANGEL: I don't want coffee! I want champagne! We're celebrating! Aren't we celebrating?

DELIA: Come on now. Let me help you . . . Just relax, okay?

ANGEL: Relax? How can I relax? I just got fired! I got fired, Deal!

DELIA: Fired? She got fired? You didn't tell me she got fired.

GUY: The night is young. The whole sordid story has just begun to unfold.

ANGEL: I thought when he came backstage to tell me he was married, he'd go on home to his wife and leave me in peace to do the show. He must have known my heart was broken, but when we came out to do "Wild about Harry," he was sitting right in the front in his regular seat with Frankie and that other scary guy and they were toasting him and celebrating . . . They were having a party right up in my face! What could I do?

GUY *(Bringing coffee)*: Next time ask me that before you go onstage.

ANGEL: I hate coffee. Put some brandy in it.

GUY: Drink it!

DELIA: What did she do?

GUY: When they got to the part where they say, "The heavenly blisses of his kisses fill me with ecstasy," Miss Angel broke out of the line, walked over to his table and told Nick all about his sorry self.

DELIA: From the stage?

GUY: Centerstage, thank you. She read his titles clear for about two minutes, then she burst into tears and the stage manager came and took her away. He threw her and her stuff out into the middle of Lenox Avenue. We've been "celebrating" ever since.

DELIA: They can't fire her for that, can they?

GUY: For cussing out a short-tempered gangster in the middle of an up-tempo production number?

ANGEL: I didn't curse him. I couldn't curse Nicky. I love him.

GUY: Okay, Sweetie. Time for bed before we start back down that road.

ANGEL: I don't want to go to bed. What kind of dreams am I gonna have, huh? No man. No job.

GUY: There are still plenty of clubs in Harlem looking for a fine woman who can sing.

ANGEL: I can't sing anymore. My heart is broken.

GUY: You can sing the blues.

ANGEL: Everybody in Harlem is singing the blues.

GUY: Then you can come to Paris with me. Give Josephine some competition.

(Guy covers Angel with a blanket. She snuggles down like a child and draws the covers up to her chin. She is fading fast.)

ANGEL: Are we really going to Paris, Big Daddy?

GUY: Oui, ma chérie. We are really and truly going. Any day now.

ANGEL: What's the boat going to be like?

GUY: A ship. Not a boat. It's too elegant to be a boat.

ANGEL: And are we elegant too?

GUY: We are très, très élégant!

ANGEL: You gonna save me again, Big Daddy?

GUY: Every chance I get.

> *(Guy kisses Angel's cheek. Guy and Delia talk quietly,*
> *but Angel is already sleeping.)*

GUY: Sorry we woke you up. Want some champagne? *(He*
takes out a bottle and two glasses)

DELIA: It's three o'clock in the morning!

GUY: You are going to have to get over this primitive idea you
have that the world shuts down between 10 P.M. and 7
A.M. *(He hands her a glass)* Cheers!

DELIA: Do you think she really loved Nicky?

GUY: I don't think that was part of their deal.

DELIA *(Looking thoughtfully at the sleeping Angel)*: Maybe I
can teach her how to type.

GUY: Teach who how to type?

DELIA: Angel. I've got this typing correspondence course.

GUY: You don't have a typewriter.

DELIA: They sent a folding chart so I can practice until I get
one.

GUY: What makes you think Angel wants to learn how to type?

DELIA: I think she's scared she won't be able to find another
singing job.

GUY: She better be scared. Half the singers in Harlem are
looking for work.

DELIA: You just said there were plenty of places . . .

GUY: She already got dumped and fired. I figured that was
enough bad news for one Saturday night.

DELIA: Well, thanks for the champagne. I'm going back to bed. Church in the morning.

GUY: Adam Powell must be preaching.

DELIA *(Blushing guiltily)*: As a matter of fact, he is.

GUY: You all need to leave that poor man alone. Finish your champagne.

DELIA: I want to tell him about the clinic. You should come go with me. Help me get my nerve up.

GUY: You've got nerve to spare already. Besides, young Reverend Powell is not my type, thank you. The truth of the matter is, the finest young thing I've seen in ages walked home with me and Angel.

DELIA: The man with you downstairs? Was he a friend of yours?

GUY: Never saw him before in my life. He saw me struggling down 125th Street with a drunken woman in my arms and took pity on us.

DELIA: A friend of Angel's?

GUY: He's a stranger is what I'm trying to tell you. A mysterious gentleman who came to our aid and then melted back into the Harlem night.

DELIA: That's very romantic.

GUY: I thought so. That's one of the secrets of life, Young Miss. Don't forget it. Learn to spot the romance. For example . . . *(He presents a new costume sketch with a flourish)* Voilà!

DELIA: It's wonderful! When did you . . . ?

GUY: Last night. I dreamed it. I saw Josephine walking down the center staircase of one of those fabulous Folies Bergère sets in this very dress. And feel this. *(He gently hands her a carefully folded piece of brilliant magenta satin)* Satin. Isn't it wonderful?

DELIA *(Awed by the richness of the fabric)*: Can you imagine sleeping on satin sheets?

GUY: I understand your pastor is partial to them.

DELIA: Who told you that?

GUY: I run in international circles, girl. I have my sources. Look at you! I don't know how you can traipse around Harlem all day talking about opening birth control clinics and then blush when I tell you your pastor sleeps on satin sheets.

DELIA: I just never thought about it.

GUY *(Suddenly)*: Deal, can I ask you something personal?

DELIA: What if I say no?

GUY: I'll ask you anyway.

DELIA: Then go ahead.

GUY: Are you a virgin?

DELIA *(Flustered and indignant; she clearly is)*: I'm twenty-five years old!

GUY: That's what I thought! How wonderful! To be present at the awakening of another young fawn!

DELIA: What makes you think I'm awakening?

GUY: You're already drinking French champagne with a notorious homosexual at three o'clock on Sunday morning! What more proof do you need?

DELIA: Just don't tell Angel. She already treats me like I'm her little sister.

GUY: She treats everybody like they're her little sister. Drink up! *(He pours more champagne and raises his glass to the photograph of Josephine Baker)* To Josephine. Paris has never seen costumes like the ones I'm designing for La Bakaire!

DELIA: Do you ever think you won't go?

GUY: I'm going. Besides I have no choice. The matter is now officially out of my hands. Angel wasn't the only one who got fired last evening.

DELIA: You? Why?

GUY: Well, I couldn't hardly stand by and let Bobby toss her bodily out into the street, could I?

DELIA: What are you going to do?

GUY: I'm going to drive Josephine crazy until she sends for me. She promised she would and I'm going to take her at her word.

DELIA: I've got a little money saved if you need anything.

GUY: Aren't you sweet? *(Kisses her)* I'm fine for now. I've got a couple of jobs working on the outside, thank God! Do me a favor?

DELIA: Sure.

GUY: Don't tell Angel. I don't want her to panic. I can take care of both of us if I have to. It won't be the first time.

DELIA: I promise.

GUY: Thanks.

(Delia looks at Angel sleeping soundly.)

DELIA: Maybe I'll bring that typing chart by after church anyway. She might want to . . . try something new.

GUY: Forget the charts. Come by after service and finish this champagne with us.

DELIA: Does it have to be either-or?

GUY: Everything is either-or, Sweetie. Good night.

DELIA: Good night. *(A beat)* Do you really think I have nerve to spare?

GUY: No question.

(He kisses her cheek. Delia crosses the hall to her own apartment, removes her shoes and robe and gets back into bed. Guy closes his door. He walks quietly over to check on Angel and fixes her covers gently as the lights go to black.)

Scene Two

Later that afternoon. Guy's apartment is quiet. Angel is still curled up on the sofa. Guy enters carrying a small overnight bag and comes upstairs. He opens the door to his apartment and sees no signs of life. He sets the bag down and peers at Angel, then goes over and shakes her gently. No activity. He removes his coat and hat, puts on coffee and shakes her again. She groans.

ANGEL: Go away!

GUY: Rise and shine!

ANGEL: Are you crazy? What time is it?

GUY: Half-past noon, Sweetie.

ANGEL: Are you kidding? God! I feel like hell.

GUY: You look pretty bad, too.

ANGEL: Thanks. What have we got to drink?

GUY: Coffee.

> *(She glares at him.)*

> But since you asked so nicely, I'll put some brandy in it for you.

ANGEL: Aspirin?

GUY: We're out. Again.

ANGEL: Where were we last night anyway?

GUY: Don't you remember?

ANGEL: If I remembered I wouldn't be—oh!

GUY: I thought it might come back to you.

ANGEL: Did I—?

GUY: You did.

ANGEL: Did they—?

GUY: They did.

ANGEL: Fired me?

GUY: Like you stole something.

ANGEL: They'll take me back though, won't they? I mean, if I go down and talk nice to Bobby, he'll understand. I didn't throw anything, did I?

> *(A beat. He looks at her. Clearly, she did.)*

GUY: Drink your coffee before you get yourself all worked up.

(Angel drinks the coffee slowly.)

ANGEL: Do you think they'll take me back? Really, I mean.

GUY: Truth or solace?

ANGEL: Truth.

GUY: Not a chance.

ANGEL: What the hell am I gonna do now?

GUY: We'll think of something.

ANGEL: Like what? The Depression has killed all the nightlife in Harlem and nobody's gonna hire me downtown after what I said to Nick.

GUY: You can always come to Paris with me.

ANGEL: Sure I can.

GUY: I'm serious.

ANGEL: I know you are, but you being serious doesn't pay the rent.

GUY: Which brings us to my last little piece of good news.

ANGEL: I can hardly wait.

GUY: I went by your place.

ANGEL: This morning?

GUY: I figured Nicky's Catholic, he should be in church on Sunday morning . . .

ANGEL: With his wife.

GUY: . . . so that might be a good time to go get your stuff with a minimum of confusion.

ANGEL: What kind of confusion?

GUY: I don't think the details are particularly important except to say that the doorman let me go up for a fast five minutes to get what I convinced him were irreplaceable and exotic medicines which you had to have or die an agonizing and immediate death which would be on his conscience forever, especially if you expired on the Sabbath. *(He hands her the small bag)* I grabbed what I could.

ANGEL: This is it?

GUY: I only had five minutes, Sweetie.

ANGEL: He told me I could stay there as long as I wanted to. Think of it as your place, that's what he told me!

GUY: Think of it as your old place. And welcome to your new one.

ANGEL: I can't stay here. You know last time we tried that we stopped speaking to each other for a month.

GUY: Okay. *(He waits)*

ANGEL *(Quietly)*: Go to hell.

GUY: Don't worry about it. It'll be just like old times. Tripping over your stuff on the way to the toilet. Worrying about you wearing all my good clothes. You're over here half the time anyway. What's the big deal?

ANGEL: Guy . . .

(She looks at him without speaking. He sees/senses her fear. They have had this kind of conversation many times before.)

GUY: Look, even in your current sorry state, you're better off than most of the Negroes in Harlem. You've got a place to stay and I'm not gonna let you starve to death. We'll figure it out.

ANGEL: I should be figuring things out for myself.

GUY: Shoulda, coulda, woulda.

ANGEL: My head hurts too bad to argue.

GUY: Have I ever let you down?

ANGEL: You know you haven't.

GUY: I know I haven't, but I'm asking you.

(A beat. He waits.)

ANGEL: No, you have never let me down.

GUY: You think I'm gonna start now?

ANGEL: No, I don't think you're gonna start now.

GUY: Then stop worrying and pull yourself together. Big Daddy's gonna keep everything fine and mellow. Just like always.

ANGEL: But I'm so broke. I owe everybody . . .

GUY: Just . . . like . . . always. Okay?

ANGEL: I love you.

GUY: I love you too, Sweetie.

(Delia enters from church and knocks loudly on their door. Angel groans and falls back, holding her head. Delia pokes her head in.)

DELIA: How is she?

GUY: She's alive.

DELIA: How are you feeling?

ANGEL: How do I look?

DELIA: Well . . .

ANGEL: Never mind. Do you have any aspirin?

DELIA: I think I've got some across the hall. I've got something else to show you, too, but I'll wait until you're feeling better.

(Delia winks conspiratorially at Guy and goes to get the aspirin. During the dialogue that follows, Delia looks around for aspirin, but finds none. On her way out, she picks up the typing chart and book and takes them back across the hall with her.)

ANGEL: I can hardly wait. What is she talking about?

GUY: She wants to teach you how to use a typewriter.

ANGEL: What?

(Throughout this scene, Guy works at his sewing while participating fully in the conversation. This is his habit, and his friends are all used to it.)

GUY: Since you said you couldn't sing anymore because of your broken heart, Deal thought you might want to take advantage of the growing opportunities in the secretarial pool.

ANGEL: Tell me it hasn't come to that.

GUY: It hasn't come to that.

ANGEL: Swear it.

GUY: I swear it.

ANGEL: My head is killing me. Where is that child with the aspirin?

GUY: Sam's coming by this afternoon. He'll have some.

ANGEL: When did you see Sam?

GUY: We saw him. Last night at Small's.

ANGEL: God! I don't even remember being at Small's. Was I already drunk?

GUY: Let's just say, the question was already beside the point.

ANGEL *(Remembering vaguely)*: Did he walk home with us?

GUY: No. We left him at the club. He delivered five babies yesterday. He was celebrating their arrival.

ANGEL: I thought there was somebody else . . .

GUY: A brother walked with us part of the way from 125th Street. Saw a damsel in distress and offered his assistance. A real Southern gentleman from the accent. Beautiful silk suit, too.

ANGEL: A silk suit? I thought you said he was Southern.

GUY: I didn't say Southern bumpkin.

ANGEL: Who was he?

GUY: I never saw him around before.

ANGEL: Didn't you ask him?

GUY: I was a little preoccupied.

(Delia returns to the apartment.)

DELIA: I'm sorry. I guess I'm out too.

(Angel groans.)

ANGEL: Well, let's pray for Sam. *(She lies down and closes her eyes)*

DELIA: Is Sam coming?

GUY: Any minute now.

DELIA: Oh, well. I'll go on then.

GUY: Why? Doc's family.

DELIA: He's just so . . .

GUY: What?

DELIA: Sometimes he doesn't seem like a doctor. He's out as much as you and Angel.

GUY: Are we now the standard of dissipation?

DELIA: No, but he's a doctor.

GUY: Doctors can't like jazz?

DELIA: It's not the music. It's the way he acts. Whoever heard of a doctor going around hollering . . .

GUY: "Let the good times roll!" And he doesn't holler. He speaks with conviction.

DELIA: Does that sound like a serious physician to you?

GUY: Relax, Sweetie. Sam's the best doctor in New York City. He'll work his magic on Angel and we'll all go out to eat.

ANGEL: Don't talk about food!

DELIA: Angel? *(No response)* Can I show you something?

ANGEL: No!

DELIA: Oh, well. *(A beat. She decides to plow ahead anyway. She lies out the typing chart and book)* I can just leave it for you, then. You can look at it later. Whenever you feel like it. I don't need it back right away or anything. *(A beat)* I just thought maybe you . . . last night . . . you sounded like . . . you might want to try something new . . . and there are expanding opportunities in the secretarial pool.

(Angel groans loudly.)

GUY: Your timing is lousy, Deal. Come tell me what the good Reverend Powell was up to this morning.

DELIA: He was wonderful! He got so worked up at the end of his sermon, he came out of the pulpit, walked straight down the middle aisle and right up Seventh Avenue. His robe was billowing out around him like wings . . .

GUY: That Negro ought to quit preaching and go on into full-time show business.

DELIA: By the time he turned around and came back he had picked up twenty new members and the choir was still singing the invitational hymn. And guess what else?

GUY: A dove landed on his shoulder and a voice said . . .

DELIA: I talked to him about the clinic.

GUY: You did?

DELIA: And I wasn't even nervous. I was in line to shake his hand after service and he said he was happy to see I had decided to make Abyssinian my church home. And I said I was proud to be a part of a church that had a sense of responsibility to the masses.

GUY: Not those Negroes again.

DELIA *(A little defensive)*: He knew what I meant! The people of Harlem. The women who need . . .

(Angel groans.)

ANGEL: Please don't get her all worked up! I can't take the history of the downtrodden without some aspirin!

GUY: Our apologies, Madam. We forgot the presence of the infirm in our midst. *(To Delia)* Go on.

DELIA: So then I said I was working with Margaret Sanger to open a family planning clinic right here in Harlem.

GUY: You said "family planning" in the fellowship line at Abyssinian? *(Laughs)* I hope none of those high-tones from Sugar Hill heard you.

DELIA: Then Reverend Powell said it sounded like a very interesting idea and to come by the church office on Monday so I could tell him more about it.

GUY: Well, all-reet! You hear that, Angel?

ANGEL *(Groaning)*: I want Sam!

(Sam enters from the street and comes in their open door.)

SAM: Ask and ye shall receive! It's a boy!

GUY: My favorite Harlem healer! Come on in, Doc.

DELIA: How's the mother?

SAM: You didn't let me finish. It's also a girl.

DELIA: Twins?

SAM: Mother and babies are doing fine.

ANGEL: Just what Harlem needs. Two more mouths to feed.

GUY: Don't listen to the cynic. Congratulations!

SAM: Thank you on behalf of all concerned. Especially the proud father who also happens to be a successful boot-legger. *(He pulls a bottle from his coat pocket)*

GUY *(Going to get glasses or cups for everybody)*: I'm liking this family more all the time.

SAM *(To Angel)*: How're you feeling?

ANGEL: Tell me you have aspirin or shoot me.

SAM: Here, try this. *(He hands her some pills from his pocket)*

ANGEL: What is it?

SAM: Just aspirin. Hospital-strength. I've found it to be very effective in treating the Harlem hangover. *(He hands her a glass of the bootleg liquor, and she swallows it with the pills)*

DELIA *(As Sam pours for the others)*: Is it really safe for us to drink it?

GUY: Just enough to toast the new arrivals.

DELIA: Aren't you afraid we'll go blind or something?

SAM: Don't worry. I'm a doctor. *(He holds up his glass)* To the two newest citizens of Harlem! Long life, good health, and let the good times roll!

GUY: Amen!

(They all drink.)

SAM: Feeling anything yet?

ANGEL: Not yet.

SAM: It just takes a minute. I promise. *(He drains his glass)* Seven babies in two days. I think it's a record. Even for me!

GUY: Then you deserve another drink.

SAM: Thank you, kind sir. *(Pouring another for himself and for Guy)* You know, that woman almost didn't make it.

DELIA: The mother?

SAM: They didn't even know she was carrying twins and one of them was coming breech. When I let her husband know what the risks were, he broke down and cried. He kept saying, "That's the best woman in the world in there, Doc. That's the best woman in the world."

DELIA: If she's so precious to him, why didn't he take her to the doctor?

SAM: He did. He just took her a little late, that's all.

GUY: Why didn't she take herself? If she's old enough to have two babies at one time, she ought to be able to figure out how to catch the subway.

ANGEL *(Suddenly)*: It worked!

SAM: I told you.

ANGEL: It's a miracle! You're a genius, Sam! They ought to put you in charge of Harlem hospital.

SAM: That's not my reward, is it?

GUY: No. Your reward is you get to take us all out for Sunday dinner. Can you come, Deal?

DELIA: Well, I . . .

SAM *(Interrupting her quickly before she can refuse)*: Great idea! What do you think, Angel? Ready for solid food yet?

ANGEL: Not a chance. You all go on though. I'll be fine.

DELIA: Want us to bring you back a plate?

GUY: If you think I'm going to join the Sunday promenade carrying a plate of leftover collard greens, you could not be more wrong!

SAM: Let's go. Now that you said "food," I'm starving!

DELIA: Give me five minutes.

GUY: Take ten. I need to freshen up myself.

SAM: Good. I'll take a quick nap.

(Delia exits to her apartment, Guy to the bedroom. Sam sits slumped in his chair with his eyes closed. Angel watches him. He speaks without opening his eyes.)

So how is it, Angel Eyes?

ANGEL: It's been better.

SAM: Well, look on the bright side.

ANGEL: What bright side is that?

SAM: I met a bootlegger and found a cure for hangover in the same week.

ANGEL: Nice work if you can get it.

(Angel is pacing around restlessly. Sam opens his eyes and watches her.)

SAM: Why don't you sing me some Sunday morning blues?

ANGEL: Didn't your mama teach you not to sing no blues on the Lord's day?

(Sam leans back and closes his eyes again wearily.)

SAM: My mama taught me that man was the beginning and end of his own misery and that calling on God to fix it once you broke it was a comfort we were not allowed.

ANGEL *(Sitting beside him and stroking his forehead maternally)*: Your mama said a mouthful to answer a simple question, huh?

SAM: The curse of the Negro intellectual.

(A beat.)

ANGEL: You look like hell.

SAM *(Eyes still closed)*: The pot calling the kettle . . .

ANGEL: But you're supposed to be respectable.

SAM: Our recent population explosion didn't leave me much time to get my suit pressed. I don't look that bad, do I?

ANGEL: Terrible. You need somebody to take care of you, Doc. I'm looking for a job. Let's get married.

SAM: Wait 'til I tell you what my mother said about marriage.

ANGEL: Too bad. I'd be a great wife. You'd come home from a hard day's work, and I'd be there with a hot, home-cooked meal on the table and your slippers by the fire.

SAM: Can't you be there in a red satin shimmy singing "St. Louis Blues" and drinking bathtub gin?

ANGEL: That's not the wife! That's the girlfriend.

SAM: Okay. Lose the shimmy. Lose the gin. Keep the blues.

(A beat.)

ANGEL: Why didn't we ever get together?

SAM: Because you deserve better.

(A beat. She is moved by the directness of his response, but then she laughs as if he was only teasing.)

ANGEL: All right, smooth talker! If I go to hell, it's on your conscience. *(She begins to sing "St. Louis Blues")*

111

I hate to see
the evening sun go down.
I hate to see
the evening sun go down.
It makes me think,
I'm on my last go 'round . . .

(Delia reenters. Angel sings her way over to Delia and begins dancing with her as she sings. Delia is shy, but delighted. Sam watches them affectionately.)

SAM: I didn't realize your revolution left a space for dancing.

ANGEL *(Still dancing)*: All revolutions leave a space for dancing. They just like to pretend they don't.

(Delia stops dancing.)

DELIA *(Defensive)*: I'm not trying to make a revolution. I'm just trying to give women in Harlem the chance to plan their families.

SAM: From what I hear, your Mrs. Sanger said that's where the whole thing begins. Women's bodies out of their control. Sickly kids and sorry men everywhere you look.

(Delia is becoming more agitated. She doesn't know Sam well and she's never sure when he is teasing her.)

And she's right, of course! *(He raises a glass, still teasing)* Here's to victory for your side.

GUY *(Reenters dressed to go out)*: I leave for five minutes and you all are choosing up sides. What did you do, Angel?

ANGEL: Me? I didn't do anything. I sang "St. Louis Blues" for Doc and . . .

GUY: Well, there you go. What did your mama tell you about singing those low-down blues on Sunday morning?

ANGEL *(To Sam)*: I warned you!

GUY: Change your mind and come with us.

ANGEL: Where are you going?

GUY: Probably down to Ike Hines's.

ANGEL: Chinese food?

SAM: I have the feeling Delia's changing her mind about going anywhere with me.

DELIA: It's just not funny to me, that's all. Women are dying . . .

GUY: Don't pay Sam any mind. He can't help it. *(To Angel)* Coming?

ANGEL: It's too early in the day for chop suey.

GUY: Well, try to behave yourself until we get back. Everybody ready?

SAM *(To Delia)*: It's not funny to me either. I apologize. I was just teasing because I didn't know how to tell the two of you how beautiful you looked dancing in the sunlight. It won't happen again.

(Sam extends his arm and after a slight hesitation, Delia takes it.)

GUY: Well, la dee dah! Now can we eat?

DELIA: I'm starving.

(The rest of the conversation takes place as they exit.)

DELIA: Do you want to go by the reading at the "Y" afterward?

GUY: Not unless Langston is going to be there.

SAM: Langston's not back yet, is he?

GUY: There's your answer!

(They exit. Angel watches them go from the window. She walks absentmindedly around the apartment. She looks at the typing chart and open typing book. She holds her

*hands over the chart as if preparing to type, then shud-
ders and moves away. She picks up a fan and fans herself languidly. When she passes the window, she leans
out, still fanning, hoping for something to catch her eye.
Leland enters. He is well dressed in a dark suit, white
shirt and tie. She sees him as he sees her, but she does not
remember him from last night. He looks at her without
embarrassment. She smiles at him, intrigued, fanning
seductively.)*

ANGEL: Hot enough for you?

LELAND: Yes, ma'am.

ANGEL *(Amused by his formality)*: You're not from around
here, huh?

LELAND: I'm from Alabama.

ANGEL: You a long way from home, Alabama.

LELAND: My name is Leland.

ANGEL: First or last?

LELAND: I beg your pardon?

ANGEL: Leland your first name or your last one?

LELAND: First one. Leland Cunningham's my full Christian
name.

ANGEL: And are you a Christian, Mr. Leland Cunningham?

LELAND: I try to be.

ANGEL: Good for you. *(A beat)* I'm Angel. You looking for
somebody, or you just looking.

LELAND: I was looking for you.

ANGEL: I think you've got me confused with somebody else.

LELAND: Last night. *(A beat)* With your . . . friend. He was taking you home and I . . .

ANGEL: You're not my Southern gentleman, are you?

LELAND: I guess I am . . .

ANGEL: Well, thank you for your assistance. *(A beat)* But what
are you doing here today?

LELAND: I just wanted to see if you were feeling all right.

ANGEL: I'm feeling fine. Just fine . . . thanks.
LELAND: Well, good. I just wanted to be sure everything was . . . that you were okay.

(A beat. She watches him, fanning herself slowly.)

ANGEL: So how hot does it get in Alabama?
LELAND: It's pretty near always this hot down there. One way or another.
ANGEL: Well, it's not always this hot in Harlem, but today it is. *(A beat)* Do you know what I mean?
LELAND: I'm not sure that I do.
ANGEL: What I mean is, it's a little too hot today for a lady to take a stroll with a gentleman friend even if the idea presented itself to her.

(He looks at her. A beat. He wants this to be the right answer.)

LELAND: It's supposed to be a lot cooler by the weekend.
ANGEL: You keep up with the weather, do you?
LELAND: I grew up on a farm. Old habits are hard to break.
ANGEL: All right, Alabama, why don't you come by next Sunday evening and we'll take us an old-fashioned Southern stroll.
LELAND: Around seven?
ANGEL: Apartment Two.
LELAND: I won't be late.
ANGEL: I know you won't, Alabama. It's not in your nature.
LELAND: Call me Leland.
ANGEL: Leland.

(He tips his hat and exits. She smiles after him as the lights go to black.)

Scene Three

Wednesday, late afternoon. Delia is unwrapping a box that has arrived in the mail. On top of the tissue paper inside is a note in a small envelope. Delia reads the note, smiles and puts it aside. She folds back the tissue paper and pulls out a dress. It is a bright color and very different from the plain suits Delia usually wears. She looks at it, holds it up against herself and smiles. She even twirls a little, imagining herself in the dress. She lays it carefully aside and returns to the table where she was working earlier. She picks up her pen and begins to work. She stops suddenly, looks up at the dress, smiles again and then focuses completely on her work.

Angel enters downstairs and walks slowly up the stairs. She kicks off her shoes and drops her hat as soon as she enters the apartment door. Guy is not home, and the apartment is empty. She is wearing a fairly dressy suit. She sighs and then begins looking around for something. She looks under cushions, chairs and in drawers. Not finding what she is looking for, she stops in frustration, looks around the room. She thinks hard as she looks at the sewing corner, listens, looks out the window to see who might be coming. Seeing no one, she moves swiftly to the sewing area, opens a drawer; nothing. She listens again. Opens another drawer. Victory! She holds up a bottle of liquor with guilty relief. She grabs a glass, pours a shot and gulps it, eyes closed. She relaxes a little, then pours another drink. Carefully, she puts the bottle back. She sits down and holds the drink close to her. Guy enters downstairs. She hears him on the steps, gulps down her drink and puts the glass under the chair.

Guy enters with several bolts of fabric. He is pleased to see Angel, who stands guiltily, holding her hat.

GUY: Well, hey, Sweetie! *(Kisses her on both cheeks)* Comment ça va? You just walk in the door?

ANGEL: Just this minute. Where've you been?

GUY: Over at the Hole in the Wall measuring these chubby little chorus girls who keep trying to lie about their weight when I'm sitting right there with a tape measure.

ANGEL: Why are you working at that dive? What's Bobby gonna say?

GUY: The money was too good to turn it down. I sound like a whore, don't I?

ANGEL: Not yet.

GUY: Thanks for the vote of confidence. And how was your day?

ANGEL: Terrible, thanks.

GUY: No luck, huh?

ANGEL: There are no singing jobs in Harlem. Period.

GUY: Well, it's not too late to take Deal up on her offer to teach you typing.

ANGEL: That isn't funny. I've been all over Harlem and nobody will even give me the time of day. There aren't any jobs doing anything, especially singing for your supper. Whole families sitting on the sidewalk with their stuff set out beside them. No place to sleep. No place to wash. Walking all day.

GUY: Listen, Sweetie . . . I saw Nick.

ANGEL: You spoke to him?

GUY: He asked me where you were working and I had to confess you were between engagements.

ANGEL: It's all his fault, the sorry bastard.

GUY: He said he felt bad about what had happened and he gave me a number for you to call about an audition. A club downtown.

ANGEL: Really? Which one?

GUY: Here.

(Guy pulls a piece of paper from his pocket and hands it to Angel. She reads it, face falls for a minute, then she regroups and looks on the bright side.)

ANGEL: I know this guy. He's a friend of Nick's. You know Tony T.

GUY: I've seen him around . . .

ANGEL: Why'd you say it like that?

GUY: I just don't think he's looking for a singer.

(A beat. She looks stunned.)

ANGEL: Nick wouldn't do that.

(Guy is silent.)

He said an audition, right?

(A beat.)

GUY: You can't make it real just because you want it to be.

ANGEL: Are you really going to Paris?

GUY: It's not the same thing.

ANGEL: Why isn't it? Because you're some kind of genius with a dream and I'm just a colored woman out of a job?

GUY: Is that your dream? Singing for gangsters? And then what?

ANGEL: Then I'll have to figure out something else. Isn't that what you always tell me? "One step at a time."

GUY: Okay. One step at a time. Audition. Sing your heart out and if he acts a fool, me and Sam will cut his heart out for him.

ANGEL: It's a deal.

GUY: Just don't ask me to make you anything to wear. I don't have time and I can't make time. You're on your own.

ANGEL: You can make twelve outfits for those Hole in the Wall floozies and not one little dress for me?

GUY: They're not floozies and their boss is paying enough to get me halfway to Paris.

ANGEL: How long can it take to run up one little dress?

GUY: Wear your suit. It still looks great on you.

ANGEL: Everybody's already seen it!

GUY: You're not going to let me say no, are you?

ANGEL: Not if I can help it.

GUY: I'll alter the suit . . . slightly! And I'll make you a hat. That's my final offer.

ANGEL: I swear I will never ask you for anything again!

GUY: Let's have a drink before you make any more promises you can't possibly keep.

ANGEL *(Innocently)*: Do we have anything? I thought we drank the last of that.

(He goes to the bottle Angel has recently restashed. He squints at the level of the alcohol.)

GUY: Well, we didn't, but we're working on it. *(He pours two drinks and hands one to Angel)*

ANGEL: You know everywhere I went this week there were twenty people in line ahead of me. I've never seen things this bad all over. Nobody's working and nobody's got prospects.

GUY: For prospects, you gotta look past 125th Street. No law says we gotta live and die in Harlem, USA, just 'cause we happened to wind up here when we finally blew out of Savannah. The world is a big place!

ANGEL: Getting smaller every day.

GUY: No it isn't. I can look out of this very window and see us walking arm in arm down the Champs Élysées.

ANGEL: Remember how you used to take those old broke-up binoculars whenever we'd go to the beach at home? The only Negro in the world ever tried to see Paris from the coast of Georgia.

GUY: I am not! Langston said he used to . . . oh, my God! I almost forgot! He's back!

ANGEL: Langston? Since when?

GUY: Since last Saturday. I ran into Bruce Nugent and he said the group is gathering at his place later for a welcome home. Everybody is going to be there. Want to go preen?

ANGEL: Can I wear your tux?

GUY: I'm wearing my tux! Why don't you go very femme? You'll probably be the only lady at this affair. Show them what they're missing.

ANGEL: I hate being the only girl. You always abandon me the first time some sweet young thing flutters his eyelashes at you, then I'm stuck the rest of the night making small talk with guys who are still pretending not to know why they came there.

GUY: Okay. Let's take Deal.

ANGEL *(Laughing)*: Deal's not ready for one of Bruce's parties and you know it.

GUY: Well, it's time she got ready. Go ask her. We all deserve a night out!

ANGEL: I can return her chart, too, thank God!

GUY: I'm going to take a quick nap since Bruce's parties require one to be both ravishing and alert. Wake me at seven if you don't hear me up, will you? Dinner's at eight.

ANGEL: Dinner? How rich is Bruce's new lover?

GUY: It's just buffet, darling. He may have long money but he's not going to try and feed the entire Negro demimonde!

ANGEL: I'll wake you in plenty of time.

(She crosses the hall to knock at Delia's apartment door. Guy goes into the bedroom for his nap. Delia is working. She answers the door reluctantly.)

Are you busy?

DELIA: Well, I'm working on some stuff for Reverend Powell.

ANGEL: But don't you want to hear the news?

(Delia pauses.)

It's good news.

DELIA: All right.

ANGEL: I'm not going to learn how to type. *(She hands the chart back to Delia)* Want to know why?

DELIA: Why?

ANGEL: I got an audition!

DELIA: That's wonderful! Where?

ANGEL: A place downtown. The owner's a friend of Nick's. He's always wanted me to sing there so I think the audition is pretty much just for show.

DELIA: You should do that song you were singing on Sunday.

ANGEL: Those Italians don't care nothin' about no blues. They like hotsy-totsy girls, grinnin' and shakin' and singin' all at the same damn time. *(A beat)* Can I tell you something?

DELIA: Sure . . .

ANGEL: Guy got fired.

DELIA: How do you know?

ANGEL: I went to the club today to beg Bobby for my job back.

DELIA: What did he say?

ANGEL: They fired him the same night they did me!

DELIA: I mean about your old job.

ANGEL: Not a chance. Of course, he let me beg for a while before he said no. *(A beat)* I couldn't figure out why Guy was taking work from dives like the Hole in the Wall, but he hasn't got any choice.

DELIA: He says it won't be for long. Just until . . .

ANGEL: Don't say it! The myth of the magical Josephine. She practically lives with us but so far I haven't seen her share of the rent money!

DELIA: Guy says he expects to hear from her by the end of the month.

ANGEL: Guy says, Guy says! He's been sending her sketches for a year but have you seen a return cable? A letter? A postcard of the Eiffel Tower? Nothing! Nothing but that damn picture hanging up there grinning at me all day and all night! *(A beat)* Guy's a dreamer. He always was and he always will be, but I'm gonna hitch my star to somebody a little closer to home. *(Suddenly brightens)* I almost forgot the rest of my good news! Langston's back and you have to come with us to the welcome home party!

DELIA: I don't even know Langston Hughes.

ANGEL: Half the people there don't know him either. That's what makes it fun. To see the ones who don't try to pretend to be the ones who do.

DELIA: I can't tonight. Sam's coming over.

ANGEL: Sam's coming here? When?

DELIA: In a little while. Reverend Powell suggested I ask him to help me get ready for the deacons meeting next week. Some of them aren't crazy about the clinic. *(A beat)* I didn't even know Reverend Powell knew Sam.

ANGEL: Everybody knows Sam, this is just his first time calling on you.

DELIA: He's not calling on me. We're working together.

ANGEL: He thinks you're adorable.

DELIA: What are you talking about?

ANGEL: You don't think he was grinning at me dancing in the sunshine, do you?

DELIA: Then why is he always teasing me?

ANGEL: It's just his way. *(Notices the new dress)* Deal . . . you don't have anything I can wear, do you? For the audition? I've worn this to death and I lost all my other stuff at Nicky's.

DELIA: I don't think so. Most of my stuff is . . . plain.

ANGEL: I know!

DELIA: Social workers are supposed to blend in, otherwise we scare people.

ANGEL: Those suits they make you wear are what scare people. I begged Guy to make me something new, but he's
crazy trying to get Josephine's things done and these
new costumes for . . . *(As if she just noticed the dress)*
Deal! What about this? Is it new?

DELIA: My aunt just sent it to me. She doesn't like my suits
much either.

ANGEL: It's beautiful. Do you think it would fit me? I know
we're not exactly the same size, but I think I could . . .
can I try it?

DELIA: Well, I guess so.

(Angel stops suddenly.)

ANGEL: What is wrong with me? This is a brand-new dress,
isn't it? You're probably saving it for something special.

DELIA: An audition is something special, isn't it?

ANGEL: Thanks, Deal. Really. *(She puts on the dress immediately)* Zip me up!

(The dress looks great.)

How do I look?

DELIA: Better than I ever will in it!

ANGEL: It's perfect! I can't lose! I'll be a big star in no time
and we'll both go to Paris and drink champagne and
marry two rich old Frenchmen who will die immediately
and leave us everything!

DELIA: Sounds wonderful, but I've got to get back to work.

(A beat.)

ANGEL: Look at you, Deal. You got bags under your eyes like
an old woman. All tired and frowned up.

DELIA: I do look tired, don't I?

ANGEL: Sit down here for a minute. Can I take your hair aloose?

DELIA: Angel . . .

ANGEL: This will only take a minute, I promise.

(Delia sits, and Angel begins to massage her head expertly. As Angel talks, we see Delia's body relax.)

A New Orleans Voodoo woman showed me how to do this when I was a little girl back in Savannah.

DELIA: What was she doing in Savannah?

ANGEL: The Voodoo woman? What does anybody do anywhere? How does that feel?

DELIA: Wonderful.

ANGEL: You have to use your whole hand. All the fingers at the same time, but not too hard. Just enough.

DELIA *(Her eyes closed)*: It feels like everything is just . . . floating away.

ANGEL *(Massaging Delia's head expertly and gently as she speaks)*: When I was working at Miss Lillie's, as many of those old men would pay me for this as would pay me for the other.

DELIA: I don't know how you can talk about it like that.

ANGEL: Talk about what like that?

DELIA: About what happened to you.

ANGEL: It was better than living on the street.

(Delia doesn't respond.)

Look, I'm none the worse for wear and a whole lot smarter than most women will ever be. There's nothing a man can do to surprise me. *(A beat)* At least I didn't have to wear old lady suits to work.

(Delia laughs in spite of herself.)

DELIA: Aren't there any colored gangsters you could fall in love with?

ANGEL: They're married, too, just like the Italians.

(Sam enters and comes upstairs.)

DELIA: That feels wonderful.

ANGEL: See? Those old guys still got their money's worth.

SAM *(Standing at the open door)*: And that's important to us old guys!

ANGEL: Hey, Doc!

DELIA: Oh! You startled me!

SAM: I'm sorry. I thought we were going to work on your speech.

DELIA: Yes, yes! Of course we are. *(She reties her hair back from her face)*

SAM *(To Angel)*: Can you do me?

ANGEL: Sorry. For ladies only. I'll leave you two to your hard work since I can't talk you into coming out to celebrate with us.

SAM: Too bad. What are we not celebrating?

ANGEL: I've got an audition downtown, and Langston's back!

SAM: It's about time. I thought that Negro had put us down for good.

ANGEL: Welcome back party tonight at Bruce's. Guy's across the hall getting his beauty winks right now.

SAM: He'll have to go aways to outshine you in that dress. It looks like it was made for you.

ANGEL: It's Deal's!

SAM *(Surprised)*: Really?

ANGEL: Turn your back, Doc, so I can return this dress and leave you two in peace.

DELIA *(Quickly)*: Keep it. You can give it back after your audition.

ANGEL: I'll take good care of it. I promise.

DELIA: I believe you.

ANGEL: And don't pay me any attention, Doc. We promise to have a terrible time without you and, knowing Langston, he probably won't do anything but sit on the fire escape and laugh at everybody.

SAM: Tell him to laugh loud enough for me, will you?

(Angel exits to her apartment. She goes into the bedroom to wake Guy.)

SAM: That's a very beautiful dress.

DELIA: It was a gift. I don't know what my aunt was thinking.

(A beat. Sam smiles, but remains at the door.)

If you want to go out, it's all right. I don't want you to feel obligated.

SAM: I'm glad to have a chance to help. May I come in?

DELIA: Of course. I'm sorry. Please . . . come in.

(She starts to close the door, then leaves it partially open. Sam observes this.)

SAM: If Reverend Powell hadn't told you to ask me, I'd have been forced to volunteer.

DELIA: Why didn't you?

SAM: I thought you might be suspicious of my motives. A middle-aged man with a bad reputation offering to help a beautiful young woman?

DELIA: Do you have a bad reputation?

SAM *(Smiling)*: In some quarters.

DELIA: Yes . . . well. Let me take your hat. Sit down.

SAM: Thank you.

DELIA: Why don't I tell you about our planning so far and then you can read what I've been working on?

SAM: I'm all ears. *(He suddenly yawns widely)* Please excuse me. I've been working double shifts this week. We're still shorthanded.

DELIA: Would you like some coffee?

SAM: Thanks. Maybe that'll wake me up.

(As the following scene progresses, Delia shows Sam some papers, pointing out things to him. She finally hands him a sheaf of pages and as he reads, she stands up to make coffee. She is trying to give him time to read. We see his head jerk several times. He is trying not to fall asleep. He finally loses the battle, his chin sinks to his chest over the pages in his hand and he sleeps.

Across the hall, Angel comes out of the bedroom. She is carrying shoes and a shawl. When she comes out, she puts these down and finds the other things she wants among her scattered belongings: several pairs of earrings, other jewelry to try and another pair of shoes. She still has on Delia's dress, but during this scene, she accessorizes it into something so glamorous, it is barely recognizable. Guy comes out of the bedroom wearing a beautiful, perfectly cut tuxedo and a formal white shirt. He goes to the mirror and fiddles with his tie. Angel stands at the mirror too, putting on her makeup.)

ANGEL: Let me do it.

GUY: Don't get lipstick on my collar!

ANGEL: Hold still. *(She fixes it expertly)* Voilà!

(He slips on his jacket.)

GUY: How do I look?

ANGEL: You look positively Parisian!

GUY: Merci, mademoiselle. I'm sorry Deal's not coming, but that dress is perfect for you. I can't believe she let you walk out the door in it.

ANGEL: Sam said it looked like it was made for me.

GUY: That's your special talent. Everybody's clothes look better on you.

ANGEL: I should wear this on Sunday.

GUY: And where are we going on Sunday?

ANGEL: I'm going for a stroll with my mystery man.

GUY: What mystery man?

ANGEL: The guy who walked home with us the other night.

GUY: You saw him again?

ANGEL: He came by Sunday after you all went to Ike Hines's. His name is Leland Cunningham. From Alabama.

GUY: What did he want?

ANGEL: He wanted to make sure I was okay. A real gentleman.

GUY: Which is exactly why you need to leave the boy alone.

ANGEL: He's a grown man. And a good-looking one too.

GUY: All right, "He's a grown man." Remember that when he's howling outside the window after you get tired of that down-home charm.

ANGEL: I thought you wanted me to stop hanging around with gangsters.

GUY: I do.

ANGEL: Well, he's definitely not a gangster and we're only going for a walk, if it's okay with you.

GUY: No skin off my nose. I'd have winked at him myself if I thought he was open to persuasion.

ANGEL: Not a chance!

GUY: By the way, who did you tell your country boy I was?

ANGEL: My baby sister.

(They exit to the hallway. Delia's door is still partially open.)

GUY *(Whispering)*: Should we let them see how beautiful we are?

ANGEL *(Also whispering, but suggestively)*: They're working. *(She takes his arm and smiles)* We are beautiful, aren't we?

GUY: We are très élégant.

(They exit together. Lights back up on Delia, finishing her tea. Sam's back is to her. She looks at him expectantly.)

DELIA: Well, what do you think?

(Sam makes no response, and she gets up to walk around to his front. She sees that he is asleep. She is taken aback. At first she is offended, then she is curious, then sympathetic. She sits down across from him and shakes his hand gently. He wakes with a start and blinks guiltily at Delia.)

SAM: Was I sleeping?

(Delia nods.)

How long?

DELIA: Long enough. *(She takes the pages from where he has dropped them)* Pretty bad, huh?

SAM: No, no! It's my fault. I haven't had much sleep lately.

DELIA: Maybe you should cut back on your nightlife.

SAM: That's the one thing I should not do.

DELIA: And why is that?

SAM: Because it helps me remember that we're not just a bunch of premature labors and gunshot wounds. In a choice between a couple of hours sleep and a couple of hours of Fats Waller, I'd have to let the good times roll!

DELIA: Don't you ever stop teasing?

SAM: I don't want to work so hard on the body I forget about the soul. *(A beat)* Besides, I've already cut back on my nightlife. My longtime partners in crime are out right now terrorizing our mutual friends and I'm here with you, working tirelessly to save the race!

DELIA: Maybe not so tirelessly . . .

SAM: The clinic is a great idea. Your speech is fine and if the good Reverend Powell endorses it, the deacon board probably will too, but . . .

DELIA: But what?

SAM *(Gently)*: I deliver babies everyday to exhausted women and stone-broke men, but they never ask me about birth control. They ask me about jobs.

DELIA: What does that mean?

SAM: It means we still see our best hope in the faces of our children and it's going to take more than some rich white women playing missionary in Harlem to convince these Negroes otherwise.

DELIA *(Angrily)*: Why can't we take help wherever we can find it?

SAM: Because it's more complicated than that. The Garveyites are already charging genocide and the clinic isn't even open yet.

DELIA: Genocide?

SAM: And they're not the only ones who feel that way. What does family planning mean to the average colored man? White women teaching colored women how to stop having children.

DELIA: A woman shouldn't have to make a baby every time she makes love!

(A beat.)

SAM: Is that what you're going to tell those deacons at Abyssinian?

(She realizes he has been preparing her for the possibility of these hostile questions from the deacon board. She calms down and answers carefully.)

DELIA: No. I'm going to ask them for their help in building strong families with healthy mothers, happy children and loving fathers all over Harlem. Is that better?

SAM *(Smiling)*: Much better. That's the only approach they can buy. I don't think pleasure is the guiding principle at Abyssinian yet, despite the pastor's best efforts in that direction.

DELIA: Reverend Powell thinks very highly of you. Everyone does.

SAM: Do you?

DELIA: We all do. The work you've done at the hospital . . . in the community. People are always very impressed that I've met you . . .

SAM *(Embarrassed)*: That sounds so respectable, I'm about to make myself sick.

DELIA: You're teasing me again.

SAM: I apologize. It's late. I'd better go.

DELIA: Thank you for your help.

SAM: Now you're teasing me.

DELIA: No. I mean it.

SAM: Did I say something helpful in between resting my eyes?

DELIA: Yes, you did.

SAM: Maybe I was talking in my sleep.

DELIA: Maybe you should try it more often.

SAM: But who'll be there to remember what I say?

DELIA: Good night.

SAM: Good night.

(He exits. Delia gathers her papers thoughtfully and gets ready for bed as the lights fade to black.)

Scene Four

Sunday evening. Guy is sewing on the couch. Angel enters from the street. She is moving quickly, kicking off her shoes, looking for accessories, changing into Delia's dress again.

GUY: Where have you been? I thought I was going to have to entertain your beau all by myself.

ANGEL: This is the only day the guys could get together to rehearse for the audition.

GUY: How'd it go?

ANGEL: Great! They sounded so good they make me think I can really sing! *(She puts on some very delicate high heels)* I thought you were going to the theatre with Deal.

GUY: We're probably going to miss it, thank God! I do not think my nerves are strong enough for an evening with the literati. Everybody is sure to be abuzz with the news.

ANGEL: What news?

GUY: Bruce and some stallion were holding hands on the street the other night and a group of those young hoodlums knocked the wind out of them for their trouble.

ANGEL: Where were they?

GUY: Right around the corner.

ANGEL: Are they all right?

GUY: Mother and baby both doing fine. Bruce was barefoot, as usual, and they kept trying to stomp on his feet, but he was too quick.

ANGEL: I'm telling you, this Depression is making people mean.

GUY: People been mean. Bruce needs to get himself a straight razor . . . I thought you two were going for a walk.

ANGEL: We are.

GUY: You're not going very far in those shoes.

ANGEL: Far enough. Where's Deal?

GUY: They changed the deacon's meeting at the last minute. She had to give her speech tonight.

ANGEL: Tonight? Was she ready?

GUY: She was nervous as a cat. Sam went along for moral support.

ANGEL: Good old Sam! *(She holds up two different pairs of earrings)* These or these?

GUY: Those.

ANGEL: Do you think so? I thought these might be better with it.

GUY *(Exasperated)*: Why not wear one of each? What is wrong with you tonight?

ANGEL: The terrible truth is, I don't remember quite what to do when a gentleman comes to call.

GUY: Open the door, extend your hand and drag him in.

(She leans to look critically at her face in the mirror. She touches the area around her eyes and at the corners of her mouth and neck.)

ANGEL: How old do you think he is?

GUY: Younger than you'd like him to be. Stop worrying. You look beautiful.

ANGEL: The whole time I was going around with Nicky, the whole time I was singing at the Club, I kept thinking something wonderful was going to happen, but it never did. In my mind, I could see myself doing all these things with Nick—riding around in fancy cars, wearing furs, him giving me diamonds. I even saw us getting married. But mostly all we did was go to his place after I'd do the last show. Half the time, his friends would come with us and they'd all sit around drinking and playing cards like I wasn't even there. Then when I'd ask him to take me home, he'd tell me he wanted me to stay around to bring him luck. I remember wishing I could bring myself some luck once in a while. *(A beat)* This guy feels like luck to me. I don't know why, but he does. That's not so bad, is it?

GUY: Just remember, Sweetie, Alabama isn't just a state. It's a state of mind.

(Sam and Delia enter the building talking excitedly.)

SAM *(Laughing)*: I thought Deacon Johnson was never going to come around.

DELIA: Until he remembered you delivered all his grandchildren.

GUY: Brace yourself. Here come the rebels.

DELIA *(Bursting in, excited)*: Sam was wonderful. He convinced everybody . . .

SAM *(With exaggerated courtliness)*: . . . who hadn't been convinced already by the brilliance of your speech.

DELIA: Tease me as much as you want. We're going to have the best clinic in New York City right up on 126th Street!

SAM: My practice doesn't stand a chance.

GUY: I take it this means you birth control fanatics will now be free to roam around Harlem at will?

DELIA: Not only that. They're going to list the clinic name, address and services in the church bulletin and I've got an interview with the *Amsterdam News*.

GUY: All that in one night? I am impressed!

SAM: She was amazing. I stayed awake the whole time.

ANGEL: High praise from a man who can sleep anywhere.

SAM: I rose to the occasion.

ANGEL: I'll bet you did!

DELIA: Do you deliver every grandbaby born in Harlem?

SAM: I do my best.

ANGEL: Looks like you owe Doc one, Deal.

DELIA *(Flustered)*: One what?

GUY: One evening out for dinner with a few of his closest friends.

DELIA: That sounds good to me.

SAM: Me, too, but don't you have tickets to the opening at the Lafayette?

DELIA: I had forgotten all about it!

GUY: Thanks a lot, Doc!

DELIA *(To Sam)*: Can you come with us? I'm sure they have tickets left.

GUY: Doc has never stayed awake through a theatrical performance in his life.

SAM: I took a nap this afternoon. I'm good until midnight.

GUY: Well, I stand corrected . . .

DELIA: Want to come, Angel?

GUY: She can't! She has a gentleman caller arriving momentarily.

DELIA: Really? Who?

ANGEL: His name is Leland Cunningham.

GUY: And he's the prettiest young country thing for miles.

SAM: Is this an official date or just a friendly visit?

ANGEL: We're just going for a walk.

SAM: A Sunday stroll? Angel, this is a new you.

GUY: That's what I told her.

SAM: I can't wait to meet him.

GUY: No time like the present. We've got a minute, don't we, Deal?

(Delia looks at her watch nervously.)

Of course, we do. He won't be late. No gentleman caller worth the name comes late for a Sunday stroll.

ANGEL: Well, sit down then so you all won't scare him to death the minute he walks in.

GUY: Perfect! We can be casually engaged in pleasant conversation.

(A beat. No one can think of a neutral topic.)

Okay. I'll start. *(To Angel, with exaggerated interest)* Wherever did you get that beautiful dress?

ANGEL: Go to hell!

DELIA: What did you decide to do for your audition?

ANGEL: Thank you! I took your advice. I'm singing blues.

DELIA: I thought you said Italians don't like blues.

ANGEL: They don't have to like blues. They just have to like me. Plus, I'm singing it real fast, almost double-time.

(She snaps her fingers and begins to sing while she talks, performing for them. Leland enters downstairs and comes up to the door. He checks the number, but before he knocks he listens to her singing.)

And I've got on Deal's beautiful dress, again, and a hat specifically designed for me by none other than Monsieur Guy de Paree and I'm dancing just a little and singing the best I've sung in years and everything is right on time!

(She completes the song with a flourish. They applaud as Leland knocks on the door.)

What did I tell you?

(Angel goes to the door. Leland immediately removes his hat. He is wearing a dark suit, a white shirt and a tie.)

Hello, Alabama.

LELAND: Good evening.

ANGEL: Come on in and say hello. *(She draws him in)* You met Guy.

GUY: Thanks again for your help the other night.

LELAND: My pleasure.

ANGEL: This is Delia. She lives across the hall. This is her dress.

LELAND: It's beautiful.

DELIA: Thank you.

ANGEL: And this is Sam, but we call him Doc.

LELAND: Are you really a doctor?

SAM: Harlem Hospital. Fifteen years Christmas.

LELAND: It's an honor. I've never met a Negro doctor before.

GUY: Well, stick around. Who knows what else new you might find!

SAM: Where in Alabama are you from?

LELAND: Tuskegee.

SAM: Home of the world-famous Institute.

LELAND *(Pleased)*: You're familiar with Dr. Washington's work?

SAM: I'm an admirer.

DELIA: I hate to rush everybody, but we're trying to make an eight o'clock curtain.

GUY: The literati wait for no man!

SAM: Good to meet you, Leland.

LELAND: Same here.

GUY: Bye, Sweetie!

(Sam, Delia and Guy exit.)

LELAND: I didn't know you were a singer.

ANGEL: You heard me?

LELAND: Through the door.

ANGEL: What did you think I was?

LELAND: Nothing. I mean, I didn't think about you working.

ANGEL: What did you think about me doing?

(He doesn't answer, and she laughs at his discomfort.)

Do I make you nervous, Alabama?

LELAND: I knew somebody . . . *(A beat)* You look a lot like somebody I used to know back home. I keep expecting her voice to come out of your mouth.

ANGEL: Was she your sweetheart?

LELAND: She was my wife. She died eight months ago giving birth to our son. She was always frail, but she said the Lord said be fruitful and multiply and that's what she intended to do. I lost them both.

ANGEL: How long were you married?

LELAND: Two years last May. We grew up together. I knew her all my life.

ANGEL: That's a long time to know somebody and not get tired of them.

LELAND: I couldn't get tired of Anna. It'd be like getting tired of your arms. *(A beat)* When I passed you and your friend on the street that night, I thought you were a ghost.

ANGEL: Did I look that bad?

LELAND: You looked beautiful. I thought my Anna had come back to me. You've got her eyes, her mouth, her smile . . .

ANGEL *(Interrupting him)*: Listen, Alabama, I may look like her, but I'm not her. Don't let's get things confused.

LELAND: I'm not confused. *(A beat)* I'm real glad to be right here.

ANGEL *(Softening)*: I didn't mean to snap at you. It's just hard enough to find a gentleman you want to spend some time with and if he's already got another woman's face in his mind, well . . . *(She shrugs)* It's still a little hot for a stroll, I think. Would you like to sit here in the window and see if we can catch a breeze?

(She gets her fan and, he pulls up two chairs.)

LELAND: Are these all right?

ANGEL: Fine.

(They sit. As the scene progresses, darkness falls.)

I feel like I've been asking all the questions. Now you ask me something.

LELAND: What do you want me to ask?

ANGEL: What do you want to know?

LELAND: Is that really your name?

ANGEL: Yes. My turn again. What are you doing in Harlem?

LELAND: I'm visiting.

ANGEL: Visiting who?

LELAND: Isn't it my turn?

ANGEL: Sorry. Go ahead.

LELAND: Do you ever sing church music?

ANGEL: No. Visiting who?

LELAND: A cousin.

ANGEL: You're not a big talker, huh?

LELAND: I wanted to get out of Tuskegee for a while. Everybody kept asking me if I was okay about Anna and my boy. How could I be okay about it? I missed her all the time. I started feeling like if I turned around real fast, she'd be standing there, looking at me . . . laughing the way she used to . . . I have a third cousin on my mother's side living up here. He needed some work done on an old brownstone he got cheap.

ANGEL: Your cousin bought a brownstone?

LELAND: I sent him a letter and he sent me a train ticket.

ANGEL: One-way or round-trip?

LELAND: I haven't decided yet.

ANGEL: Your turn.

LELAND: Do you have a church home?

ANGEL: A what?

LELAND: A church home. I still haven't found anyplace up here to . . .

ANGEL: Try Abyssinian.

LELAND: Is that where you . . .

ANGEL: I don't go to church.

LELAND: I've already been there.

ANGEL: Didn't you like it?

LELAND: It didn't feel like church to me. The pastor was talking more about this world then he was the next one.

ANGEL: What should he be talking about?

LELAND *(Hesitates, then speaks urgently)*: About sin and salvation. About the presence of hellfire. Reverend Horace, my pastor back home, says . . .

ANGEL *(Quickly)*: Hold on, Alabama.

(Leland stops abruptly.)

Church is over for the day, okay?

LELAND: I'm sorry.

ANGEL: Your turn again.

LELAND: I don't know what to ask you.

ANGEL: Ask me what's the worst thing that just happened to me and what's the best one.

LELAND: I can't think about anything bad happening to you.

ANGEL: Twice! Two bad things. Right together. Bam! Bam! Just like that.

LELAND: What were they?

ANGEL: I'm out of a job and I lost all my clothes.

LELAND: Lost your clothes?

ANGEL: Every stitch, except Deal's dress, which doesn't really count, and a few odds and ends I got from Guy.

LELAND: Was there a fire?

ANGEL: Sort of . . . but the good news is . . .

(She waits for him to ask. He's confused and silent. She prompts him.)

"The good news is . . . "

LELAND: What's the good news?

ANGEL: I've got an audition on Friday and the job is as good as mine!

LELAND: Where do you sing?

ANGEL: In nightclubs. You've been in a juke joint, right?

LELAND: I've seen a couple back home . . .

ANGEL: Places like that, but with a little more class.

LELAND: Maybe I could come and watch you sometime. Listen to you sing.

ANGEL: It's not going to be church music.

LELAND: Then I won't come on Sunday.

ANGEL: What do you want from me, Alabama?

LELAND: I want to make you laugh.

ANGEL: You talk real pretty for a country boy.

LELAND: The other night, that first night, when you went inside, you dropped this.

(He reaches into his pocket and hands her the scarf. She searches his face for a long moment. She raises the scarf to her face, smelling it gently.)

ANGEL: It smells like you.

(She drapes the scarf around his neck. Straddling his leg, she lowers herself onto his lap slowly as she speaks softly.)

Did you take it to bed with you? Did it make you think about me? Was I laughing in your dreams, Alabama?

(She kisses him as the lights go to black.)

Scene Five

Friday evening. Delia is standing on a small stool, swathed in a brightly colored piece of silk. The fabric has been draped and wrapped around her by Guy who is pinning it this way and that distractedly while he talks. Delia stands with her arms held out stiffly at her sides. There is a transatlantic cable propped underneath the picture of Josephine in the place of honor.

GUY: I knew they'd love my sketches! Now all I have to do is send Josephine three or four finished pieces so they can actually see them on her and . . . look up, Sweetie!

DELIA: I thought you invited me over here to celebrate.

GUY: I know, I know! But I just had a brilliant idea and I don't want to lose it. Hold still a minute.

(Delia moves her arm and sticks herself.)

DELIA: Ow!

GUY *(Laughing)*: Your fault!

DELIA: I'll bet you don't stick Angel like that.

GUY: That's because she doesn't squirm, unlike some people who can take the most beautiful fabric in New York City and reduce it to sackcloth over a pinprick or two. *(He lifts the fabric off Delia)* You may step down.

DELIA: Thank you!

GUY *(Picking up the cable reverently)*: This is what we've been waiting for, Deal, and it's going to make me crazy until I can tell her everything!

DELIA: Maybe the audition went so well, they asked her to stay and do a show.

GUY: Maybe . . . *(He knows this isn't what happened. He looks at the cable)* Well, hell! Let's pop the cork on this champagne anyway! She can catch up when she gets here. *(He pours two glasses, but his mind is still on Angel)* We've slowed down now, but me and Miss Angel used to terrorize these streets. When we first got to Harlem, we specialized in gowns for discriminating gentlemen. Don't look so shocked, Deal. You don't think these six-foot queens buy off the rack, do you?

DELIA: I never thought about it.

GUY: Well, I did. The first time I went to the Hamilton Lodge Drag Ball, I knew I was looking at a gold mine. Once they saw Angel in my special creations, I couldn't work fast enough to fill the orders we were getting . . . Once I made us matching tuxedos. I even painted a little mustache on her.

DELIA: I would have paid to see that.

GUY: I never could make her really look like a man, though. Probably a good thing, too. As it was, she made half the queens who saw her second-guess their stated sexual preference.

DELIA: Did you ever think you and Angel could be . . . you know . . .

GUY *(Gently)*: I like boys, Deal. Remember?

DELIA: Do you think it's because of your grandmother?

GUY: My grandmother wasn't particularly fond of boys, as I recall.

DELIA: I mean being raised by your grandmother. Being so close to her and all . . .

GUY: Maybe I'm just lucky.

(Delia yawns widely.)

GUY: You keeping Doc's late hours?

DELIA: We're trying to get the clinic open next week and now the landlord says he wants to cancel the lease.

GUY: Why?

DELIA: He got some phone calls, unsigned letters. Now he thinks we're a bunch of free-loving suffragettes out to destroy the Negro race.

GUY *(Lightly; he doesn't want to get too serious)*: Too late! Mission already accomplished.

(Delia yawns again.)

DELIA: I'm sorry!

GUY: Don't be sorry. Go get some sleep. We'll continue our celebration later.

DELIA: Goodnight, and congratulations.

GUY: Merci, ma chérie. Bon nuit.

DELIA: Bon nuit.

(Delia exits to her apartment, closes the door, yawns again, kicks off her shoes and exits to her bedroom. Guy pours himself another glass of champagne, goes to the portrait of Josephine Baker and raises the glass in a toast. He drinks slowly and with great peace and satisfaction. Leland enters, climbs the stairs and knocks at the door. He is carrying a dress box. Guy answers.)

GUY: Well, good afternoon. Evening, I guess it is.

LELAND: Good evening. Is Angel here?

GUY: She's not back from the audition yet. You're welcome to come in and wait for her.

LELAND: I can just wait out front.

GUY: Don't be silly. Come on in.

LELAND: Thanks. It is pretty warm out there.

GUY: Want a drink?

LELAND: Is that liquor?

GUY: Champagne.

LELAND: It's still prohibition, isn't it?

GUY: Not in Harlem it isn't, but don't let me corrupt you. *(He puts on his shirt and tie as they talk)* You and Angel doing something special tonight?

LELAND: I'm going to help her celebrate her new singing job.

GUY: Be sure you let her tell you how it went before you pop the cork on that champagne, or whatever it is you do.

LELAND: What do you mean by that?

GUY: I mean it's a rough business. Things don't always go the way you plan them.

LELAND: Thanks. I'll remember that. *(Looking around)* You a working man?

GUY: Aren't we all?

LELAND: Not these days. We're two of the lucky ones, I guess. What do you do?

GUY: Costumes.

LELAND: Like for Halloween?

GUY: No. Nightclubs. Cabarets.

LELAND: People pay you to do that?

GUY: I scrape by. And what do you do?

LELAND: I'm a carpenter.

GUY: Just like Jesus.

LELAND: I didn't mean to offend you. I don't know very much about show business.

GUY: And I hope you never do.

LELAND: That depends on Angel.

GUY: Then you're home free.

LELAND: Angel told me what happened with her clothes burning up in the fire and all.

GUY: The fire?

LELAND: At her old place?

GUY: Oh, right. That fire.

LELAND: I know how important clothes are to a woman, so I . . . *(He holds up the box awkwardly)* I bought her something.

GUY: Something to wear?

LELAND: It's a dress, and since she's your cousin and you know her a lot better than I do, I thought maybe you could tell me if you think she'll like it.

GUY: Okay. Let's have a look.

(Guy carefully opens the box, folds back the tissue paper and pulls out a long, shapeless navy blue dress with a prim white collar and cuffs. A heart-shaped card falls out. Leland picks the card up quickly before Guy can look at it. Guy looks at Leland's hopeful face and speaks gently.)

I think she'll love it.

LELAND: You're not just shining me on, are you?

GUY: I think what she'll like most is that you were thinking about her. Angel likes to know she's on your mind. *(He folds the dress carefully and puts it away)*

LELAND *(Laughing nervously)*: Well, no problem there.

GUY: Listen. I just got some good news from Paris and I'm going out to spread joy. You're welcome to stay here and wait for Angel as long as you like. Just do me one favor.

LELAND: If I can.

GUY *(Amused)*: A healthy suspicion of open-ended questions. I like that in a man.

LELAND *(Confused)*: Look, I don't think you . . .

GUY: I don't think anything about anything. As far as I can see, all's right with the world. My dreams are about to come true! Just tell Angel to read that cable, will you? Tell her I tried to wait for her, but I had to answer the call of the wild.

LELAND: I'll tell her.

GUY: No offense. *(He extends a hand)*

LELAND: None taken.

(They shake hands. Guy exits. Leland walks around looking at everything, touching nothing. He looks out the window. No Angel. He seats himself to wait. Angel enters, walking rapidly. She strides into the house angrily. Leland stands quickly, but she doesn't see him. She grabs the champagne bottle, takes a big gulp, rinses her mouth and spits it into the wastebasket. She tosses the bottle in the same basket and rubs her mouth vigorously with the back of her hand.)

Angel?

(She is completely startled.)

ANGEL: Are you spying on me?

LELAND: No, we've having dinner, remember?

ANGEL: How did you get in?

LELAND: Guy was here. He told me to tell you . . . to give you this. *(He hands her the cable)*

ANGEL: From Josephine? *(She grabs it and reads quickly. When she is finished, she speaks sarcastically)* She says she just loves everything, of course. She can't really commit to a job or anything, of course, but if he can just send three or four finished pieces, she's almost certain they might be able to at least think about giving him a try. *(She crumples the cable and tosses it down)*

LELAND: He said it was a dream come true . . .

ANGEL: I'm tired of Negro dreams. All they ever do is break your heart.

LELAND *(Very gently)*: Didn't you sing well?

ANGEL: I never sang at all. Not a note. It wasn't necessary. The job he had open was mine when I hit the front door.

LELAND: I don't understand.

ANGEL: It doesn't matter.

LELAND: Yes, it does. Tell me.

ANGEL: Tony T. called the guys and told them the audition was canceled so when I got there, the place was empty. It was just me and him. So he says they must be caught in traffic or something and he offers me a drink while we're waiting and right then, just that quick, I felt it.

LELAND: Felt what?

ANGEL: The truth of it. Me trying to play headliner. Guy trying to play Paris. The whole truth of it. Tony kept saying he could look out for me. Offer me some protection in these hard times. *(A beat)* He didn't want a singer any more than you do. He wanted to keep a colored woman stashed up in Harlem so he could come by every now and then and rub her head for luck.

LELAND: That son of a . . . *(He reaches for her protectively)*

ANGEL: Don't!

LELAND: No Negro woman should have to . . .

ANGEL: No Negro woman should have to anything, and so
what? Do you even understand what I'm talking about?
When I was sitting there at Tony's this afternoon, I saw
him looking like he could see right through my clothes,
and I knew he had talked to Nick about me. I didn't
have to imagine what they said. I've heard them talk
about women. I know what they say. But I wouldn't let
myself think about that. I pushed it right on out of my
mind because I know how to take care of myself! I'm not
going to be a broke old woman, begging up and down
125th Street, dreaming about fine clothes and French
champagne. So, I drank with him and listened to him
telling me how long he'd been wanting to get to know
me better and I watched him put his hand on my knee
like I wouldn't notice and I pretended not to. And I
laughed and laughed just to keep up some noise in that
room. It was so quiet . . . Then I stood up to pour another drink and I saw myself in the mirror . . . and I thought
what is that poor, crazy colored woman laughing about?
(A beat) When I turned around, there was Tony, waiting
for his answer, so I gave it to him . . .

LELAND: You never have to see him again.

(A beat.)

ANGEL: We had a good time the other night, Alabama. But the
party's over. Go home.

LELAND: I love you.

ANGEL: I don't love you.

LELAND: But you will. You had a run of bad luck, but it's over
now. I'm going to take care of you.

ANGEL: Why? So you can call me by some other woman's
name?

(A beat.)

LELAND: I know you're not my Anna. I know that! But I still have all the love she gave me. And if I can't shape it new to protect and cherish and keep you, if I can't save you any more then I could save her, then that love isn't worth a damn thing.

ANGEL: All I can do for you is drive you crazy.

LELAND: You can't drive me anyplace I don't want to go.

ANGEL *(Suddenly overwhelmed)*: I'm tired.

LELAND *(Picking up his hat)*: Should I come tomorrow?

ANGEL: Yes.

LELAND: Good night, then.

(A beat.)

ANGEL: Good night. *(As he starts out the door, she calls out to him)* Leland?

(He turns to her. She tries to smile.)

You gonna be my lucky charm?

LELAND: I'm gonna be your man.

(He turns and exits downstairs. She closes the door and leans against it wearily. She sees the dress box, opens it, picks up the card and reads it, folds back the tissue paper and looks at the dress. She sees how horrible it looks, sighs in resignation, withdraws it from the box slowly and holds it up against her body as the lights go to black.)

Act Two

Scene One

Two weeks later. It is early Sunday afternoon. Things are arranged for a "high tea" to celebrate Guy's readiness to mail his costumes to Paris. There are flowers, china plates and cups arranged on a silver tray. Guy's package of costumes, wrapped for mailing, is sitting under the photo of Josephine as if waiting for a blessing. Angel is putting out spoons and napkins. She is wearing the dress Leland gave her, but she has improved upon it slightly with a belt or other visible adjustments. Guy enters downstairs. He is wearing tuxedo pants, a formal shirt with an ascot and a silk smoking jacket. He is disheveled. He is carrying a small bag from the grocery store. He bursts into the apartment angrily. He puts down the bag and goes to the mirror to check himself for damages.

ANGEL: What happened to you?

GUY: Young hoodlums down the street trying to prove their manhood.

ANGEL: Are you all right? You're bleeding!

GUY: Where? *(He checks himself, then grins)* No, I'm not. But somebody is! Damn! This shirt is brand-new! *(He makes sure the jacket covers the small stain, reties his ascot and smoking jacket sash as they talk)*

ANGEL *(Relieved)*: You scared me to death!

GUY: Relax, Sweetie! If you ever see me in a fight with a bear, you help the bear.

ANGEL: I can't believe these Negroes are out robbing people on Sunday morning.

GUY: They weren't robbing me. They didn't like the way I was dressed. I was a little too continental for their uncouth asses.

ANGEL: Did you recognize any of them?

GUY: What difference does it make? They are a temporary inconvenience. In Paris, a well-turned gentleman does not have to be subjected to the barbarism of street thugs! *(He finishes his neatening up)* Good as new! And, I didn't drop the sugar! *(He takes it out of the bag and fills the china sugar bowl)*

ANGEL: I wish you'd be more careful.

GUY: Walking up to the corner in broad daylight?

ANGEL: Leland knows some of these guys and he said . . .

GUY: What guys?

ANGEL: Like the ones who . . . stopped you at the store.

GUY: They didn't stop me. They offered to kick my ass.

ANGEL: You know they'll spot you dressed like that!

GUY: Spot me? I'm not hiding! Look, I'm leaving this place as fast as I can, but until I do? I plan to walk where I please, wearing what I please, whenever I please. What's Leland doing hanging around with those hoodlums anyway?

ANGEL: He just met some of them at a prayer meeting or something . . .

GUY: Nothing like a God-fearing man.

ANGEL: I don't know what I'd do if something happened to you.

GUY: Likewise, I'm sure.

(A beat.)

ANGEL: I talked to Bobby last week.

GUY: Lucky you.

ANGEL: When were you going to tell me they fired you?

GUY: As the ship pulled away from the dock and not a minute before.

ANGEL: Don't you think I have a right to know?

GUY: Why? So you can worry yourself to death and drive me crazy?

ANGEL: I'm serious!

GUY: I'm serious too! I've been working like a young slave to get this stuff ready for Josephine. I'm sewing for whatever clubs are left in Harlem and I got two weddings coming up if all else fails. We'll make it, Angel. I promise.

ANGEL: You're a hell of a provider, Big Daddy.

GUY: You wouldn't dismiss it all so fast if I was a straight man offering to take you to Paris.

ANGEL: But you're not that, are you?

(Sam and Delia arrive.)

GUY: Bonjour! Bonjour! Comment ça va? Comment ça va? *(He kisses Delia on both cheeks)*

DELIA: Everything looks beautiful.

SAM: I've never been invited to high tea before. I didn't know Negroes were allowed to partake.

GUY: I won't tell if you don't tell.

SAM: So when is the great international launch actually taking place?

GUY: I'm going to put this package containing five—count 'em!—five, brand-new, breathtaking, Guy de Paree originals on a freighter tomorrow morning at ten o'clock, then hold my breath for three weeks!

DELIA: Tell him about Langston's friend.

GUY: Langston knows a Negro in Paris who has a lover at the French Embassy. He'll come to pick it up so it won't get held up in customs.

DELIA: Langston had to promise him that he could personally deliver the package to Josephine.

SAM: He'll probably arrive in top hat and tails.

GUY: All of Josephine's admirers arrive in top hat and tails!

SAM: Why so quiet, Angel Eyes? Cat got your tongue?

ANGEL: I hate that expression.

GUY: Angel and I have been fighting about my effectiveness as a provider.

SAM: A provider of what?

ANGEL: Let's talk about something else.

DELIA: Is Leland coming?

ANGEL: Any minute now.

SAM: Should I be asking about this Negro's intentions?

GUY: Maybe you should ask him if he's a good provider.

SAM: He seems to be an honest, hardworking man. You can't hardly ask for more than that, can you?

(Leland enters downstairs.)

DELIA: Do you love him?

GUY: Out of the mouths of babes!

(Leland knocks on the door.)

ANGEL: Sh-h-h-h!

(She opens the door for Leland.)

LELAND: Good afternoon.

ANGEL: Good afternoon yourself. Come in and say hello to everybody.

LELAND: Hello, everybody.

SAM: Good to see you again.

LELAND: Thank you. Miss Patterson . . .

DELIA: Call me Delia.

GUY: We were just talking about you.

LELAND: I hope some good things were said on my behalf.

ANGEL: The best. Sit down.

(There is an awkward silence.)

LELAND: I seem to have interrupted something.

SAM *(Quickly)*: We were just congratulating Delia. Margaret Sanger addressed the congregation at Abyssinian this morning.

GUY: I completely forgot this was the day! I have been working too hard. Sorry, sorry, sorry! Tell me everything.

DELIA: I don't think Margaret had ever been around that many colored people at one time, but she was wonderful!

SAM: She even had a couple of converts in the amen corner.

LELAND: I'm sorry to have to ask, but who is she?

DELIA: She's an advocate for family planning. She has two clinics in New York already and now we're going to open one right here in Harlem.

GUY: They'll probably put Doc out of business in a couple of years. Tea, or shall we just put some gin in these cups and call it square?

SAM: Is that why they call it high tea?

LELAND: You're talking about birth control, aren't you?

DELIA: Aren't you in favor of it?

GUY: I vote for the gin. How about you, Doc?

LELAND: The cure for mothers who don't want babies is fathers who do.

ANGEL: What else happened at Abyssinian? Was Isabel there?

GUY: Did she sit in the third pew on the right and gaze at Adam Junior like he just hung the moon?

SAM: From the expression on his face when she walked down the center aisle, I don't think Reverend Powell Senior has resigned himself to having a showgirl in the family.

GUY: Isabel can always be counted on for high drama.

ANGEL: She told me the most romantic story I've ever heard.

DELIA: I didn't know you knew Isabel Washington.

ANGEL: We were in the Cotton Club chorus together. Then she got that part in a Broadway show where Adam saw her and they fell in love.

GUY: L'amour, l'amour!

ANGEL: He was still in school up at Colgate and his father was determined to keep them apart.

LELAND: Every woman is not cut out to be a pastor's wife.

(There is an awkward silence.)

SAM: I'll say amen to that!

ANGEL: They had a big fight about something and all the way up there on the train, she was planning to break off their relationship for good. By the time the train pulled into the station, it was dark outside and snow was starting to fall.

GUY: High drama!

DELIA: Go on, Angel!

ANGEL: Even worse, she didn't see Adam at all. She was fit to be tied. She grabbed her suitcase, determined to catch the next train back to Harlem, but when she stepped onto the platform, there he was at the end of it with snow in his hair and his arms full of long-stemmed red roses.

GUY: You've got to be born with a talent for finding roses in the middle of December!

ANGEL: He walked the length of the platform . . .

GUY: And knowing Isabel, she waited right there for him to walk it, too!

ANGEL: Then he dropped the roses at her feet, swept her up in his arms and kissed her right there for all the world to see. *(A beat)* And they've been together ever since.

DELIA: Snow roses!

GUY: Snow job is more like it. *(Melodramatically, as if reading from a bad novel)* And in the sudden darkness, he felt that he was lost inside her.

DELIA: What's the most romantic thing you ever saw?

GUY: I thought you'd never ask! It was just the other night so it's fresh in my mind. Angel was there.

ANGEL: Where?

GUY: Langston's party at Bruce's place.

ANGEL *(Nervously)*: That's too new to qualify as a memory.

GUY: The question was what is the most romantic thing you ever saw. Is there a statute of limitations?

SAM: Not that I know of. Fire when ready.

GUY: There were a million people there. Young and not so young. Rich and poor. Well, not that poor. You know Bruce is a snob. But everyone was acting very sophisticated and unimpressed with the stars who were floating around. The beautiful young men in their own tuxedos were arranged at strategic points throughout the room, as usual, but their attention was focused on a tall, slender young man with a poetic mouth and the body of a sepia Adonis. They couldn't hardly welcome Langston home for eyeballing this handsome stranger, when in walks . . .

LELAND: Excuse me. The men were looking at another man?

ANGEL: Maybe you should save this story for another time. You tell one, Deal.

LELAND: I just don't think I understood you right. Did you say these men at your party were making . . .

GUY: It wasn't my party. I was a guest. Just like Angel.

LELAND *(To Angel)*: Did you see those men looking at that other man?

ANGEL: It was just a party, Leland. Nothing happened.

LELAND: What did you mean when you said eyeballing?

SAM: Maybe I can . . .

GUY: Eyeballing. Admiring. Sizing up. Flirting.

LELAND: Men flirting with men?

GUY: They were homosexuals, for God's sake. What's wrong with you?

LELAND: Don't put God's name in the stuff you're talking about! I don't know how sophisticated New York people feel about it, but in Alabama, there's still such a thing as abomination!

GUY *(Standing)*: Get out.

ANGEL: Guy! Don't!

GUY: Then I think you better.

ANGEL *(Looking at Leland helplessly)*: Will you wait for me downstairs for just a minute, honey?

(Leland hesitates.)

ANGEL: I'll be right down. I promise. Please?

LELAND *(Stiffly)*: Good afternoon, Miss Patterson. Dr. Thomas.

(Leland exits.)

SAM: I'll talk to him.

(Sam exits. Delia goes quietly with him and, with a look to the others that acknowledges the awkward moment, goes to her apartment. Sam goes downstairs to where Leland stands stiffly by the stoop. Upstairs, Guy and Angel face each other angrily.)

GUY: He's exactly the kind of small-minded, ignorant, judgmental bastard I left Savannah to get away from!

ANGEL: He didn't deserve that!

GUY: Who gave him the right to vote on my love stories?

ANGEL: Who gave you the right to vote on mine?

(Sam and Leland are talking on the stoop.)

SAM *(To Leland)*: I'll tell you, Brother Leland, we're an opinionated group of loud talkers, but we truly do love Angel.

LELAND: I would die for Angel.

SAM: Live for her, man. It's a much better bargain.

LELAND: I just don't believe in those things they were talking about. *(A beat)* Do they kill babies at that clinic, too?

SAM: No.

LELAND: There was a white doctor at home used to do that when girls got in trouble. Their mamas would bring them to the back door after hours. I thought a doctor was supposed to save lives.

SAM: It's not always that clear a question.

LELAND: You don't do those operations, do you?

(A beat.)

SAM: It's against the law.

LELAND: That doesn't seem to matter up here! Isn't it against the law for one man to eyeball another man?

SAM: Didn't you know Guy was homosexual?

LELAND: She said he was her second cousin from home. She didn't say anything about him being that way and I never thought to ask her. Did you know he was that way?

SAM: Of course. We've been friends for ten years.

LELAND: You're not . . . ?

SAM: No, but you're not going to meet a better man than Guy. He's saved Angel's life more than once and probably mine, too.

LELAND: You call him a man, the same as you or me?

SAM: He is a man.

LELAND: Well, he may be what you call a man, but he ain't the same as me and the sooner I get Angel out of there, the better it will be for all of us. Would you please tell her I'll be back later?

SAM: All right.

LELAND: I'm surprised you can accept something like that.

SAM: I'm just a doctor. I'm not God.

(Leland exits. They are still arguing upstairs.)

ANGEL: Sometimes I think you're jealous.

GUY: I'm always jealous, but I just don't get what you see in this guy.

ANGEL: A rent check that won't bounce.

GUY: Is that it?

ANGEL: Isn't that enough?

GUY: Listen, Sweetie, everything's about to change. As soon as Josephine's producer sees these costumes, they're going to send me a ticket as fast as they can get to the American Express office. Come with me, Angel! Paris is another world away from here. Everywhere you've been looking lately there's nothing but a bunch of sad-eyed souls wondering who pulled the rug out. But Paris won't be like this. I promise. We'll sleep on satin and dress in silk and drink so much fine French champagne we'll get tired of it.

ANGEL: I can't go to Paris with you. You love me, but you don't want to take me home.

GUY: I always take you home.

ANGEL *(Only half teasing)*: But you can't get lost inside me.

GUY *(Surprised)*: Do you want me to?

ANGEL: I've thought about it.

GUY *(A little uncomfortable with the turn the conversation has taken)*: I've thought about it, too, but you're just not my type.

ANGEL: Leland wants to take care of me. I'm going to let him try.

GUY: You don't love him.

ANGEL: He'll never know the difference.

GUY: Yes, he will.

ANGEL: And then what?

GUY: He'll never be able to forgive you for the lie.

ANGEL: Just like you.

GUY: No. I forgive you everything. That's what we've always traded.

ANGEL: And why is that?

GUY: Because you let me see how beautiful I was.

(Sam enters alone.)

ANGEL: Where's Leland?

SAM: He said he'll be back later.

ANGEL: Maybe I can catch him. *(She exits quickly)*

GUY: The story of my life, Doc. Always the bridesmaid, never the bride. You want to finish this high tea with me?

SAM: I thought I might look in on your neighbor.

GUY: L'amour, l'amour! Well, I'm too pretty to spend Sunday afternoon all alone. I think I'll go over to the Kit Kat Klub and see what trouble I can get into.

SAM: You know I had your back earlier.

GUY: I'd-a sliced that country fool six ways 'til Sunday.

SAM: Maybe we'll catch up with you later.

GUY: I wouldn't count on it.

(Guy exits behind Sam, who taps on Delia's door. She answers immediately.)

SAM: The coast is clear. May I come in?

DELIA: Of course. *(She doesn't close the door completely)* Did you talk to Leland?

SAM: I did. He thinks we're a bunch of amoral Philistines.

DELIA: I don't know anybody like him.

SAM: Most of the people I see think like that.

DELIA: About birth control?

SAM: About life.

DELIA: What do you say to them?

SAM: I ask the mother if she is watching her diet. I tell the father to bring her fruit instead of candy.

DELIA: I mean about what they think.

SAM: Nothing.

DELIA: So now what?

SAM: She's going to break his heart.

DELIA: Leland or Guy?

SAM: Both.

DELIA: I don't want to be in love like that.

SAM: Do you want to be in love?

DELIA: Yes. Don't you?

SAM: How old are you?

DELIA: Angel says once you're grown, what difference does it make?

SAM: And are you grown?

DELIA: There's no way to answer a question like that.

SAM: There's no way to answer the one you asked me either.

DELIA: That one should be easy.

SAM: I'm forty years old. I work too hard and I drink too much.

DELIA: But would you like to be in love?

SAM: I've been waiting all my life to be in love.

DELIA: Me, too. *(She kisses Sam gently)*

SAM: May I close the door?

DELIA: Yes.

SAM: Should I lock it?

DELIA: Yes.

SAM: Good.

DELIA: I didn't think I'd be so nervous. I talk about this all the time. Not specifically about you, of course, just in general.

SAM: Don't worry about a thing. I'm a doctor.

DELIA: I know everything about birth control.

SAM: Good.

DELIA: But, I mean, it's all theoretical. I've never . . .

SAM: Do you want to get married first?

DELIA: I thought we were talking about falling in love.

SAM: We are.

DELIA: I promised myself I'd never marry a doctor.

SAM: I'll stop practicing. I'll wear two-tone shoes and play the baritone sax.

(A beat.)

DELIA: Will you do everything real slow?

SAM: As molasses . . .

(He puts his arm around her, and they exit to the bedroom. Angel enters and sits on the stoop. Leland enters almost immediately and stands watching Angel, who looks up suddenly to see him standing there.)

ANGEL: I thought maybe you weren't coming back.

LELAND: I wasn't sure you wanted me to.

ANGEL *(Teasing gently)*: You think I'd be sitting out here in my new dress if I didn't?

LELAND: No, I guess you wouldn't. *(A beat)* What did you do to it?

ANGEL: I just fixed it up a little. Don't you like it?

LELAND: I liked it the way it was before.

ANGEL: Come here. *(She stands, embraces him and then steps back, surprised)* What's that?

LELAND *(Removing a pistol from his waistband)*: I'm sorry. I went by to check on my cousin's place and I always . . . *(He sticks the gun in the back of his belt quickly)* You never know who's gonna walk up on you in Harlem. A man has to be prepared, even on Sunday!

ANGEL: I hate guns.

(A beat.)

LELAND: Listen, Angel, I'm not like you and your friends. I believe there's a right and a wrong of it.

ANGEL: Guy's family.

LELAND: That doesn't make it right!

ANGEL: I think you're just scared.

LELAND: Scared of what? We had his kind back home, but we didn't hang around with them.

ANGEL: And what kind is that?

LELAND: I told you I was a God-fearing, Christian man the first time you ever laid eyes on me.

ANGEL: I thought you said you weren't afraid of anything.

LELAND: Reverend Horace, my pastor back home, he said sometimes when we think we hear the voice of God, it isn't that at all. It's something else, something we want to put up in God's place, like money or lust or gambling. He said sometimes the voice of that other thing can sound so sweet, we swear it's the heavenly choir. But it's not.

(A beat.)

ANGEL: You know what I'm afraid of? Nothing so grand as losing my soul, of course. All I'm afraid of is trying to lean on one more weak Negro who can't finish what he started!

(Leland hesitates, starts to speak, changes his mind. He exits. Angel watches him go as the lights go to black.)

Scene Two

Two weeks later. Sam is sitting patiently on the stoop outside the apartment. Angel enters. She is wearing the same dress she had on at the start of the play, but it, and she, look a bit worse for wear. She is pleased to see Sam.

ANGEL: Hey, Doc.

SAM: You're a sight for sore eyes. Where are you going all dressed up?

(Angel sits beside him.)

ANGEL: I've been where I'm going, and just between me and you? It doesn't pay as good as it used to.

SAM: Things are tough all over.

(She takes off her high heels and rubs her feet.)

ANGEL: How did we ever get this old?

SAM: One day at a time. Brother Leland still missing in action?

ANGEL: I must have been crazy to let that Alabama Negro walk out of here.

SAM: Your test came back.

(A beat.)

ANGEL: How far gone am I?

SAM: Almost eight weeks.

ANGEL: Well, it never rains but it pours, right?

SAM: I'm sorry this isn't what you want.

ANGEL: Yeah. Me, too. *(A beat)* What are you doing out here, anyway?

SAM: Deal's still down at the clinic. That woman works so hard, I barely see enough of her to be a bad influence.

ANGEL: Well, come on upstairs. Maybe I can scare us up something to drink.

SAM: Not me. I've got to go back to the hospital, but . . .

(Angel sees an official notice tacked to the door. She takes it down and reads it with some agitation.)

SAM: What is it?

ANGEL: It's an eviction notice. We're going to be set out on the street!

SAM: Let me see it.

(He reads the notice. It confirms what Angel has said.)

ANGEL: Guy told me he paid it two weeks ago!

SAM: It might be a mistake. Why don't you wait and see what Guy says?

ANGEL *(Angrily)*: What does he ever say? Comment ça va? Comment ça va?

SAM: I can probably come up with fifty or sixty bucks. *(Apologetically)* My patients clean me out the first of every month, but . . .

ANGEL: I'll figure something out. *(She turns away from him)*

SAM: Okay, Angel Eyes. Call me if you need me.

(Sam exits. Angel goes to her purse, opens it, dumps out the contents and separates out the money. There are only a few bills and some coins. She checks to make sure she didn't miss anything. She didn't. She stuffs the money back into her purse. She is not pleased. She picks up the notice again and looks at it as if the intensity of her gaze could change the words. Guy enters carrying an armful of flowers.)

GUY: Bonjour, chérie! Comment ça va? Look at these! I couldn't resist them.

ANGEL: Have you seen this?

(Guy reads the notice, lays the flowers near Angel.)

GUY: Sorry, Sweetie. I'll take care of it.

ANGEL: With what? How much have you got?

GUY: Almost enough.

ANGEL: Almost enough?

GUY: I never said my name was Rockefeller. How much have you got?

ANGEL: Fourteen dollars and seventy-two cents.

GUY: Every little bit helps. Don't worry. Big Daddy is on the case. I've been feeling Josephine in the air all day!

ANGEL: Stop it! Just stop it! Don't you understand? They're going to put us out on the street in seven days! One week!

GUY: Then I better hustle on down to the cable office and see if there's anything there for me.

ANGEL: Whatever presence you're feeling hasn't got anything to do with Josephine. We're not in Paris. We're in Harlem. We're not strolling the boulevard. We're about to be evicted!

(A beat.)

GUY: Do you want to walk down with me? Maybe we can scare up some dinner.

ANGEL: I think it's time for me to look out for myself. *(Sarcastically)* Big Daddy.

GUY: You always do, Angel. One way or another. *(He exits)*

(Angel begins to cry in anger and frustration. Leland enters, comes upstairs and knocks gently. She opens the door and looks at him. He is the last person she wants to see.)

ANGEL: What do you want? *(She turns away from him and he follows her)*

LELAND: Angel, please, listen to me . . .

ANGEL: I'm listening.

(A beat.)

LELAND: The night I found you, I went to bed early, like I always do, but I couldn't sleep. I was just laying there, wide awake. So I got up and went out for a walk. I was missing that Alabama sky where the stars are so thick it's bright as day. So, I looked up between the buildings and I thought I was dreaming. Didn't even look like Harlem. Stars everywhere, twinkling at me like a promise. And then I saw you. And that was all I saw. Just you. *(A beat)* Marry me, Angel. I'll never leave you again.

ANGEL: Swear it.

LELAND: I swear it.

ANGEL: I was hoping you would come.

LELAND: You were?

ANGEL: Yes. I want your son to grow up with his father.

LELAND: What did you say?

ANGEL: We're going to have a child.

LELAND: Are you sure?

ANGEL: I'm sure.

LELAND *(Suddenly agitated)*: What time is it?

ANGEL: About four, I think . . .

LELAND: We can get the license today!

ANGEL: Now?

LELAND: Right now! I think this is our lucky day. Don't you?

ANGEL: Maybe you can convince me.

(He quickly embraces her as the lights go to black.)

Scene Three

The next day. Sam and Delia are in her apartment. Delia is quite agitated.

SAM: It's not going to do any good to get yourself all worked up again.

DELIA: Somebody could have been killed!

SAM: But nobody was.

DELIA: You know what some of them are telling Margaret, don't you? They're telling her to forget about a clinic in Harlem. It's too dangerous.

SAM: Not if we move it someplace safer.

DELIA: Everybody knows that fire was set to run us out. Who's going to rent to us now?

SAM: I am.

DELIA: What are you talking about?

SAM: The ground floor of my parents' brownstone was my first office when I got out of medical school. It's not very big, but it's completely independent of the house with an entrance on the street, three examining rooms and some basic equipment.

DELIA: How long would it take to get it ready for patients?

SAM: Probably the end of the week with what's already there and what you can salvage from your place.

DELIA: That would show them something, wouldn't it?

SAM *(Embracing her protectively)*: You can't let them think they scared you!

DELIA *(Laughing with relief)*: They did scare me!

(Guy enters from outside. He is resplendent in new hat, suit, shoes and spats. He is carrying a bottle of champagne and an overseas cable. He takes the steps two at a time and bursts upon Delia and Sam.)

GUY: Listen to this! *(Reading from the cable)* "To Mr. Guy Jacobs . . ."

DELIA: You heard from Josephine?

GUY: Just sit down and listen!

DELIA: All right, all right!

GUY: "To Mr. Guy Jacobs . . ."

SAM: You already read that part!

GUY *(With great dignity)*: I'm starting from the beginning so you two can get the full effect, unless you haven't got the time to hear the words that are going to change my life forever.

DELIA: We'll be quiet. I promise!

GUY: "To Mr. Guy Jacobs, Harlem, New York, from Mademoiselle Josephine Baker, the Folies Bergère, Paris, France. Ma chérie . . ." Ma chérie . . . music to my ears!

DELIA: Read it!

GUY: "Ma chérie, your costumes fabulous! All here green with envy. Must use all five in next show." Can you believe it? All five!

SAM: Go on, man! You're killing me!

GUY: "Looking forward to seeing you in Paris as soon as you can make the crossing! Au revoir, ma chérie! Je t'aime! Je t'aime! Je t'aime!" She wrote that three times and she sent a first-class ticket and enough cash to get whatever I need for the trip, including this beautiful ensemble. Get the glasses!

DELIA: I don't have any.

GUY: You're hopeless! Follow me!

(They go across the hall. Guy gets glasses.)

GUY: She said they loved everything. Every single piece fit perfectly.

SAM: Of course they did. You're a genius.

GUY: I'm a realist. I added two inches to the measurements she sent me! Women always lie about their ages and their hips!

DELIA: And what do men lie about?

GUY: Men lie about everything else. *(Toasting the photograph)* To Josephine, the magnificent! Merci, merci, merci! It is my intention to run the streets of Harlem tonight until everyone who ever crossed me has heard the news and turned pea green with envy. I will expect you two to accompany me if I'm going to have any chance of returning home alive.

SAM: I would consider it an honor as well as my sacred duty as your personal physician!

DELIA: I wouldn't miss it.

SAM: Let the good times roll!

DELIA: I need to change.

GUY: Thank God. That suit has a life of its own, but it's not a nightlife.

DELIA: I'll just be a minute.

SAM: Don't rush. I have to stop by the hospital, anyway.

GUY: Why don't you meet us at Ike Hines's? We'll start the evening with some celebratory chop suey and see where the spirit leads us!

SAM: If I'm not back in ten minutes, I'll meet you there by eight-thirty.

DELIA: Be careful.

SAM: Careful as I can. *(He kisses her and exits)*

GUY: L'amour, l'amour!

DELIA: Have you told Angel?

GUY: I haven't seen her.

DELIA: She won't believe it.

GUY: She'll believe it when I hand her first-class passage to Paris. Then she can stop looking out the window for that long-gone Alabama fool like he's her ticket to Paradise.

DELIA: This suit isn't that bad, is it?

GUY: Worse than that, but what the hell? Maybe I'll send you back a dress from Paris.

DELIA: Would you?

GUY: I'll send a dozen dresses, all with shoes to match and tiny little hats with veils.

DELIA: I always wanted to see Paris.

GUY: In the springtime?

DELIA: Anytime. I won't be but a minute.

GUY: Good! I'm ready to move out amongst 'em!

(Delia exits to her apartment bedroom to change. Guy pours himself another glass of champagne. Angel enters wearing Leland's dress without adornment and very little makeup.)

Comment ça va, chérie? *(He kisses her on both cheeks)* That dress is more dreadful every time I see it, but all is forgiven!

ANGEL: Where did you spend last night? Shoplifting at Saks Fifth Avenue?

GUY: I didn't get there 'til this morning and I paid cold, hard cash.

ANGEL: Well, it must have been a big night.

GUY: Bigger than that. Are you ready?

ANGEL: I want to tell you something . . .

GUY: My news first!

ANGEL: All right, go ahead.

GUY: I heard from Josephine. They are going to use every single piece I sent them, and she sent so much real live spending money that I was able to pay off everybody we owe and still purchase you first-class passage to Gay Paree!

(He hands her a folder with the necessary papers and tickets.)

GUY: We sail a week from Friday! Now aren't you glad I made you get your passport? Otherwise we'd have to wait a month and you know how mean Josephine gets when you keep her waiting! Don't look so surprised. Say something!

ANGEL: You're really going.

GUY: We're going.

(Angel does not respond.)

GUY: Aren't we?

ANGEL: Bad timing, Big Daddy. I'm pregnant.

(A beat.)

GUY: Accident or insurance?

ANGEL: Yes.

GUY: Does Leland know?

ANGEL: He asked me to marry him. And I told him I would.

GUY: Well, I guess we missed the moment big time, didn't we?

(A beat.)

ANGEL: No, we didn't. I don't even love him! You said so yourself!

GUY: What about the baby? What about Leland?

ANGEL: I can get rid of it! I'm not that far along! I'll tell him I had a miscarriage.

GUY: So you're going to tell him you miscarried his baby and oh, by the way, the wedding is off because you're sailing for France next Friday?

ANGEL: I thought you were the one who could forgive me everything.

(He takes the folder and lays it on the table beside her.)

GUY: Sometimes you wear me out, Miss Angel. Sometimes you just wear me out.

(He closes the door behind him as Delia steps out into the hallway. He smiles at her.)

Ready?

DELIA: How do I look?

GUY: We'll work on it.

(They exit out the back door of the building as Sam enters downstairs. Angel picks up the ticket and holds it in her hand. She savors the possibilities that it represents. It is clear that she has already settled the questions involved and is headed for Paris. Sam sticks his head in the door.)

SAM: Did I miss the celebrants?

ANGEL: They just left.

SAM: I was hoping I could catch them. You've heard the big news?

(Angel nods.)

SAM: So how is it, Angel Eyes?

ANGEL: It's been better. *(A beat)* Leland came by last night.

SAM: Is that good or bad?

ANGEL: He asked me to marry him.

SAM: So you two patched things up after all?

ANGEL: I don't want to have this baby, Sam.

(A beat.)

SAM: What about Leland?

ANGEL: What about him? *(A beat)* I don't know. I just know
I'm going to Paris. Guy booked passage for me and we
sail next Friday.

SAM: Did you tell him about the baby?

ANGEL: Of course I told him. He was surprised at first, maybe
a little mad at me. He sounded like you. "What about
Leland? What about Leland?" What about me?

SAM: This will kill him, Angel.

ANGEL: No, it won't! He'll live through it just fine. And so will I.
(A beat) This is my chance to live free, Doc, and I'm
taking it.

SAM: Freedom's such an abstract thing. That baby's flesh and
blood.

(A beat.)

ANGEL: It was flesh and blood the last time, too, but it didn't
seem to bother you. What's the difference? How come a
little half-Italian baby didn't tug at your heartstrings
like this one does?

SAM: It wasn't the same thing.

ANGEL: Yes, it was. I was carrying a baby I didn't want from a
man I didn't love and I wanted to get rid of it without
bleeding to death on somebody's kitchen table.

SAM: You told me you'd go crazy if you had to have Nick's
child.

ANGEL: Is that what you want? Then will you save me?

SAM: You're asking me to do something I don't think I'm prepared to do.

(A beat.)

ANGEL: So is that how it works? You can help as long as the
poor, ignorant woman is at her wit's end and could
never survive the birth. As long as all she's going to do

after you save her is go home and feel guilty enough or scared enough to keep the next one so you can deliver it and bring us all a bottle of champagne to toast the newest citizens of Harlem . . . and let the good times roll? *(A beat)* Don't worry about it. I'm sure Tony T. can find me a number if I tell him that the baby's his.

SAM: It doesn't have to be this hard.

ANGEL: It already is, Doc. Just not for you.

(A beat.)

SAM: I'll be in my office tomorrow morning first thing.

ANGEL: Why? Because I made you feel guilty?

SAM: Because you're right. Everybody's got to kill their own snakes.

ANGEL: Thanks, Doc. I'll never ask you again. I promise!

(Sam sits wearily.)

What have we got to drink around here?

(She rummages through the cabinets as Sam watches her. The lights fade to black.)

Scene Four

The following day. It is midmorning. Guy is hanging up some costumes prior to delivering them. Angel enters. She is walking slowly. She comes upstairs and enters the apartment.

GUY: You're out early. I didn't even hear you get up.

ANGEL: I took care of it.

GUY: What are you talking about?

ANGEL: I saw Sam.

GUY: This morning?

ANGEL: Just now. *(A beat)* There is no more baby.

GUY: My God, Angel! Did he bring you home?

ANGEL: I caught a cab. He's coming by later.

GUY: Do you want to lie down? Can I get you anything?

ANGEL: I'm all right.

GUY: My God, Angel!

ANGEL: Stop saying that! *(She sits down and closes her eyes wearily)*

GUY: I'm taking the last of these costumes over to the club, but I'll be right back. Will you be okay?

ANGEL: You're not sorry, are you?

GUY: Are you?

ANGEL: I'm sorry in about twenty different ways and I don't give a damn about any of them.

GUY: I won't be long.

(He exits. Angel remains motionless, eyes closed. Leland enters carrying a small rocking chair. He struggles up the stairs with it and knocks on Angel's door. She opens the door, and is startled to see the chair in front of her.)

ANGEL: Oh! I thought it was Sam.

LELAND: May I come in?

ANGEL: Of course.

LELAND *(Putting the chair down gently)*: It's a rocking chair. *(He rocks it)* I made it for you. I started on it that first night I saw you . . .

ANGEL *(Stops the chair from rocking)*: My grandmother said death rocks an empty chair!

LELAND: Then sit in it. I want you to rock all of our children in this chair.

(Angel turns away quickly, but Leland embraces her.)

I just came from my cousin's place. I had those guys hoppin' up there today! We're going to be able to move in a lot sooner then I thought. Maybe next month. Right after the wedding. Would you like that?

ANGEL: Yes, I . . .

LELAND: And, I have something else for you. *(He reaches into his pocket and brings out a small box)* Open it.

(She opens it. Inside is a small diamond ring.)

ANGEL: It's beautiful, but . . .

LELAND: It was my mother's. And then Anna . . . I thought at first we should bury it with her, but my mother said no. Let the dead bury the dead and pass this on to the living.

(She hands it back to him.)

What's wrong?

ANGEL: I have to tell you something.

LELAND: Are you all right?

ANGEL: I had a miscarriage. I lost the baby.

LELAND: Lost . . . the baby?

ANGEL: Sam says there was nothing he could do. Sometimes nature takes care of things that weren't supposed to be.

(Leland sits in the rocking chair and puts his head in his hands. She watches him closely.)

LELAND: I was so happy when Anna told me she was carrying my son. She never had a sick day the whole time she carried him. They still don't know what went wrong. She just stopped breathing in the middle of her labor and by the time they got to him, he wasn't breathing either. They laid them out side by side like they were both just

sleeping. *(A beat)* I'm so sorry. I know how much the
baby meant to you. I'm just thankful you're safe.

ANGEL: I'm fine.

LELAND: What did Sam say?

ANGEL: He said I just need to take it easy for a while.

LELAND: Did he say we can try again?

ANGEL: I didn't ask him.

LELAND: Don't you want to?

ANGEL: I can't think about that yet, Leland. It's too soon.

LELAND: I know, but the sooner the better.

ANGEL: Sam said it would be good if I got away for a while. So
I wouldn't keep thinking about the baby.

LELAND: That's a good idea. Where should we go?

ANGEL: I don't think that's the kind of trip he meant.

LELAND: What did he mean then?

ANGEL: Just me.

LELAND: You want to take a trip alone?

ANGEL: Well, no. I have a friend to go with me.

LELAND: You're not making any sense.

ANGEL: I want to go to Paris with Guy.

LELAND: To Paris? What are you talking about?

ANGEL: He's . . . scared to go alone. And I need to get away.
Sam says . . . to get my strength back. We'll get married
as soon as I get back. I might even be able to talk Guy
into making me a wedding dress.

LELAND: It's because of the babies, isn't it? Because of both
my sons dying. *(A beat)* It was a son, wasn't it?

ANGEL: What difference does it make?

LELAND: I always wanted a son first so he could take care of
the younger ones. I always could see myself with a son.
(A beat) You don't hold it against me, do you?

ANGEL: Listen to me, Alabama. This isn't about you and it
isn't about all the dead mamas and all the dead babies
and all the things that are supposed to move me. I'm not
that kind of colored woman! I just don't want to think

about all that anymore. I'm tired of it! I'm going away. From you. From Harlem. From all those crying colored ghosts who won't shut up and let me live my life!

LELAND: Don't talk like that, Angel! We'll have lots of beautiful babies. I promise.

ANGEL: I don't want any babies. Not yours or anybody's.

(A beat.)

LELAND: What do you mean?

(A beat.)

ANGEL: Leave me alone.

LELAND: Tell me what you meant.

ANGEL: Nothing.

LELAND: You're lying.

ANGEL: You want me to lie! That's all you ever wanted. Pretend I'm Anna. Pretend I love you. I'm through with it!

(Leland grabs her arms and turns her toward him roughly.)

LELAND: Look at me!

ANGEL: I didn't lose the baby. I got rid of it.

LELAND: You got rid of my son? How . . . *(A beat)* Dr. Thomas? You let Dr. Thomas take my son? *(He grabs her by the shoulders as if to shake her, but he stops himself and releases her)* If you didn't have Anna's face, I'd kill you.

(He exits. Angel closes and locks the door after him, leaning against it and closing her eyes wearily. Sam enters downstairs and meets Leland outside the house.)

SAM: Brother Leland . . .

LELAND: I'm not your brother.

(Sam hears the agitation in Leland's voice and recognizes immediately that Leland knows.)

SAM: All right. My mistake.
LELAND: Where are you going?
SAM: Angel . . . wasn't feeling well. I told her I'd stop by.
LELAND: She's not here.
SAM: Then I guess she's feeling better.
LELAND: Angel told me what you did.

(A beat.)

SAM: What did she tell you?
LELAND: She told me that you killed my son!
SAM: Go home, man. It's over.

(Sam turns and starts away. Leland pulls a gun from his belt and points it at Sam's back. There is an immediate blackout, followed by the sound of one gunshot. In the darkness, one small spot comes up on Angel's horrified face in the darkness. This spot stays on for just a few seconds and then the lights go to black.)

Scene Five

Two weeks later. Delia enters from her bedroom. She is looking at a newspaper. Guy enters from his bedroom. He has a small suitcase which he places by the door. There is a champagne bottle resting in a silver ice bucket with two glasses nearby. He gently turns the bottle. Delia finishes reading the story and folds the paper slowly. She picks up her coat and hat and a small photograph and crosses to Guy's apartment. He is looking at the photograph of Josephine and doesn't notice her at first. He looks up and sees her watching him.

GUY: It's not time to go yet, is it?

DELIA: No. I was just rattling around over there driving myself crazy, so I thought I'd come over here.

GUY: And drive me crazy, too? Well, come on and sit down. I'm trying not to forget anything. I've sent the rest of my luggage ahead and paid the landlord through the end of next month in case ... she comes back to get her things.

DELIA: Have you seen the paper?

GUY: Not today.

DELIA *(Reads)*: "Murdered physician accused of performing illegal abortion on missing Harlem showgirl."

GUY: Why do you keep reading that stuff?

DELIA: Everybody in Harlem is reading it!

GUY: Hardly a recommendation!

DELIA: They make it sound so tawdry.

GUY: It is tawdry. And so what? So are we all! Tawdry and tainted and running for our natural lives! *(Sees the photo of Sam)* You got a picture of Sam. Good.

DELIA: They had one at the hospital. It isn't a very good one. Look how young he is ...

GUY: It doesn't matter. He has to be here for the send-off.

(Delia hands him the photo of Sam, which he props up under the photo of Josephine. He pours a glass of champagne for himself and Delia.)

GUY: Drink up, Sweetie. Sam's spirit requires champagne to ease the journey.

(Delia turns away.)

Are you okay?

DELIA *(Looking at Sam's photo)*: We only had a chance to ... be together three times ... and I just keep thinking about it. I don't even know I'm thinking about it, and there it is. Pictures in my mind and everything. *(A beat)* I'm sorry . . . I didn't mean to embarrass you.

GUY: You can't embarrass me.

DELIA: I just didn't know how much I'd miss him. There isn't a single place in Harlem where I don't think about something we did, something he said . . . *(A beat)* I thought after the funeral, I'd be able to move on, but . . .

GUY *(Gently)*: It's only been a couple of weeks, Sweetie. Give it time.

DELIA: Margaret offered me her place in the mountains. I might just take her up on it.

GUY: Are you serious?

DELIA: Well, you're leaving and the trial isn't for another month at least.

GUY: If you're going away for a month, what's the point of moping around the Catskills? Come with me!

DELIA: To Paris? You're mixing up your lady friends, aren't you?

GUY: Not a chance! Listen to me for a minute. Harlem was supposed to be a place where Negroes could come together and really walk about, and for a red-hot minute, we did. But this isn't the end of the world, you know. It's just New York City.

DELIA: What if Angel comes back?

(A beat.)

GUY: When I first met Angel at Miss Lillie's, she was already saving her getaway money. She had her little coins and crumpled-up dollar bills all knotted up in somebody's great big silk handkerchief. She was headed up to Harlem as fast as she could get there and she believed it so hard, I believed it, too. So I got my own white silk handkerchief and started putting those coins in there everyday and counting them every night. And I'd be lying there with my eyes closed, letting those old men

183

touch me wherever they felt like it, but it didn't matter, because in my mind, I was stomping at the Savoy! But I never told Angel. I just kept my ears open so when she was ready to make a move, I'd be ready too. One of the other girls told me she was leaving one night late, so I got my little suitcase and met her at the train station. She was happy to see me, but she sure would have left without me. *(A beat)* Angel doesn't like to say good-bye.

DELIA: I want her to say she's sorry.

GUY: Sorry ain't worth waiting for, trust me. All sorry can do is sit there. It can't ever make it right. We got our hearts broken, Deal, but we don't have to pay for it with our lives. Sam already took care of those dues.

DELIA: I don't even have a ticket!

GUY: Do you have a passport?

DELIA: Yes, but . . .

GUY: It's never crowded this time of year. We can book your passage at the dock. I've got plenty of money and a huge stateroom. If worse comes to worse, we'll tell them you're my little sister and you can bunk with me.

DELIA: I can't just pick up and . . . what about the clinic?

GUY: Don't tell me those suffragettes down there can't figure out what to do for a couple of weeks without you!

DELIA: I'm not even packed.

GUY: We'll buy you whatever you need on the ship! Including a new hat!

DELIA: I love this hat!

GUY: I know! *(He opens the door and grabs his suitcase)* Ready?

(She clearly wants to go, but she hesitates, amazed at her own boldness.)

DELIA: Can I really do this?

GUY: What would Sam say?

(She hesitates, then smiles slowly.)

DELIA: Let the good times roll!

GUY: Then get your passport and meet me at the corner! I'll get us a cab.

DELIA: I won't be a minute!

GUY: You better not be! We're going first-class, but I don't think they'll hold the ship for us.

(He exits quickly. Delia goes over to her apartment, rummages quickly through her desk looking for her passport, doesn't find it. She stops, thinks, then exits to the bedroom. A beat. Angel enters cautiously through the back door, listens to be sure they have gone and then lets herself into Guy's apartment, leaving the door open behind her. The two champagne glasses are still there. Sam's picture is still propped under the photo of Josephine. She picks the photo up and stands looking at it quietly.

Delia comes out of her bedroom with her passport and a small overnight bag. She is moving rapidly. She moves into the hallway and sees Guy's open door, stops, enters cautiously. Angel, still holding the picture of Sam, looks up and sees her standing there. In that moment, both understand that things have changed forever between them. Angel crosses to Delia and hands her the photograph. Delia takes it.)

ANGEL: Good-bye, Deal.

DELIA: Good-bye, Angel.

(Delia exits quickly without looking back. Angel picks up the bottle of champagne and refills one of the glasses. She walks over to the open window and sits down, looking out calmly in a moment that is clearly reminiscent of the afternoon she first encountered Leland. She has been

faced with these same difficult decisions about how she will live many times and although she would have avoided this moment if she could have, she is not in a state of panic, confusion or even remorse. She is thinking—figuring out what is, and what is next. She raises her glass and drinks slowly as the lights fade to black.)

END OF PLAY

Bourbon
at the Border

Bourbon at the Border was originally commissioned by The Alliance Theatre Company in Atlanta, Georgia (Kenny Leon, Artistic Director; T. Jane Bishop, General Manager), where it premiered in 1997 under the direction of Kenny Leon. Sets were designed by Marjorie Bradley Kellogg, lights by Ann G. Wrightson, costumes by Susan E. Mickey, sound by Brian Kettler and musical composition was by Dwight Andrews. The cast was as follows:

MAY THOMPSON	Carol Mitchell-Leon
ROSA ST. JOHN	Andrea Frye
CHARLES THOMPSON	Terry Alexander
TYRONE WASHINGTON	Taurean Blacque

Characters

MAY THOMPSON, an African-American woman, late 40s

ROSA ST. JOHN, an African-American woman, late 40s

CHARLES THOMPSON, an African-American man, late 40s

TYRONE WASHINGTON, an African-American man, late 40s

Time and Place

September 1995; Detroit, Michigan

Setting

All action takes place in May's apartment. There is a living area and a small kitchen separated from the larger room by a counter. There is also a door to an unseen bedroom. Located in an area of the city's downtown that is neither particularly fashionable or particularly safe, the apartment's most striking feature is its view of the Ambassador Bridge connecting Detroit to Windsor, Ontario, Canada. On clear days and at night, when it is lit, the bridge is almost a presence in the apartment.

Act One

Act Two

Playwright's Note

In the summer of 1964, the Student Nonviolent Coordinating Committee (SNCC), the Congress of Racial Equality (CORE), the Southern Christian Leadership Conference (SCLC), the Council of Federated Organizations (COFO) and the National Association for the Advancement of Colored People (NAACP), brought together grassroots organizers, students and movement veterans for a massive voter registration drive. The goal of the drive was the enfrancisement of thousands of Mississippi Negroes who had been systematically and violently denied their right to vote. The activists who went South called it the Mississippi Summer Project—Freedom Summer. Their experiences that summer—including the murders of Summer Project workers James Chaney, Andrew Goodman and Michael Schwerner, as well as the violence against many others whose names are unknown to us—exposed the level of American racial warfare in a way that was as dramatic as it was undeniable.

That same year, black playwright LeRoi Jones's *Dutchman* was produced in New York. The anguished assertion of Clay, the twenty-year-old Negro protagonist, that murder is the only solution to African-American madness is as real and as frightening now as it was then. Somewhere in the space between the nonviolent warriors and the powerless rage of the would-be poet, is the answer to the question W. E. B. Du Bois warned would shape the twentieth century: the question of the color line.

Charlie Parker? Charlie Parker. All the hip white boys scream for Bird. And Bird saying, "Up your ass, feeble-minded ofay! Up your ass." And they sit there talking about the tortured genius of Charlie Parker. Bird would've played not a note of music if he just walked up to East Sixty-Seventh Street and killed the first ten white people he saw. Not a note! And I'm the great would-be poet. Yes. That's right! Poet. Some kind of bastard literature . . . all it needs is a simple knife thrust. Just let me bleed you, you loud whore, and one poem vanished. A whole people of neurotics, struggling to keep from being sane. And the only thing that would cure the neurosis would be your murder. Simple as that. I mean if I murdered you, then other white people would begin to understand me. You understand? No. I guess not. If Bessie Smith had killed some white people she wouldn't have needed that music. She could have talked very straight and plain about the world. No metaphors. No grunts. No wiggles in the dark of her soul. Just straight two and two are four. Money. Power. Luxury. Like that. All of them. Crazy niggers turning their backs on sanity. When all it needs is that simple act. Murder. Just murder! Would make us all sane.

—*LeRoi Jones*
Dutchman

Act One

Scene One

May's apartment. Friday, early evening. The apartment is already neat as a pin, but May is nervously plumping pillows, straightening pictures, slightly altering one chair or another. She surveys her work and, finally satisified, sits down, picks up a magazine, flips through it, puts it down, gets up, paces, sits again, picks up an envelope, withdraws several snapshots, looks at them as if searching for the answer to a familiar question.

The doorbell rings. Although this is what she's been waiting for, she takes a moment to gather herself together, then goes to the door and opens it quickly. Rosa St. John is standing there. She is dressed to the nines—high heels, full makeup, after-five dress. Rosa sweeps into the apartment and strikes a pose in the middle of the room.

ROSA: Well?
MAY: I thought you were going out.
ROSA: I am. Tell me the truth.

MAY: About what?

ROSA: This outfit! I got it at the resale shop but you know how little that dressing room is down there, if you can even call it that, and Doris will tell you anything makes you look like Miss Black America if you give her five dollars for it! I think she purposely angles that mirror so you can't see your behind!

MAY: It looks great on you.

ROSA: I know that, but is it, you know . . .

MAY: What?

ROSA: Is it too young for me?

MAY: How young is too young?

ROSA: Tyrone thinks I'm forty-five . . .

MAY: You told him you were forty-five!

ROSA: That is neither here nor there. The point is, the only way to pull off forty-five is not to go overboard and start pretending thirty-five.

(Rosa is vain, but insecure about her looks at this age. Throughout this scene, she fixes her makeup, applies more lipstick and fusses with her dress.)

MAY: How old is he?

ROSA: He ain't no child, but it's different for men.

MAY: Why is that?

ROSA: Because they make the rules.

MAY: Then why don't you tell him the truth?

ROSA: Oh, sure. That would be a great way to start the evening: "Hey, baby! Guess what?" I don't think so.

MAY: What do you always tell me?

ROSA: What?

MAY: Age ain't nothin' but a number.

ROSA: I don't know why I'm even asking you. It's been so long since you went out, you don't have anything to compare it to.

MAY: I'm out all the time!

ROSA: Going to work does not count.

MAY: You look beautiful. Tyrone won't know what hit him.

ROSA: He's already seen it.

MAY: What did he say?

ROSA *(Grinning)*: He said I looked good enough to eat.

MAY: Then what are you doing down here harrassing me?

ROSA: Trying to get a second opinion. You know men will tell you anything when they want something.

MAY: What time is the show?

ROSA: Eight o'clock, but Tyrone wants to get there early so we can park close to the club. I told him if he's so worried about that Cadillac, he needs to go on and get him an old raggedy Ford so he can relax.

MAY: Where is he?

ROSA: He went to the liquor store. I told him I had to finish fixing my face and to pick me up down here.

MAY: Oh. Well . . .

ROSA: Am I interrupting something?

MAY: No, I was just thinking I might be going out in a minute, too . . .

ROSA *(Immediately suspicious)*: Going out where?

MAY: I don't have to get your permission, do I?

ROSA: Hell no, honey! I've been trying to get you outta here for months. *(A beat)* You got a date?

MAY: Of course not!

ROSA: Don't say of course not. Charlie's been gone almost all summer.

MAY: He's coming home.

ROSA: Sure he is, honey, but you're only human and when the cat's away, who knows what the mice might do?

MAY: He's coming home today.

ROSA: Today?

MAY: I thought it was him when you rang the bell.

ROSA: Why didn't you tell me?

MAY: I know how you feel about all this . . .

ROSA: You're not picking him up?

MAY: He asked me not to.

ROSA: Then who's bringing him?

MAY: He's on the bus.

ROSA: The bus?

MAY: He said if he can't get home by himself, he doesn't need to be out.

ROSA: I heard that.

MAY: But he should be here by now.

ROSA: Don't worry. He can find this place in his sleep.

MAY: I guess you're right.

ROSA: I'm always right. *(A beat)* May?

MAY: Yeah?

ROSA: Don't get mad when I say this, but it might be good for us to wait with you until he gets here.

MAY: Why?

ROSA: To make sure he's . . . okay.

MAY *(Sharply)*: He's coming home, isn't he?

ROSA: They sent him home last time, too, and said he was fine. Next thing you know he's back up on the roof.

(A beat.)

MAY: Maybe you should wait for Tyrone upstairs.

ROSA: You don't have to put me out, honey. I'll give you my opinion all day and all night, but once you make your choice, I'm on your side. Whichever way it comes out.

MAY: I know. I didn't mean to snap at you.

ROSA: Are you nervous?

MAY: A little. It's just sort of sudden, you know? He hadn't been doing good at all. I couldn't get him to talk to me. Sometimes I wasn't even sure he knew I was there. It was like he was going in deeper and deeper and there wasn't any way to make him come back. I kept trying to get the doctor to tell me something, but they didn't know anything either. They kept on asking me what did I think had set him off this time and I kept on telling them if I knew what set him off, I'd know how to keep him away from it!

ROSA: Why they asking you? I thought you were paying them every dime you got to figure it out.

MAY: I told them that, too. But then about a month ago, he changed. He started talking and laughing again. He took the medicine they wanted him to try on the schedule they gave him. When I went to see him last time, he even—

ROSA: What? He even what?

MAY: He was flirting with me.

ROSA: In the hospital?

MAY: Well, it's not like he's in bed with one of those ass-out gowns on. We're in a regular room, sitting on a couch, talking like regular people.

ROSA: They let you be alone with him?

MAY: He's not dangerous, Rose. The only person he ever tries to hurt is himself.

ROSA: What did he say?

MAY: He said he had figured it out and he was going to be a new man. He said he was going to come home and get a job and make up for everything.

ROSA *(Skeptical)*: He's going to be *a making up something* if you ask me.

(A beat.)

MAY: Be glad for me, Rose.

ROSA: I am glad, honey. I'm real glad. I just don't want you to get all worked up before you have a chance to talk to him. You know. See how he's really doing.

MAY: He said I embarrassed him last time I picked him up.

ROSA: You didn't act a fool up in the place, did you?

MAY: I couldn't help it! I was doing fine until he walked in the room and then I just . . . I just felt like if I couldn't touch him, I'd go crazy.

ROSA: Don't do that! One to a family is all that's allowed. *(A beat)* I'm sorry. I didn't mean that the way it sounded.

MAY: How did you mean it?

ROSA: I meant to say good for you and good for Charlie and I hope by the time he gets here I'll have a chance to get my foot out of my mouth long enough to say welcome home. *(A beat)* Don't be mad, honey. If I didn't say the wrong thing, I probably wouldn't say nothin' at all.

MAY: The truth of it is, I could use a little company. I've been up since six and if I pick up that magazine one more time, I'll know it by heart!

ROSA: Maybe he'll get here before we leave and we can pinch enough bourbon off Ty for a welcome-home toast.

MAY: I don't know, Rose. He might not be in the mood for company right at first.

ROSA: Just one? For the fellowship?

MAY: I guess one would be okay.

ROSA: That's all you gonna get, trust me. Tyrone got plenty of money, but he's stingy as the day is long. You know why he went to the liquor store?

MAY: To buy liquor?

ROSA: Of course to buy liquor, but why?

MAY: Why?

ROSA: When we first get to the club, he orders two bourbon and cokes, right?

MAY: Right . . .

ROSA: After that, all he'll order is plain cokes and we gotta sneak and add the taste to it from the bottle we brought in with us.

MAY: You're kidding.

ROSA: I wish I was. Last time he spilled Jack Daniels all over me trying to pour it under the table. You remember that white linen skirt I got from Doris? Stain never did come out. This time, I'm pouring. He ain't messin' up another dress of mine with his cheap self. Speaking of cheap, what you got I can nibble on real quick? I know Ty ain't thinking about feeding me.

MAY: I got some tuna fish in there.

ROSA: To be working in a cafeteria, you got the sorriest refrigerator of anybody I know.

MAY: They don't pay me in food.

ROSA: I know that, but even when I used to work in people's houses, we got to take the leftovers home.

MAY: Take it or leave it.

ROSA: Never mind. I won't be thinking about food once the show starts anyway. Johnny Taylor in a club that size? I'm going to lose my mind!

MAY: Won't Tyrone get jealous?

ROSA: He better! That's the whole point. *(Suddenly)* Sh-h-h!

MAY *(Instantly quiet and on the alert)*: What?

ROSA: Don't you hear that?

MAY: Hear what?

ROSA: My stomach is growling so loud I won't be able to hear the music! Is it too late for me to change my mind about that tuna?

MAY: I'll make you a sandwich. *(She does as they talk)*

ROSA: Don't put mayonnaise on it. I hate mayonnaise on a tuna sandwich! Guess what? My brother, the one who lives in Chicago? He called and said it snowed last night! Just barely September and they had snow! I don't see how anybody can live there. Detroit is as cold as I can stand.

MAY: My first winter up here, I almost froze to death. Charlie kept bringing me coats and sweaters, but I couldn't get warm no matter what I put on.

ROSA: When I was a kid, it used to be so cold on Halloween you'd have to wear your coat over your costume and when people opened the door for trick or treat, you'd flash 'em fast so you didn't get pneumonia.

MAY: First snow I saw was out this window. Charlie was sleep and I came out the bedroom and saw it. One of those wet, heavy snows, coming down thick. I screamed so loud, I probably woke up the whole building.

ROSA: What were you screaming about? Snow ain't never hurt nobody who wasn't out in it without enough clothes on.

MAY: I don't know. It surprised me, I guess. Just to see it coming down like that and not making a bit of noise. Like if I hadn't gotten up, I never would have known it was there at all.

ROSA: You'd know when you went out to start your car and had to spend ten minutes scraping it off the windows.

MAY: I kind of like it now. It's peaceful.

ROSA: May?

MAY: Yeah?

ROSA: You know I didn't mean anything before about Charlie. I just meant, you know, I've been living here five years and he's been in more than he's been out.

MAY: He's not dangerous, Rose. He's depressed.

ROSA: A lot of people get depressed from time to time, but Charlie is the first black person I ever knew who went all the way crazy.

MAY: Me, too.

ROSA: For real? Was it weird?

MAY: Was what weird?

ROSA: When you found out he was really crazy.

MAY: By the time I had to put a word on it, I think I already knew.

ROSA: Most folks wouldn't a stuck like you have.

MAY: Most folks won't stick if you have cancer either.

ROSA: That's different.

MAY: Why? He didn't get sick on purpose. He just got sick. *(A beat)* I wish you could have seen him before. You would have liked him.

ROSA: I like him now!

(May picks up the envelope she put aside earlier, withdraws the snapshots, hands one to Rosa.)

MAY: Recognize any of these bright-eyed, young Negroes?

ROSA: Oh, my God! Is that you?

MAY: Me and Charlie in our prime. I got a letter from my sister today. She found these in Mama's closet and sent them on.

ROSA: Look at all that hair on your head!

MAY: Going natural was supposed to set us free, but I spent as much time braiding and blowing out and Afro-picking as I ever did trying to keep a perm together.

ROSA: You all look so serious.

MAY: We were serious.

ROSA: You really got into that sixties thing, didn't you?

MAY: That's why I went to Howard in the first place. *(A beat)* Look at Charlie. He was the main one talking people into going to Mississippi. Every day at noon, he'd be standing down there on the steps of Douglass Hall, talking about how we'd be the sorriest people on the face of this earth if we let a bunch of white kids go down there to register all those black folks to vote.

ROSA: Old Charlie was fine, too!

MAY: One day I stopped to listen and when he started up on how it wouldn't be fair for us to let these white kids fight our battles for us, I said, trying to be funny, fair to who? A couple of people standing around laughed, but Charlie looked at me real serious and said, fair to the memory of our ancestors' bones.

ROSA: Damn!

MAY: That made me feel guilty as hell, of course, so I stayed around to apologize and he asked me to go for coffee.

ROSA: And the rest is history.

MAY: I don't know about all that, but I kept trying to apologize and he kept trying to ask me if I didn't want to be a part of changing how the world worked. Finally, I said, look, I can think of more interesting ways to spend my summer than trudging around Mississippi trying to register some scared Negroes to vote, and he gave me that look again. Next thing I knew, I was on the bus to Sunflower County.

ROSA: Did you already know you were in love with him?

MAY: I followed him to Mississippi. How much more proof can you stand?

ROSA: Who is this?

MAY: Those are the Hemphills, the family I stayed with.

ROSA: What do you mean stayed with?

MAY: We all stayed with families. It broke down all that stuff about them being poor and ignorant and us being missionaries coming to save them.

ROSA: This whole family in that one little house?

MAY: You could stand at the front door and see clear through to the back porch. Neat as a pin. They had nine kids and almost no money, but they took me in like I was family. See this girl?

ROSA: The one holding the baby?

MAY: That's Esther and that's her little brother, John F. Kennedy Hemphill, also known as Prez. She was the oldest and she was seriously in love with a big old country boy from down the road about six miles. They both had to work the fields every day but he always came to walk her to church on Sunday. She'd wake up real early to get eveybody fed, then she'd put on her one good dress and sit down on the front porch to watch for him coming up that road. I sat with her sometimes and I swear, I've never seen anybody in love like that in my life. When he came around that bend, she'd catch her breath like Jesus Christ himself was walking up that road.

ROSA: Maybe it was like those stories where Jesus is there in a regular place, looking like a regular person, so nobody knows it's him until most of them have treated him like a dog and then they all feel ashamed, but it's too late and only the ones who were nice to him get to go to heaven.

MAY: Well, if this boy was the baby Jesus in disguise, Esther Hemphill is guaranteed a place at the right hand of God.

ROSA *(Picking up a yellowed clipping)*: "Three Civil Rights Workers Missing, Feared Dead." Did you know them?

MAY: No. We were still in training. Up in Ohio, thinking we were going down there and they were going to roll over and play dead. My grandmother called me and started crying and begging me not to go. *(A beat)* Part of what made it so hard was that they were missing for weeks. Even after we got there, we'd be driving around, walking around, wondering if this one or that one was the killer. We knew they were dead. We weren't that naive. It was pretty scary. Some people couldn't take it. They got too scared to function.

ROSA: What happened to them?

MAY: They went home.

ROSA: But you stayed.

MAY: As long as we could, then Charlie got hurt and we came up here.

ROSA: What's this woman so mad about? Look how she's looking at that guy.

MAY: That's her husband. He had finally agreed to come down to the courthouse to register. We were so proud and he was so proud. All of his kids were excited, but his wife knew that if he really did it, there was a good chance they'd lose the little bit they had. We kept on talking about how proud her sons were going to be, but she wasn't buying it. Then, all of a sudden, he said he was tired of being scared and if the white folks were going to do something to him, they were going to have to just go ahead and do it. *(A beat)* That's the first time somebody followed us. When we left that place.

ROSA: Followed you?

MAY: A car full of young white boys saw us turn out of the plantation road and fell in behind us. People told us the best thing to do was head for town as fast as you could since they were less likely to act a fool if other folks were around, so I hit the gas. Those Mississippi back roads were pitch-black at night. We had only been driving them a couple of weeks, but I was taking those curves at sixty miles an hour.

ROSA: Were you scared?

MAY: Sure I was. They hugged our bumper the whole way back to town. Sometimes we could hear them laughing and hollering out the window. There had to be five or six of them. Once we hit town, they just turned off. I was shaking so bad when we finally got back to where we were staying, it was a shame. Charlie was trying to act brave so I wouldn't know how scared he was, but I could see it on his face. I was about ready to go home that night, but it was too late to start out anywhere, so we sat up talking. Trying to understand. By morning, it almost seemed like it had happened to somebody else, so we got up and went back to work.

ROSA: Do you ever wish you hadn't gone down there at all?

MAY: Never. Going to Mississippi was the only thing I ever did that wasn't just an ordinary day.

(The doorbell rings. Rosa starts for the door, but May stops her.)

I'll get it.

(May opens the door to Tyrone.)

TYRONE: Greetings and salutations! Is there a blues-lovin' woman on the premises who's looking for a blues-lovin' man?

ROSA: You got that right!

TYRONE: How you doin', May?

MAY: I'm good, Tyrone. You?

TYRONE: Couldn't be better. I got a brand-new Cadillac, a pocket full of money and a fine woman who likes to call me "sweet thing."

ROSA: Not necessarily in that order.

TYRONE: Let's hit the street, babe. You know those Negroes will have double-parked all the good spaces by seven-thirty!

ROSA: We got time. Guess what?

TYRONE: What?

ROSA: Charlie's coming home today.

TYRONE: Who?

MAY: My husband, Charlie.

ROSA: You know I told you about Charlie.

TYRONE *(He clearly doesn't remember)*: Oh, right! Where's he been?

MAY: In the hospital.

TYRONE: Yeah? What happened?

MAY: He got hurt in Mississippi a long time ago.

TYRONE: Mississippi?

ROSA: Charlie and May were in the Civil Rights Movement.

TYRONE: What happened?

MAY: Freedom Summer. You ever heard of it?

TYRONE: The sixties, right?

MAY: Sixty-four.

TYRONE: I always thought those Negroes were crazy going down there.

MAY: It wasn't that big a leap for me. I was born in Georgia.

TYRONE: That's why you still got that little Southern sweetness in your voice. Every girl I meet from down home sound like she been suckin' on a sugar tit.

ROSA: Tyrone! Be nice!

TYRONE: I didn't mean nothin'.

ROSA: Gentlemen do not use that word in mixed company.

TYRONE: "Tit" ain't necessarily a bad word. Depends on how you use it. All I was doin' was callin' it what they call it. No offense, May.

MAY: It's okay.

TYRONE: Where in Georgia you from?

MAY: Near Madison. It's about an hour outside of Atlanta.

TYRONE *(Laughs)*: Well, a miss is as good as a mile!

ROSA: Everybody ain't from the city like you, sweet thing.

TYRONE: Say it again.

ROSA *(Suggestively)*: Sweet thing.

TYRONE: If I hadn't paid for these tickets in advance, I'd toss them out the window and take you back upstairs right now!

ROSA: You gonna get your money's worth all the way around. Trust me.

TYRONE: Well, I don't trust nobody to hold back time and I ain't up for fighting about no parking space.

ROSA: Did you get the bourbon?

TYRONE *(He takes a pint bottle from his pocket)*: Mr. Jack Black, present and accounted for!

ROSA: Listen, Ty, I'd love for you to have a chance to meet Charlie before we go.

TYRONE: When's he coming?

MAY: He's on his way.

TYRONE: We ain't got time for all that now, Rosa.

ROSA: Then how about the three of us have a quick drink and May can tell Brother Charles we toasted him in absentia?

TYRONE: That ain't what I bought it for, whatever that means.

MAY: Maybe we should do this another time.

ROSA: When? *(She goes to the kitchen and gets four glasses)* Charlie's coming home today. If we don't do it now, it'll be bad luck to double back and try to catch up later.

TYRONE: Be bad luck to run outta booze before the second show.

(A beat.)

ROSA: I would hate to think our whole evening could be ruined over a couple a shots of liquor among friends.

TYRONE: All right, all right. *(He carefully pours three tiny shots)*

ROSA: Put some in Charlie's glass, too.

TYRONE: He ain't even here!

ROSA: It's symbolic, honey. Like communion.

(Tyrone reluctantly pours an even smaller shot in the remaining empty glass.)

To Charlie.

MAY: To Charlie.

(A beat.)

TYRONE: To Charlie.

(They drink.)

ROSA: And now, before we make our exit, in plenty of time, I have a new joke.

MAY: No, Rose!

TYRONE: We gotta go, baby.

ROSA: It's a knock-knock joke.

MAY: I'm not doing it.

ROSA: It's a short knock-knock joke.

MAY: You can't tell jokes!

ROSA: This one is so easy even I won't mess it up. Come on, Ty, please?

TYRONE: Okay. Go ahead.

ROSA: Knock-knock.

TYRONE: Who's there?

ROSA: Banana.

TYRONE: Banana, who?

ROSA: Knock-knock.

TYRONE: You already said that.

ROSA: I know, but I have to say it again. That's part of the joke.

TYRONE: Oh.

MAY: Don't look at me. I'm not in it.

ROSA: So you have to answer again, too.

TYRONE: Oh. *(Clearly confused)* What is it?

ROSA: Knock-knock.

TYRONE: Who's there?

ROSA: Banana.

TYRONE: Banana who?

ROSA: Knock-knock.

MAY: Rosa!

ROSA: This is the end part! Just one more. Knock-knock.

TYRONE *(Exasperated)*: Maybe we should just catch a cab 'cause there will be no place to park.

MAY: Who's there?

ROSA: Orange.

MAY: Orange who?

ROSA: Orange you glad I didn't say banana?

(Tyrone laughs. May groans.)

TYRONE: Now can we go?

ROSA: Yes! Now we can go.

TYRONE: Nothing against you about the liquor, May. It's just that I'm watching my money pretty close these days. I'm getting ready to make some moves and I gotta bring some to get some, you know what I mean?

MAY: Sure, Ty. No problem.

(Tyrone turns to go and sees Rosa looking at him disap-
provingly. A beat.)

TYRONE: Ah, what the hell! *(He gives May the rest of the bour-*
bon) Tell your old man I said welcome home.
MAY: You don't have to do that.
TYRONE: What's a pint among friends?
ROSA: You sweet thing! *(She kisses him)* Drinks at the club
are on me!
TYRONE *(Grinning)*: Say it again.
ROSA: Sweet thing.
TYRONE: No, I mean the part about who's buying the drinks!
ROSA: Call me in the morning.
MAY: I will.
TYRONE: Okay, okay! Let's get a move on else we gonna have
to park in Cinncinati!

(Tyrone and Rosa exit. May closes the door, clears away
the glasses and the bourbon. Now that Tyrone and Rosa
are gone, she is again left with nothing to do but wait.
She goes to the window and stands looking out. As she
watches, the bridge lights are illuminated for the night.
Time passes.
The sound of a key in the lock as Charlie enters. He
has a slight limp. May stands, but does not move toward
him. He closes the door, but does not move toward her.
They stand looking at each other for a beat. Although
they will not touch each other until the end of this scene,
it is obvious that they are longing to do so from the time
he enters.)

CHARLIE: Hello, May.
MAY: Hello, Charlie.
CHARLIE: I didn't mean to worry you.
MAY: Are you all right?

CHARLIE: Yes.

MAY: It got so late.

CHARLIE: I figured it out, May. The only way they win is if they make me too crazy to be with you.

MAY: Oh, Charlie.

(May begins to cry. He embraces and caresses her.)

CHARLIE: Don't cry, baby. It's over now. It's all over. Daddy's home. Daddy's home . . .

(May returns his caresses as the lights fade to black.)

Scene Two

The next morning. Charlie, fully dressed, is up drinking a cup of coffee and looking out the window. May comes out of the bedroom wearing a robe. Her manner is casual, but she is completely focused on getting a clear reading on Charlie's mental state. There is between them an intangible but undenial air of desire unfulfilled.

MAY: I didn't hear you get up.

CHARLIE: You weren't supposed to.

(She joins him at the window.)

MAY: You sleep all right?

CHARLIE: Like a baby. You?

MAY: Yeah, until you woke me up with those big old cold feet!

CHARLIE: Tonight I'll wear socks.

MAY: That's all right. Once I was awake, I had a chance to take a look at you without you knowing it.

CHARLIE: Did I pass inspection?

MAY: So far, so good.

CHARLIE: Maybe we can ride over to Canada next weekend and get a cabin for a couple of days so you can complete your examination.

MAY: Let's do it today.

CHARLIE: Can't do it today. I gotta go over to Northland. They're hiring at Hudson's warehouse.

(A beat.)

MAY: You don't have to do that.

CHARLIE: Yes I do.

MAY: Why don't you wait until Monday?

CHARLIE: What's going to happen between now and then, do you think?

MAY: You'll have a chance to rest.

CHARLIE: I've been resting.

MAY: I think the warehouse is a bad idea.

CHARLIE: I've only got a couple of choices. I can sit here and let you take care of me because I'm too crazy to be moving around out in the world, or I can get off my black, insane ass and figure out how to take care of my wife like a man is supposed to do.

MAY: Who gets to decide what a man is supposed to do?

CHARLIE: Only the man in question, otherwise it's all bullshit. I gotta get a job, May. I can't let you talk me out of it for my own good.

MAY: What did the doctor say?

CHARLIE: The doctor said I'm no crazier than most of the folks walking around out here and they're doing fine. Plus, I've got lots of new medication. I've got pills for when I get up in the morning and pills for when I go to bed at night. I've got pills that can chase the blues and pills to soothe the savage beast. Stop worrying.

MAY: Did he say anything about whether or not you should be working?

CHARLIE: Listen, May. Three weeks ago, they put me in with a new doctor. I'm not making much progress but they think maybe I'll do better with this guy than I'm doing with the other one. So I'm sitting in the office, talking to him and he's an Indian, an India Indian, not a Native American brother, and he was asking me questions and scribbling down notes when I answered, I mean lots of notes, like everything I said was critical to him understanding my problem, whatever they had told him my problem was. And I'm thinking to myself, this guy is really taking this serious. Maybe he can help me figure this stuff out, even if he is an Indian. I mean, I'm damn near fifty years old. Time should be on my side, right? And I been in a lot of shrinks' offices and I don't remember one of them writing down a single word. Then the guy got an emergency phone call and practically broke his neck running out to take it, but he left that pad, so I went over and picked it up to see what he'd been writing about me and it said: "My darling, please forgive me for what I've done. I love only you and always will. Please, my angel, can't we start again?" He wasn't writing about me at all. He wasn't even thinking about me. He was trying to beg some woman for her forgiveness and that was more important than anything I had to say. And you know what? It didn't even make me mad. It was like a sign or something. A sign to me about what's really important. About love and how easy you can fuck it up by being too selfish or too mean or too crazy to see the cure is standing right beside you.

(A beat.)

MAY: At first, when they wouldn't let me in to see you, I'd drive out there anyway and make them tell me no every day like I didn't remember what they said the day before. Then I'd go walk around outside the building for an hour as close as I could get so maybe you would pass by a window and see me.

CHARLIE *(Quietly)*: There were no windows . . .

MAY: No windows?

CHARLIE: Not at first.

MAY *(Quickly recovering)*: I always wore that dress you like.

CHARLIE: The green one?

MAY *(Quoting him)*: The one that floats on me like water . . .

CHARLIE: Did you have the hat?

MAY: Yes.

CHARLIE: And those shoes with the high heels?

MAY: You sure you didn't see me?

CHARLIE: I felt you.

MAY: Promise me something?

CHARLIE: What's that?

MAY: If the foreman has a Confederate flag in his office, on his cap or anywhere on his person, you won't take the job.

CHARLIE: I promise!

MAY: Do you really have to go?

CHARLIE: Yes! I won't be late. Even if I get it, they won't start me today.

MAY: I love you, Charlie.

(Charlie closes his eyes, puts one hand over his heart, sighs dramatically, grins, blows May a kiss and exits. Phone rings.)

Hello? Hey, Rose. Yeah. Last night. He's gone out. Where's Ty? Sure, come on down.

(May makes more coffee. Rosa rings the bell almost immediately.)

ROSA: I thought you were going to call me.

213

MAY: Charlie just left a minute ago. I'm surprised you didn't see him in the hall.

ROSA: I wasn't sure if you had left a message and I never play them back when Ty stays over. All I need is for some old fool to resurface feeling frisky and leave me a message for old time's sake.

MAY: You ought to quit!

ROSA: So where is he?

MAY: He went out to look for work.

ROSA *(Surprised)*: On Saturday morning?

MAY: He said they're hiring at Hudson's warehouse. Just until he can find something better.

ROSA: I saw that Hudson's notice in the paper yesterday, too. I started to go down there myself.

MAY: To the warehouse?

ROSA: Sonny's insurance ain't going as far as I hoped it would, rest in peace, and me and Tyrone drank up half my savings at the club last night. Now I know why he's always sneaking something in. Five dollars for bourbon and coke! And it's a crime what they're charging for a shot of cognac!

MAY: How was the show?

ROSA: Girl, don't get me started! We were so close when he started singing "Disco Lady," I could see the sweat pop out on his face. And guess what?

MAY: I'm scared to.

ROSA: When he sang "I Believe in You," he came over and picked up my hand and started singing it straight to me. I almost passed out.

MAY: That was probably all the expensive bourbon you were drinking.

ROSA: I swear that Negro is so fine if I'd a been by myself he'd a had a helluva time getting rid of me. But enough about my night. What time did Brother Charles finally make his appearance?

MAY: Not long after you left.

ROSA: And?

MAY: And what?

ROSA: So how is he?

MAY: He's fine.

ROSA: That's it? He's fine?

MAY: That's it. He's fine.

(A beat.)

ROSA: Do they think he'll try it again?

(A beat.)

MAY: He won't try it again.

ROSA: How do you know?

MAY *(Sharply)*: Because I won't let him. *(A beat)* Want some coffee?

ROSA: Sure.

(A brief silence. Rosa cannot think of a way to get May to talk about Charlie, so she abandons the effort for the moment.)

You hear what happened?

MAY: What?

ROSA: They found a body downtown.

MAY: A body? Where?

ROSA: Right near the park.

MAY: No kidding? What happened?

ROSA: They don't know. No motive. No suspects.

MAY: Probably some more gang stuff.

ROSA: Not hardly. This was a white guy.

MAY: Really?

ROSA: An old white guy. Still had his wallet and his car keys on him.

MAY: What was he doing downtown?

ROSA: They still do business around here.

MAY: Not after this they won't.

ROSA: The cops are going to arrest everybody they even think might have done it.

MAY: All the men living in that park, they ought to have a field day.

ROSA: Tyrone said for me to be careful walking around by myself.

MAY: He's right.

ROSA: I'm always careful. I been running these streets all my life and I'm not about to quit now.

MAY: It's going to get worse before it gets better.

ROSA: You sound like that guy preaching in front of the grocery store. "There will be wars and rumors of wars."

MAY: I don't know about all that, but me and Charlie are not going to stick around for it, whatever it's going to be.

ROSA: Where are you going?

MAY: We're moving to Canada.

ROSA: To live?

MAY: Soon as I can talk Charlie into it.

ROSA: Have you ever been there?

MAY: It's right across the bridge. Haven't you?

ROSA: I went a couple of times, but what's the point, you know? Windsor ain't that much different from Detroit if you ask me.

MAY: It's different if you go out in the country.

ROSA: You moving to the woods?

MAY: Don't say it like that. It's beautiful.

ROSA: I can just see you and Charlie out there for about two weeks, then you'd come running back to the good old USA.

MAY: Not a chance. Charlie's different over there. One time we rented a cabin. We woke up in the morning and there was so much snow we couldn't hardly see the car. The sun was out and the air was so clean you wanted to

drink it like water. You'll have to come and visit us.
Tyrone can come, too.

ROSA: Tyrone ain't hardly interested in no weekend in the
woods.

MAY: You'd be surprised how different a man will act out in
nature.

ROSA: Different how?

MAY: It brings out something good in them. Being in nature,
knowing they're connected to something bigger.

ROSA: Bigger than what?

MAY: Say what you want, you'll be knocking on our door when
the city gets too crazy to live in.

ROSA: It's already too crazy to live in, so what can you do?

MAY: You weren't really thinking about going down to the
warehouse, were you?

ROSA: I surely was. Once I pay my rent and buy a couple bags
of groceries, I'm all in.

MAY: They're hiring at the city.

ROSA: In the cafeteria?

MAY: No, night work.

ROSA: Night work doing what?

MAY: Clean-up or security.

ROSA: I am not hardly ready to start scrubbing floors and you
know I ain't shooting nobody over something that don't
even belong to me!

MAY: Suit yourself.

ROSA: If I tell you something, will you promise not to tell
Tyrone?

MAY: What is it?

ROSA: You have to promise!

MAY: I promise.

ROSA: I interviewed for a phone sex job.

MAY: What?!

ROSA: Don't sound so shocked. You don't actually do anything. You just talk about it.

MAY: What did you say?

ROSA: Well, first they asked me if I had any hang-ups about anything. I said not as far as I know, then the guy started asking me—

MAY: A man interviewed you?

ROSA: He owns the place.

MAY: Go on . . .

ROSA: He asked me if I had ever faked an orgasm.

MAY: What'd you tell him?

ROSA: I told him no!

(May raises her eyebrows.)

Force of habit, okay? But I told him I was sure I could do it, so he started asking me about specific stuff and, girl, I swear, it was all I could do to keep from putting my fingers in my ears and running out the place.

MAY: Stuff like what?

ROSA: You know, animals and stuff.

MAY: Animals?

ROSA: It's a big world, honey. Everybody got a right to do their own thing.

MAY: Yeah, but animals?

ROSA: Don't worry. I told him I didn't know nothing about no animals and he said that was fine. They didn't get much call for that during the day anyway—I told him I could only work in the daytime—and how did I feel about S and M?

MAY: Did you tell him you were a Baptist?

ROSA: I told him I was a meat and potatoes kind of gal and if they specialized in all that freaky-deaky stuff I should probably take my business elsewhere.

MAY: Good for you!

ROSA: So he said everything was everything and asked me if I'd do an audition.

MAY: I thought you said it was just on the phone.

ROSA: It is, but you still got to audition. They aren't going to hook you up with a paying customer if you can't come through, no pun intended.

MAY: So what did you do?

ROSA: He put me in this little cubicle, like a telephone operator, you know, and then he called me up.

MAY: Jesus, Rose! Weren't you embarrassed?

ROSA: I'm too broke to be embarrassed.

MAY: What did he say?

ROSA: Nothing too weird, you know, he would tell me what he was gonna do to me and I had to moan and groan and act like it was driving me crazy to hear about it and then he started breathing real hard so I started breathing real hard and that was about it.

MAY: I can just hear you huffin' and puffin'. "I think I can! I think I can!"

ROSA: I know I can! I even hollered a little at the end.

MAY: I can't believe you did this.

ROSA: You know guys like it when you scream. Makes them feel like they got you to give up something you been holding back.

MAY: Are you going to take the job?

ROSA: I told him I had to think about it. He told me I was a natural.

MAY: A natural what?

ROSA: Whatever! The weirdest part about it was—don't laugh!—I really got into it.

MAY: I don't want to hear this.

ROSA: It was like dancing or something. All I had to do was follow his lead.

MAY: I think you can do better.

ROSA: Yeah, how? Sweeping up at City Hall after you unionized day workers have gone home?

MAY: Clean-up isn't so bad. At least it's quiet and you get to work by yourself.

ROSA: I don't see you running down to apply for the job.

MAY: I already did.

ROSA: Did what?

MAY: Applied for night crew. I been working three nights a week all summer. With Charlie being away, I needed something to do and we can use the extra money.

ROSA: I ain't never loved no man enough to work two jobs for him.

MAY: It won't be long. Soon as Charlie gets something, I'll quit.

ROSA: You want me to ask this guy at the sex shop if he's got another opening?

MAY: No, thanks. I couldn't do that.

ROSA: You too high-class to fake it?

MAY: It's not that. I just think some things are private.

ROSA: You're a romantic, May. You know that? All for love!

MAY: That's not a bad thing, is it?

ROSA: No. It's kind of sweet actually. Impractical, but kind of sweet. I don't think I ever felt that way.

MAY: Not even about Sonny?

ROSA: Maybe at the beginning, but not enough to be scrubbing no floors to prove it.

MAY *(Defensive)*: I'm not proving anything.

ROSA: Then what are you—May! I've got a proposition for you.

MAY: I'm fine, really.

ROSA: Charlie's looking for a job, right?

MAY: Right.

ROSA: And the doctor says it's okay, right?

MAY: Right.

ROSA: Well, last night, Ty was talking about how his boss was looking for a couple of new drivers and did he know anybody.

MAY: Are you serious?

ROSA: Serious as a heart attack. This guy and Ty were in the war together and to hear him tell it, they thick as thieves. Ty thinks the guy might even take him on as a partner pretty soon.

MAY: He wouldn't have to be out on the road a lot, would he?

ROSA *(Amused)*: You really got it bad, girl, you know that? Don't worry, he'd be right here in town. They always start the new guys off local.

MAY: Do you think Tyrone would really put in a good word for him?

ROSA: If I asked him to, but there's eomthing I gotta ask you first and you gotta tell me the truth.

MAY: What is it?

ROSA: Is he really okay?

MAY: Rose, you know I got no reason to lie to you. This morning when we were talking, he seemed like his old self again. He was really Charlie.

ROSA: But how can they be sure?

MAY: I'm sure.

ROSA: Oh, you're sure. The man is home one night and you're sure?

(A beat.)

MAY: I'm not trying to talk you into anything. You brought it up to me, remember?

ROSA: You're right, you're right! Okay, honey, here's what we'll do. Ty's coming by after work. Did you two kill that bourbon he left here yesterday?

MAY: We didn't touch it.

ROSA: Good. I'll bring him down to meet Charlie, we'll drink up that bourbon with you and see how they get along, then Ty can decide.

MAY: Should I tell Charlie?

ROSA: Of course. Make sure he's on his best behavior.

MAY: How much does Ty know?

ROSA: Not much. I told him Charlie had a bum leg they had to put a pin in. Rehab took longer than they expected it to.

MAY: Nothing else?

ROSA: I figure everybody got a right to tell their own business without no help from me. Besides, Charlie never tries anything on the job, does he?

MAY: No. He always comes home.

ROSA: So! No problem.

MAY: Thanks, Rosa.

ROSA: Don't thank me 'til he gets the job. What time is it?

MAY: Almost eleven.

ROSA: Already? I got a hair appointment at eleven-thirty and if I miss this girl, she won't wait for me. I'll see you later!

MAY: Around three?

ROSA: Make it four. I'll make sure he's in a good mood when we get down here.

MAY: Why don't you just call him?

ROSA: Go to hell!

(Rosa exits as lights go to black.)

Scene Three

That night. The radio is playing "The Way You Do the Things You Do" by the original Temptations. Charlie enters.

MAY *(Calling from the bedroom)*: Charlie?

CHARLIE: It's me.

MAY: I'll be right out!

(Charlie is enjoying the music; he snaps his fingers a little, sings a few lines. He notices a small tray with bourbon and four glasses on the counter. He lowers the music and calls to May, still in the bedroom.)

CHARLIE: We having company?

(May enters from the bedroom. She is wearing the green silk dress she described earlier.)

MAY: Rosa wants to come down and say welcome home.

CHARLIE: Fine as you look in that dress, she better talk fast.

MAY *(Teasing; pleased at his response)*: You still like this old dress?

CHARLIE: I used to dream about you in this dress. I used to close my eyes and try to remember how it felt sliding across your skin.

MAY *(Only half kidding)*: Maybe I should call and tell them to come another time.

CHARLIE: Them?

MAY: She's got a new man. Tyrone.

CHARLIE: She's always got a new man. You met him?

MAY: He's okay. He left this bourbon for you yesterday.

CHARLIE: For me?

MAY: They came by here on their way to the club. Rosa told him you were coming home.

CHARLIE: What else did she tell him?

MAY: Nothing much. Said you had to go to rehab for your leg.

CHARLIE: Good for her! I don't need no strange Negro looking fish-eyed at me because of some stuff he heard from Rosa. *(Picks up the small bottle)* At least he got the good stuff. He didn't get much of it, but what he got is top of the line.

MAY: You have any luck today?

CHARLIE: Well, depends on what you mean by luck.

MAY: What happened?

CHARLIE: Must have been two hundred people down there by ten-thirty and they weren't even giving out applications until noon.

MAY: For how many jobs?

CHARLIE: Twenty-five, but I figure, hey! I'm here early. There's only seventeen people in front of me and the ones behind me are of no concern.

MAY: Good for you!

CHARLIE: I haven't got to the good part yet. I stood there for an hour and finally they let in the first group of us. So, I filled out the application, walked over to where they were processing everybody and got in another line until they called me over to sit down in front of this young sister in a power suit and one of those wigs that sits way up on top of your head if you fool enough to wear it, and she looked at my application and she looked at me and then she kind of rolled her eyes and sighed like I was the last thing she wanted to see on a Saturday afternoon.

MAY: What was wrong with it?

CHARLIE: She didn't tell me at first. She asked me about some of the jobs I'd listed and I told her. She asked me about some of the gaps and I told her I'd been in the hospital a couple of times, but I was fine now. She rolled her eyes again when I said that and I assured her that the demands of stacking boxes would probably not be more than I could handle and she said that wasn't the problem. "Well," I said, "what is the goddamn problem?"

MAY: Did you say, "goddamn"?

CHARLIE: Only to myself, of course. To the sister, I just said, "What is the problem?" And you know what she said?

MAY: What?

CHARLIE: She said I was too old. *(He laughs)*

MAY: Too old?

CHARLIE: Too old to be stacking boxes for a living. They figure I'll be *(As if reciting from memory)* slow, unreliable and prone to work-related injury.

MAY: That's against the law!

CHARLIE: That's what I told Miss Sweetness and she referred me to her supervisor, who was out to lunch at the time.

MAY: Did you wait for him?

CHARLIE: I started to, but the more I waited, the more I couldn't think of anything I wanted to say when the guy showed up. I couldn't see spending the rest of the afternoon trying to talk somebody into letting me have a job I didn't even want.

MAY: I told you not to go down there in the first place.

CHARLIE: But not because you thought I was too old. Because you thought I was too good, so it's not like you get to say I told you so.

MAY: I never say I told you so.

CHARLIE: You don't think I'm too old, do you, May?

MAY: I think you're in your prime.

CHARLIE: Which is why I love you! When are they coming?

MAY: Any minute now.

CHARLIE: Do I have time to change my shirt?

MAY: Sure.

(Charlie exits to the bedroom. A beat, then May calls to him.)

Charlie?

CHARLIE: Yeah?

MAY: Rosa said they might be hiring on Tyrone's job.

CHARLIE: What job is that?

MAY: He drives a truck.

CHARLIE *(Comes out buttoning his shirt)*: Yeah? Local or long-distance?

MAY: Local. You know I asked her that first!

(He embraces her.)

CHARLIE: If I ever do another thing that makes me have to leave your side for longer than eight hours at a time, I want you to do me a favor.

MAY: Anything.

CHARLIE: Shoot me.

MAY: Anything but that.

(The doorbell rings. May starts to answer it, but Charlie stops her.)

CHARLIE: I got it.

(Charlie opens the door to admit Rosa and Tyrone.)

ROSA: Charlie Thompson! *(She hugs him warmly)* Welcome home and meet Tyrone! Ty, this is Charlie.
CHARLIE: Come on in.
TYRONE: Thanks, man. Good to meet you.
CHARLIE: Same here. How's it going, Rose?
ROSA: Same old, same old, but I can't complain.
MAY: Which doesn't mean she won't. Hey, Tyrone.
TYRONE: Hey, May. Looking good, girl!

(Charlie has a visibly negative reaction to Tyrone's playful compliment. No one notices except May, who glances at Charlie nervously.)

ROSA: Do you have my silver hoops?
MAY: I think so.
ROSA: I need them for this dress, honey. I'm naked without my earrings! We'll be right back.

(Rosa pulls a slightly reluctant May into the bedroom so the men can have a moment alone.)

TYRONE *(Looking after May admiringly)*: You a lucky man, brother.

(A beat.)

CHARLIE: That ain't something you got to tell me.
TYRONE *(Alerted by Charlie's tone)*: I didn't mean nothing by it.

CHARLIE: I didn't think you did. It just makes a man feel funny when some other muthafucker is as comfortable up in his house as he is.

(Tyrone is not afraid of a possible confrontation, but knows in this case he is guiltless and no confronation is required. His tone is conciliatory, but direct:)

TYRONE: It ain't like that, man. You can believe it. Rosa and May too tight for me to be trying to even think something like that. Besides, that woman loves you, man. From what Rose say, she hardly left the house since you been gone. Just sitting around, waitin' on you. This is probably only the third or fourth time I've even seen her at all.

(A beat. Charlie relaxes.)

CHARLIE: No problem, man. Everything's cool.

(Charlie extends his hand. Tyrone shakes it. Both are grateful that the bad moment has passed.)

I've just been away, that's all. Things can change.

TYRONE: I know what you talkin' about. When I was in 'Nam, brother be gone two weeks and get a letter: "Dear John Henry, love you, but love Jody more. You take care, okay?" Nigga get distracted and get his head blown off, worrying about some woman ten thousand miles away.

CHARLIE: How about a drink?

TYRONE: Don't mind if I do.

(Charlie pours two drinks and hands one to Tyrone.)

CHARLIE: Here's to good women.

TYRONE: You got that right.

(They touch glasses, drink.)

CHARLIE: Thanks for the welcome-home taste, brother. Glad you could come by to share it.

TYRONE: No problem, man. I know rehab's a bitch. When I got my arm hurt, I had so much rehab they thought I was on staff at the damn place. Shit works though. You stick with it, it pays off big-time.

CHARLIE: What happened to your arm?

TYRONE: I was out on patrol, wadn't nothin' happenin'. Quiet as you please. Sun coming up. Birds singing. I thought maybe the war was over and nobody had told us yet, but soon as you start thinking like that, that's when the shit always happens. Just like clockwork, we got hit hard coming back in. Shrapnel sliced my arm open like a grape. Sucker was hanging on by a thread so this cracker looked at it real fast and told me they were going to have to cut it off. So I picked up my weapon in my good hand and I said, "Doc, if you do, I'll be the last nigga you cut."

CHARLIE: I see he figured out something else to do.

TYRONE: Damn right! If I'd a let that cracker have his way, I'd be wearing a hook for a hand and you know women gonna run from some shit like that.

CHARLIE: I knew a guy with a hook one time. He did all right.

TYRONE: Yeah, but what kind of women we talking about? You paying a woman, she'll tell you she like whatever you got.

CHARLIE: Nice women.

TYRONE: No shit?

CHARLIE: I'll tell you what I learned from that.

TYRONE: What?

CHARLIE: They don't hang around us for our hands.

(A beat, then Tyrone laughs.)

TYRONE: You a crazy muthafucker, man!

CHARLIE *(Shares the laugh)*: You got that right.

TYRONE: May said you messed up your leg in Mississippi. What the hell happened? You weren't down there winkin' at them white girls, were you?

CHARLIE: Not me, brother. I was registering people to vote. I ran into a deputy sherriff who didn't appreciate it.

TYRONE: I never did understand that nonviolent shit. No disrespect or anything, but I ain't goin' nowhere if I gotta promise not to kick a cracker's ass if he puts his hands on me. They arrest you?

CHARLIE: Yeah. Broke my leg in three places, threw me in a hole and waited two days before they called somebody to set it.

TYRONE: Damn, man, that's ugly. You might as well have been in 'Nam, but at least when they hit us, we could hit 'em back!

CHARLIE: Sometimes, it seems like it was all one big war, you know? Some over here and some over there, but one thing guaranteed—you weren't coming out the same way you went in.

TYRONE: Mississippi got the meanest crackers God ever made. I know if it's any meaner, I don't wanna see 'em.

CHARLIE: When they threw me in that hole, they looked at me and said, "We're going to be fair about this, nigger. You gonna leave your mind down there or your nuts. You can decide." *(A beat)* So whenever a muthafucker calls me crazy, I say, goddamn right!

(They laugh and refresh their drinks as Rosa and May enter from the bedroom. Rosa is now wearing large, silver hoop earrings.)

ROSA: I think they started without us, May. What do you think?

MAY: I think if we hurry we can probably catch up.

TYRONE: It's no rush, ladies. I brought a backup just in case y'all had already put a hurtin' on this one. *(He produces a larger bottle of Jack Daniels and refreshes drinks all around)*

ROSA: Will wonders never cease?

CHARLIE: You finally found you a generous man is all.

TYRONE: Ain't no mystery about that.

ROSA: So can we finally have your official welcome-home toast?

CHARLIE: I think me and the brother have already been there.

ROSA *(To Tyrone)*: Did you say anything?

TYRONE: Like what?

ROSA: You know, remarks. Suitable for the occasion.

MAY *(Quickly)*: I'll do it.

ROSA: Thank you. Go ahead, May.

MAY: To Charlie Thompson, man of the people, light of my life, and all-around good brother. Welcome home, baby. I missed you like crazy.

(Charlie kisses May.)

ROSA: Y'all are too sweet!

TYRONE: You miss me like that when I'm hauling distance?

ROSA: I'll get used to it.

TYRONE: If I have anything to do with it, you ain't gettin' used to a damn thing.

MAY: I used to hate it when Charlie was hauling.

CHARLIE: We spent so much money on telephone bills it wasn't worth it to make the trip.

TYRONE: You drove a rig?

CHARLIE: Couple of years, off and on. I tried to get them to just let me work local, but they kept sending me on distance so I quit.

TYRONE: Distance is where the money is.

CHARLIE *(Looking affectionately at May)*: Money ain't all there is to think about sometimes.

ROSA: But it never hurts, you know what I'm saying? It never hurts.

TYRONE: That's why I keep this woman close to me, because we think the same way. She always got one eye on the flow of the cash.

ROSA: And one eye looking out for opportunities.

CHARLIE: Now you sound like an ad for the *Wall Street Journal*.

TYRONE: She's telling the truth. I asked her to do it. In sort of a semi-official way, right, babe?

ROSA: I prefer quasi-official.

MAY: Do what in a quasi-official way?

ROSA: Look for opportunities.

CHARLIE: What kind of opportunities?

TYRONE: Business, mostly. Right now, I'm concentrating on investigating the trucking business, since that's what I'm doing myself. I figure that's a good place to start.

ROSA: Business is business and I know what it takes to run one without getting taken to the cleaners. Sonny never could have made that club show a profit without me.

MAY: You're going into business?

TYRONE: Not right away, but some things are opening up for me. I might be able to get in on the ground floor of something good.

ROSA: Tell 'em, honey.

TYRONE: Hey, man, I don't mean to be taking over your party or nothin'.

CHARLIE: Don't you get nervous 'til I get nervous.

TYRONE: Cool. This guy who I'm driving for, we were in 'Nam together. He ain't no whiz kid, but his family is wired in with some people who helped him when he got back. They sold him three trucks cheap and some good routes. Now he's got more business than he can handle. But up to a year ago, I don't know any of this, right? I haven't seen this guy in twenty years. But I'm sitting in a bar one night and this guy walks in and looks at me like he knows me. This ain't a bar I frequent, so I wasn't trying to make no eye contact or nothing, but this guy keeps looking at me. I can see this out the corner of my eye, but I'm drinking like I'm alone in the room.

ROSA *(Impatiently)*: Tyrone! The suspense is killing me! Get to the point.

TYRONE: The point is, this is the guy, Neal, that I knew from 'Nam that I haven't seen in all that time, but he recognizes me and now he's telling me how great his business is doing and how much money he's making and how he's gonna buy his brothers out and be his own boss and then he starts getting all sentimental about seeing me 'cause it's like right before Christmas Eve and I saved his life once in the bush, not 'cause I knew it was him, he was just a guy down, screaming, and I grabbed his arm and pulled him in with us before they came back to finish him off and I said, hey, if you feeling so emotional and shit—pardon my French!—if you're feeling so emotional, how about giving me a job? And he was shocked that I could be out of a job, like I was in demand because I'd saved his life, but that was okay because he hired me and once I got in, I could see that there was a lot of improvements he could make. So I told him a couple of things and he tried them and they worked and so I told him a couple more and they worked even better.

CHARLIE: He ought to give you a raise and a desk job.

TYRONE: You reading my mind, man. I just look around at his operation and things jump out at me about how to fix it up first-class. Right now, I'm proving my value to this guy and then I'm going to say, hey, how about taking me in as a partner, let me have a little piece of this pie.

MAY: That sounds real good. Congratulations.

ROSA: Don't be congratulating anybody yet. All that pie is still in the sky so far, but back in the real world, I heard you got my job at Hudson's today.

CHARLIE: It's still open if you lookin' for it. They turned me down cold.

ROSA: Turned you down?

CHARLIE: Too old.

TYRONE: Too old for what?

MAY: A warehouse job downtown. Charlie was over there this morning.

TYRONE: You looking for work?

CHARLIE: Yeah.

TYRONE: Why didn't you say so? They're hiring at my place. My buddy asked me if I knew anybody since I been on him about how come I'm the only brother he got working over there. If you want the job, it's yours.

CHARLIE: Just like that?

TYRONE: Hey, man. We all went through the war together, right?

CHARLIE: Thanks a lot, brother. I mean it, but I gotta tell you something. I wasn't kidding about what I said before.

TYRONE: About what?

CHARLIE: About being crazy.

TYRONE: What you mean?

CHARLIE: They hurt my leg, that's the truth, but that wasn't shit compared to the number they did on my head.

TYRONE *(Looking at Rosa, who looks away)*: That's why you were in the hospital?

CHARLIE: Yeah.

TYRONE: All summer?

CHARLIE: Yeah.

TYRONE: What kind of crazy are you?

CHARLIE *(Grinning)*: The nonviolent kind.

TYRONE: So you feeling okay now that you out? You handling it all right?

CHARLIE: What are my other choices?

(A beat, then Tyrone laughs.)

TYRONE: You got that right! Get your ass a job like the rest of these crazy muthafuckers out here, that's what you better do. *(He takes a scrap of paper from his pocket, writes down the number of the place)* Tell him I told you to call. I'll put my name on here, too, and if he offers it, take the job, man. Just don't tell my buddy all that crazy shit. White folks don't need to know everything a nigga know!

CHARLIE: I'll drink to that!

(The men touch glasses to seal the bargain, then drink.)

ROSA: Well, now that we got that settled, I got a new joke for you, Charlie.

MAY: Oh, Lord!

CHARLIE: You think I'm ready for it, Rose?

MAY: No! Trust me!

ROSA: Ty thought it was funny.

MAY: Which shows y'all are meant for each other, but is no reason to torture the rest of us.

ROSA: Come on, Charlie. It's a good one.

CHARLIE: Okay, go ahead.

ROSA: Knock-knock.

CHARLIE: It's a knock-knock joke?

MAY: I warned you.

CHARLIE *(Laughing)*: Well, if I was ever gonna find it funny, this will be the time. Go ahead, Sister Rosa. Who's there?

ROSA: Banana.

CHARLIE: Banana, who?

ROSA: Knock-knock.

(They continue with the joke as the lights go to black.)

Scene Four

The following Saturday. Lights up on Rosa and May. May is slowly chewing a piece of pie. In front of her, there are a number of slices of pie on individual saucers. Rosa is holding a clipboard and watching May expectantly. May nods and swallows.

MAY: Mmmmmmmm. It's okay.

ROSA: So on a scale of one to ten, what?

MAY: Ten is the worst?

ROSA: Ten is the best.

MAY: I'd give it a three.

ROSA: You said, "Mmmmmmmm." You can't say, "Mmmmm-mmm," and give it a three.

MAY: I wasn't saying, "Mmmmmmmm," because it tasted so good. I was saying, "Mmmmmmmm," because I was thinking.

ROSA: What were you thinking?

MAY: I was thinking it was pretty good, but sort of bland. Needs some cinnamon. And I didn't taste any nutmeg at all.

ROSA: White folks know they can't make no sweet potato pie!

MAY: It wasn't that bad.

ROSA: Then give it a five.

MAY: What difference does it make? You don't get paid more if I like it, do you?

ROSA: I wouldn't be doing this at all if I'd a gone on and taken that 1-900 job like I had some sense.

MAY: I told you Tyrone wouldn't like that.

ROSA: He liked it fine when I did it for him.

MAY: Rosa!

ROSA: I told him the guy said I was a natural and he said he'd like to see for himself. So I told him to go on down to the pay phone and give me a buzz.

MAY: You didn't!

ROSA: I sure did.

MAY: What did he say?

ROSA: That is none of your business, but I will tell you this—
he's installing a separate line on Monday so he can call
me without standing out in the rain.

MAY: The man said you were a natural.

ROSA: Yeah, but Ty don't want me to make money off it. He
sounded like you. Some things are private.

MAY: If I had known telling you that meant I had to eat this
much bad sweet potato pie, I would have told you to go
for broke.

ROSA: You're lucky. I made Tyrone taste-test the frozen collard greens.

MAY: How were they?

ROSA: How do you think? The beauty of collard greens is the
time it takes to make them. If you cut that out, what's
the point? Do one more.

MAY: I can't do one more! I'm going to weigh a ton by the time
you get your report done.

ROSA: Just think of it this way: you'll be helping to decide
which sweet potato pie is on tables all over America.

MAY: I'd rather decide what they watch on TV.

ROSA: They got machines that do that. Sorry.

*(They clear away the pie and saucers, put away the clip-
board and questionnaires.)*

MAY: Where'd you all go last night?

ROSA: We rented a video. One of those gangster movies. Ty
loves 'em, so I'm watching it, but I'm making sure I close
my eyes so I don't see the part where they stab the guy in
the trunk of the car, I can't take that stuff, and then this
one guy is talking to his wife and she's saying how she's
worried that he might get caught doing this gangster stuff
and what would happen to her if he had to go to jail and
he tells her not to worry about it and you know why?

MAY: Why?

ROSA: Because, and these are the actual words he used, "Nobody goes to jail but nigger stick-up men."

MAY: So?

ROSA: So I didn't appreciate it.

MAY: Didn't appreciate that he said "nigger"?

ROSA: He can say what he wants but I don't have to pay three dollars to hear it.

MAY: You don't think Italian gangsters ever say "nigger"?

ROSA: In real life, I'm sure they do, but it pisses me off in the movies 'cause soon as I hear it, I get mad and miss half the movie 'til I can calm down. I hate that. I was watching this Woody Allen movie one time. It was pretty good, too. All about a bunch of sisters—blood sisters, not soul sisters—sleeping with each other's husbands and driving each other crazy, and right in the middle, when I had already picked one I sort of identified with, here comes the black maid at the party. Sister was dressed in that Hollywood maid outfit—little apron, white orthopedic shoes like a damn nurse in case somebody fell out or something. But it made me mad. She didn't have one line and nobody even said anything directly to her. They took what she was offering on that little silver tray and she glided on by and then back out to the kitchen. That was it. But I couldn't stop thinking about her. Was she pissed off 'cause she had to work? Was she tired? Were they paying her extra to work the holiday since she was there serving their Christmas dinner instead of home serving her own?

MAY *(Laughing)*: You know what I think?

ROSA: What?

MAY: I think you ought to stop going to the movies.

ROSA: I was home last night. What about that?

MAY: Maybe you should find another form of recreation.

ROSA: When I told Ty to turn it off, he had a few suggestions.

MAY: I'm sure Brother Tyrone is a man of many talents.

ROSA: Many talents and a one-track mind. All Ty's suggestios begin and end with S-E-X.

MAY: What's wrong with S-E-X?

ROSA: Nothing's wrong with it, but rationing is in effect in that area, honey.

MAY: Rationing?

ROSA: Didn't your mama ever tell you nobody buys the cow if they already got the milk?

MAY: My mama told me you catch more flies with honey than you do with vinegar.

(Charlie and Tyrone enter.)

Hey, baby!

ROSA: You two look like the cats who swallowed the canary.

CHARLIE *(Dramatically)*: The question is, what are you looking at?

ROSA: Don't get me started.

CHARLIE: And the answer is . . . tell 'em, Brother Tyrone.

TYRONE: You are looking at a Negro with a job!

CHARLIE: A good job!

MAY: You went down to Neal's today?

CHARLIE: This very day.

MAY *(Excited and very pleased)*: You didn't even tell me!

TYRONE: They hired him on the spot. I told you, I got pull down there!

CHARLIE: I start Monday. Brother Tyrone will teach me the route himself, and come Friday, I will bring you home a paycheck!

ROSA: Praise the Lord!

MAY: I knew you'd get it. *(She embraces Charlie happily)*

TYRONE: Thank you, May. Somebody around here gotta have faith in my connections.

MAY: I got faith in Charlie.

CHARLIE: Eat your heart out, man.

TYRONE *(Putting an affectionate arm around Rosa)*: I'm not doing bad.

ROSA: Thank you, sweet thing. Want some potato pie?

TYRONE: Is it any good?

MAY: I gave it a three.

ROSA: But she upgraded it to a five!

MAY: How about drinks instead? *(She brings glasses, bourbon and a bowl of ice)*

CHARLIE: Let's go get something to eat downtown.

ROSA: Listen to Mr. Rockefeller!

TYRONE: Streets are gonna be full of cops.

MAY: Why?

TYRONE: You all didn't hear about it?

ROSA: About what? We haven't been out all day.

TYRONE: They found another body. Throat cut just like the last one.

MAY: White guy?

TYRONE: Yeah. Sixty-five years old. Had money on him, too. Nothing stolen.

MAY: If he keeps going like this, ain't no white folks coming back downtown.

CHARLIE: Why'd you say "he"? What if it's a woman?

ROSA: Those guys were both in their sixties.

CHARLIE: It wouldn't have to be a girlfriend. It could be something political.

TYRONE: Like terrorists?

CHARLIE: Yeah.

MAY: Female terrorists? What country are they from?

CHARLIE: I don't know. I'm just saying, it could be.

MAY: I don't think so. Female terrorists would probably use a gun.

CHARLIE: Too loud.

MAY: But a knife makes you have to get too close. You have to actually touch the person.

CHARLIE: That's true.

MAY: Plus, I don't know any women who are mad enough to slit somebody's throat unless it's real personal.

CHARLIE: Slitting somebody's throat is always real personal.

TYRONE: Whoever's doing it, May's right. It's making folks nervous.

ROSA: It's making me nervous!

TYRONE: No, I mean white folks. Nobody mentioned it directly, but all up and down my route, they were much friendlier than usual. Smiling and saying good morning like they wanted to make sure I didn't go off.

MAY: I felt like that after the first one, too. Like the white folks at work were walking on eggs.

CHARLIE: So now we gotta start cutting people's throats to get somebody to say good morning like they got some sense?

ROSA: Let's change the subject. I got a new joke.

MAY: Oh, Lord!

ROSA: Exactly! It's a religious joke.

CHARLIE: It's not a knock-knock joke, is it?

ROSA: My brother told me this one and he's great at telling jokes!

CHARLIE: Can we get him on the phone?

MAY: I'm going to get ice. (She goes to the kitchen)

TYRONE: I'm listening.

ROSA: Thank you, sweet thing. Okay. Jesus and Moses are walking by a lake talking about how bad they both were back in the day and then Jesus says, "What was the baddest thing you ever did?" Moses thought for a second and said, "That Red Sea thing was pretty impressive. How about you?" Jesus didn't even have to think about it. He spoke right up. "Walking on water."

MAY: You didn't say it was a sacreligious joke.

ROSA: My brother said he heard it from a deacon, so hush! Anyway, Moses agreed that was truly miraculous and since they were right there by the shore and everything he asked Jesus if he could show him a few steps. "I can do better than that," Jesus said. "Let's row out to the middle and I'll walk back with you." So they rowed on out there to the deep water, Moses held the oars and Jesus stepped over the side and sank like a stone. Moses finally pulled him back up in the boat and Jesus was like, "I don't understand. I used to be really good at this." Then Moses said, "I see what the problem is. Last time, you didn't have those holes in your hands and feet."

(They all laugh, relieved and amused.)

MAY: You are going to hell, girl, sure as I'm sittin' here!

ROSA: I told you I knew how to tell a joke.

CHARLIE: You must have been practicing.

ROSA: You can tell that one to the guys at work and break the ice.

CHARLIE: Not me. If I tell one, they'll tell one and too many of their jokes got me as the punch line.

TYRONE: You got that right. When they get too relaxed, they say something you gotta hit 'em for and they didn't even mean nothin' by it. This guy in 'Nam used to like to hang out with the brothers and a couple of us had to tighten him up one time. After that, if he thought he was out of line, he'd say, "Uh, oh! How close am I to gettin' hit?"

(The men laugh.)

CHARLIE: You know this guy ain't killed but two people and we're already getting more respect. What if he really goes off and takes out ten or twelve? You'll be a partner by Christmas!

TYRONE: I'll drink to that!

(The men toast.)

ROSA: That's not funny.

MAY: They're just kidding, Rose.

ROSA: Those are innocent people.

CHARLIE: Sometimes in a war, innocent people die.

ROSA: Does this look like a war to you?

CHARLIE: Do you walk up to the corner at night by yourself?

ROSA: That's not because of any war. That's because of all those young hardheads who don't want to work for a living!

CHARLIE: Ask Brother Tyrone. He'll tell you.

MAY: I thought we were going to change the subject.

CHARLIE: Am I right, Ty?

TYRONE: About what?

CHARLIE: When you blow up a village, innocent people get blown up, too, don't they?

(A beat.)

TYRONE: Yeah. Sometimes.

CHARLIE: Sometimes innocent people get hurt. That's all I'm saying.

ROSA: You're just talking crazy.

(A beat.)

CHARLIE: I got a good job, good friends and a good woman. How crazy can I be?

MAY: Well, to have all that, this isn't much of a celebration you're throwing. We need some music!

TYRONE: They're playing old Motown on WJLB all weekend.

(May turns on the radio. It is "Pride and Joy" by Marvin Gaye.)

MAY: Come on, Tyrone! Let's show these old-time Negroes what a real bop is!

(May and Tyrone dance.)

CHARLIE: Come on, Rose. I think we been challenged.

ROSA: By two of the no-dancingest Negroes in Detroit!

TYRONE: That's not what you said at the club last Friday.

ROSA: Times change, sweet thing. Times change!

(They all laugh and dance. The phone rings. May goes to answer it.)

MAY: Hello? What? Hang on, I can't hear you.

(Charlie turns down the radio. Rosa and Tyrone move away to freshen their drinks.)

Henry? Yeah, what's up? Tomorrow? Can't Caroline go? What about Grace? I know I'm a delegate, Henry, but I'm an alternate, remember? Okay, okay. I hear you. Right. You gonna pick me up? I'm always on time! Yeah, I'll tell him. *(She hangs up the phone)*

CHARLIE: What's up, babe?

MAY: I gotta go to Chicago tomorrow for the regional union meeting. Caroline broke her ankle and Grace's kids have the mumps. I won't be back until Thursday. Henry says tell you he's sorry.

CHARLIE: Apologies accepted. *(Watching May)* So, what's the problem?

MAY: I wanted to be here for your first day down at Neal's.

CHARLIE: So you could pack my lunch and have dinner on the table when I get home?

MAY: Something like that.

CHARLIE *(Gently)*: We got plenty of time. Things ain't gonna get nothing but better.

MAY: Promise?

CHARLIE: I promise.

(Charlie turns up the music. It is "Forever" by Marvin Gaye.)

May I have this dance?

(May moves into Charlie's arms and they begin to slow dance.)

ROSA: You two are pathetic.
CHARLIE *(Laughing)*: And I ain't even 'shamed!

(Rosa moves into Tyrone's arms, and they begin to dance.)

ROSA: Me, neither!

(They all laugh and dance easily as lights fade to black.)

Act Two

Scene One

The following Friday. Lights up on Charlie alone in the kitchen. He gets a glass from the cabinet, takes an unopened bottle of Jack Daniels from a bag on the coffee table, pours a drink and sits, thinking. The doorbell rings. He ignores it and it rings again, longer. He gets up and opens the door, still holding the drink.

ROSA: Hey, Charlie! I'm on my way for Chinese takeout. Want me to bring you back something?
CHARLIE: I don't think so, but thanks . . .

(*He does not invite her in, and she glances at him, then notices the drink.*)

ROSA: You're not drinking alone, are you?
CHARLIE: I wouldn't be very good company right now, Rose.
ROSA: You'll do.

(Rosa enters, gets a glass, pours a drink and sits down. Charlie reluctantly closes the door and sits.)

CHARLIE: Don't say I didn't warn you.

ROSA: I'll keep that in mind. You talk to May?

CHARLIE: Not today.

ROSA *(Overly casual)*: Why don't you call her?

(A beat.)

CHARLIE: Relax, Rose. My plans for the evening are very simple. I'm going to lock my door, get real drunk and pass out. That's not against the law yet, is it?

ROSA: If it was, half the Negroes in Detroit would be in the penitentiary. Cheers!

(They toast and drink.)

CHARLIE: You're eating kind of late, aren't you?

ROSA: You're drinking kind of early, aren't you?

CHARLIE: Then I guess we're even. *(He pours another)*

(A beat.)

ROSA: What's up, Charlie?

CHARLIE: It's been one of those days, you know?

ROSA: Every day is one of those days, but you ain't been stopping on your way home for a bottle of Jack.

CHARLIE: How do you know?

ROSA: May would have told me.

CHARLIE: Why would she do that?

ROSA: Because we're friends. That's what friends do.

CHARLIE: Is it?

(A beat. Rosa will not be distracted.)

I haven't talked to May yet.

ROSA: You already said that.

CHARLIE: I usually talk to her at night.

ROSA: I know. Right before you go to bed.

CHARLIE: May told you that too?

ROSA: She didn't have to.

(A beat.)

CHARLIE: They gave me a drug test at work.

ROSA: So, how'd you do?

CHARLIE *(Agitated)*: How'd I do? I failed it, of course! All that shit I take for my head showed up like I was smoking crack or something!

ROSA: Did you tell them you were taking prescription drugs?

CHARLIE: I walked in yesterday morning and BAM. There they were! No talk required.

ROSA: Calm down. Talk to Neal. He'll be able to straighten it out.

CHARLIE *(Increasingly agitated)*: I tried to talk to him, but he didn't want to hear it. Pretended he hadn't been out drinking a beer with me and Ty last week like we were buddies and shit. All of a sudden he's acting like I came in to stick up the place!

ROSA: Calm down, will you? You didn't start anything down there, did you?

CHARLIE: Start anything? Like what?

ROSA: Like whatever! This job means a lot to Tyrone!

CHARLIE: This job means a lot to me! *(Struggling to regain his composure)* Listen, Rose. I been to work on time. I do my route. I say good morning and good night. I drive that damn truck all day because that's what I get paid to do, and that's all!

ROSA: Okay, okay! We both need to just calm down. This is not a big crisis. This is a small misunderstanding.

CHARLIE: That's just what I told Neal!

ROSA: Of course you did, but he needs to hear it from Ty.

CHARLIE *(Sarcastic)*: Somebody he trusts?

ROSA: He trusted him enough to give you a job, didn't he?

CHARLIE: Such as it is.

ROSA *(Standing to leave)*: You said you weren't fit company tonight. My mistake for not listening.

CHARLIE: Don't go, Rose! I'm sorry. It's just that . . . I keep telling May everything is going to be different this time. I don't want to be looking in her face if she ever stops believing me. *(A beat)* I didn't start anything. I just left.

ROSE: Good. Ty's still on the road, but I'll tell him what happened, he can talk to Neal on the phone and get things straightened around without waiting until he gets back.

CHARLIE: How long before you talk to Ty?

ROSA: About three hours from now. Right before I go to bed.

(A beat. They both relax a little.)

You not the only one with some romance in your life, you know?

CHARLIE: You really think Ty can talk to Neal? Tell him this kind of response is not required?

ROSA: I keep trying to tell you and your hardheaded wife that's what friends are for!

CHARLIE: Do me a favor and don't mention this to May. I don't want to worry her.

ROSA: Tell her once it's all squared away. Show her you knew how to handle it.

CHARLIE: Thanks, Rose.

(A beat.)

ROSA: You and May got something good, Charlie. Hold onto it.

CHARLIE: I don't deserve that woman.

ROSA: Yes, you do. Can't nobody else put up with either one of your high-strung asses.

CHARLIE: You're doing all right.

ROSA: Don't push your luck! *(She prepares to go)* So, you're not up for Chinese, how about some Cuban food?

CHARLIE: My treat.

ROSA: What's the occasion?

CHARLIE: No occasion. That's what friends do.

(They exit as lights go to black.)

Scene Two

Monday. Lights up on May vacuuming the room. A dust cloth and other light cleaning supplies are in evidence. Rosa rings the doorbell several times before May hears it and opens the door. Rosa is carrying a homemade sweet potato pie with foil over the top.

ROSA: Welcome back.

MAY: What's this?

ROSA: A real sweet potato pie. Made it myself. I figure you earned it.

MAY: Come on in. I'm just patting things. You know if you leave a man alone in a house for a week, it's a miracle it's still standing when you get back.

ROSA: Charlie home?

MAY: He's at work.

ROSA: At work?

(May takes the pie to the kitchen; she doesn't notice Rosa's surprised expression.)

MAY: He said he's been doing double shifts the whole time I was gone. What's wrong?

ROSA: Nothing. How was Chicago?

MAY: Who knows? I didn't hardly get out of the hotel. Those Negroes went there to argue, not to sightsee.

ROSA: You talk to my brother?

MAY: I did. He said call him. He's got another joke for you.

ROSA: I sure need one.

MAY: What's wrong?

ROSA: I don't know. Just seems like the world is going crazy.

MAY: I told you that a long time ago.

ROSA: You hear what happened on Belle Isle last weekend?

MAY: What?

ROSA: A bunch of people were over there, you know how they do on Sunday, drinking and smoking weed, playing music, cooking out. Same old, same old, blasé, blasé. So the day is over, time to go home and Miss Girl climbs in her car with her friends. They're driving home, talking and laughing, and she gets distracted, probably talking about some man with her girlfriends and she taps the bumper of this guy's car in front of her and he goes berserk. Jumps out, hollering and threatening to kill her, so she freaks, tries to pull around him and get away, but she taps his damn car again, still nothing major, but the guy takes this as a personal affront to his manhood, such as it is, reaches in the car, drags her out, beats her like a dog right there on the bridge and then tells his buddies to hold her while he goes to his car to get a tire iron so he can beat her some more.

MAY: My God! Where were the cops?

ROSA: Who knows? It gets worse. Of course the girl is really freaking by now, not to mention already beat-up pretty bad, and her girlfriends are screaming and begging these guys to stop, but they just laugh, and the other people on the bridge are blowing their horns or getting out to look, but ain't none of them getting near homeboy with the tire iron, so Miss Girl looks around for the help she suddenly realizes ain't there and ain't expected and she's so scared she jumps off the bridge. Can't even swim and she jumps off the Belle Isle Bridge into the river. You know what kinda fall that is? Plus, she's still so scared, when two brothers jump in to try and help, she won't let them get anywhere near her. Finally, she goes down and doesn't come up again. They didn't even find her body for two days. *(A beat)* Now how can somebody get that mad about a scratch on a damn car?

MAY: You know that wasn't about a car.

ROSA: Well, what was it about then?

(A beat.)

MAY: I don't know.

ROSA: May?

MAY: Yeah?

ROSA: I gotta ask you something, and it may sound funny, but I'm serious, okay?

MAY: Okay.

(A beat.)

ROSA: Where is Charlie working?

MAY: Down at Neal's with Tyrone, of course, where do you think?

ROSA: No, May.

MAY: No, what?

ROSA: Maybe I should let Charlie tell you.

MAY: Tell me what?

ROSA: He made me promise, otherwise you know I would have called you.

MAY: Either you tell me what you're talking about or I'm calling Neal's right now.

ROSA: Charlie doesn't work there anymore.

MAY: What do you mean?

ROSA: He got fired.

MAY: Fired for what?

ROSA: He failed a drug test.

MAY: He isn't doing any drugs!

ROSA: He said they were prescription.

MAY: You know they are! He can get a letter from his doctor. Didn't he tell Tyrone?

ROSA: Ty's been on the road, but he called Neal after he talked to Charlie.

MAY: And?

ROSA: May, I don't want to be in the middle of anything. I just stuck my head in to see if he wanted any Chinese take-out since you were gone and eveything and—

MAY: Rosa . . .

(A beat.)

ROSA: Tyrone said when he told Neal it was because Charlie was—because of a mental condition—Neal said if he was that crazy, he was too crazy to be driving a truck.

MAY: Did he say that to Charlie?

ROSA: No. Ty had to tell him.

MAY: He didn't say anything to me about it.

ROSA: Ty said Neal was really pissed off at him for even bringing Charlie around.

MAY: We talked on the phone every day. He picked me up last night. He never said a word.

ROSA: I'm sorry, honey. This isn't the way for you to hear it, but when you said he was at work—

MAY: It's okay, Rose.

ROSA: Ty's coming off the road in another couple of days. Once everything is straightened out, maybe we can all get together.

MAY: He never said a word.

ROSA: I know. *(A beat)* I'm gonna go on then. *(She goes to the door)*

MAY: Rosa? Thanks.

ROSA: Call me.

MAY: I will.

(Rosa exits. May puts away the vacuum and the dusting cloth. Charlie enters.)

CHARLIE: Hey, May.

MAY: Hey, Charlie.

CHARLIE: You okay?

MAY: Rosa told me what happened.

CHARLIE: What happened about what?

MAY: She said you got fired.

CHARLIE: I can explain about that.

MAY: Why didn't you tell me?

CHARLIE: Because I knew I could fix it.

MAY: You should have told me!

CHARLIE: But I fixed it.

MAY: How did you fix it?

CHARLIE: I called the hospital from Neal's office and they told him the medication was legal and I was okay to drive any truck he had keys for. After that, he said he was sorry he hadn't listened to me before and if I wanted my job back, I could have it.

MAY: That's not what Tyrone said.

CHARLIE: Ty's been on the road all week. I didn't talk to Neal until this morning.

MAY: Are you sure that's what he said?

(Charlie goes to the phone.)

CHARLIE: You can ask him yourself if you want to.

MAY: No. I just wish that you had told me.

CHARLIE: I didn't want to worry you. Besides, I'm telling you now.

(She moves away from him to the window. She wants to believe him, but she is still unconvinced. She speaks without taking her eyes off the bridge, almost to herself.)

MAY: When we first moved in, the thing I really liked about this place was that I could wake up every day and be someplace that wasn't here. I could just walk across that bridge and everything was different. The money, the street names, the politics. Everything. There was a whole country where not a living soul knew my name. *(Turns to him)* You know, if you ever lie to me, it changes everything.

CHARLIE: I know. *(He holds out a small brown paper bag to her)* These are for you.

MAY: What is it?

(He dumps out the contents. There are ten small packets of seeds for assorted flowers and vegetables.)

Seeds?

CHARLIE: How long you been talking about moving to Canada and planting a garden?

MAY: A long time.

CHARLIE: I just might be ready to take you up on it.

MAY: When?

CHARLIE: I only want to work for Neal for a year. He feels so bad about what happened, he'll give me all the hours I want. If we can save most of that money, we'll have a stake. We can buy a little piece of land off in the woods, where I don't have to see anybody but you. We'll plant flowers in the front and food in the back. And when it starts snowing, we'll put some logs on the fireplace and we won't come out until it's spring.

MAY: I know that dream. I used to stand here when you were gone sometimes and dream it over and over like a movie. I read books about what would grow over there and what wouldn't. I knew what phase of the moon was the best one to plant squash and pumpkins. I had a whole catalogue with nothing but tomatoes in it. I used to stand right here and say their names like the multiplication tables. Red Plum. Green Zebra. Big Rainbow. Yellow Pear. Ultra Pink. Sun Gold. Super Sweet 100. *(A beat)* I want us to get old together in peace. What do you want?

CHARLIE: That's all I ever wanted.

MAY: No, it isn't. You wanted to change the world, remember?

CHARLIE: I did a hell of a job.

MAY: You could have done worse.

CHARLIE: I could have done a lot better by you.

MAY: Okay. So in this life you owe me. In the next one, I'll make you pay through the nose.

CHARLIE: I'll never lie to you, May.

MAY *(Teasing him)*: You better not. Nonviolence was only a phase I was going through.

(The bridge illuminates, and they silently share the beauty of the lights.)

CHARLIE: They're coming, May. You know that?

MAY: What's coming, Charlie?

CHARLIE: Better days.

MAY: You promise?

CHARLIE: I promise. Now tell me what else you're going to grow in my garden.

MAY: Your garden?

CHARLIE: Our garden?

MAY: I like the sound of that.

CHARLIE: Me, too.

(He puts his arms around her gently as the lights go to black.)

Scene Three

The next day, afternoon. Lights up on May and Rosa. May is rubbing lotion into her hands. There are several small, numbered bottles of lotion in front of her. Rosa, again with a clipboard, is sitting expectantly in front of May.

MAY: This one feels pretty good.

ROSA: One to ten.

MAY: Nine.

ROSA: How about the smell?

MAY: Seven.

ROSA: How can you give the feel a nine and the smell a seven?

MAY: It feels better than it smells.

ROSA: Okay. Would you buy it?

MAY: No.

ROSA: Why not?

MAY: I don't like the smell.

ROSA: You gave it a seven.

MAY: It wasn't disgusting. I just don't like it.

ROSA: This is getting on my nerves. Enough! Wipe it off!

MAY *(Picks up another one)*: I kind of liked this one.

ROSA: It's on the house.

MAY: Thanks.

ROSA: I'm real glad everything worked out with Neal and Charlie.

MAY: Me, too. I wish he had told me, but I'm just glad it's over.

ROSA: Tyrone will be back tonight. Want to get together later?

MAY: Are you sure you want company? Ty's been gone almost a week.

ROSA: Don't worry. We won't stay long.

MAY: This job is the best thing that's happened to Charlie in a long time. It's like one good thing brings another and another.

ROSA: The opposite is true, too. Bad luck can multiply quicker than any winning streak I ever saw.

MAY: You're a pessimist.

ROSA: I'm a realist.

(A knock. May opens the door to Tyrone, who walks in quickly without being asked.)

TYRONE: Hey, May. Charlie here? *(He is very agitated)*

MAY: No, but somebody you know is.

ROSA *(Moves to embrace him)*: When'd you get back, sweet thing?

TYRONE *(Moves away from her before she makes contact)*: Six hours ago.

ROSA *(Surprised)*: Six hours? Why didn't you call me?

TYRONE: I've been talking to the police.

MAY: The police?

TYRONE: I was in Neal's office trying to be sure he wasn't holding nothing about Charlie against me and two cops came and knocked on the door. They found another body downtown this morning and there was a piece of paper lying there right next to the guy with Neal's number and my name on it! My name! Three dead crackers and the cops got my name!

ROSA: My God, Ty! What did they say?

TYRONE: They asked me a lot of questions. Where was I last night? Did I know the guy? One of them asked me if I was in 'Nam. I said yeah, I was in 'Nam, so what? And he said, the way these guys got it, looked like some Green Beret shit or something. It was clean like the guy knew what he was doing. I said that ain't me, man. We didn't do no knife stuff. We had guns, man. Guns! Only those crazy muthafuckers who like to go behind the lines and shit, that's who was cutting people's throats! Not me!

ROSA: They don't think you had anything to do with it, do they?

TYRONE: What do you think I'm talking about? I'm a suspect! They told me not to go anywhere. What do you think that means?

ROSA: But you can't help it if somebody wrote your name on a piece of paper!

TYRONE *(Rising agitation)*: But who, Rose? Who wrote my name on a piece of paper?

ROSA: How should I know? When the cops figure it out, they'll talk to him and not you. It's all just a mistake!

TYRONE: I wrote it! It's my handwriting. My fingerprints because it's the paper I wrote on sitting right here when I told Charlie about the job! When I opened my god-damn mouth and invited him to fuck up my life!

MAY: You think Charlie . . .

(Tyrone just looks at May.)

That's crazy!

TYRONE: No, he's crazy! But it's not going down like this. Not like this here!

ROSA: Just calm down, both of you! We can figure this out. You have alibis. You're innocent!

TYRONE: Listen, Rose. The cops want to arrest somebody. They don't care if it's the nigger who did it or not. They just need to say they got him. And now they got my name on the paper! No—they got me!

ROSA *(Rising panic as she realizes how serious this really is)*: Charlie can tell them, Ty. When he comes home, he can just tell them!

TYRONE: Tell them what?

ROSA: That you gave that paper to him so he could call Neal about a job.

TYRONE: Is he gonna tell them how it got down there layin' on the ground beside a dead man?

MAY: Stop it!

TYRONE: Where is he?

MAY: He's at work.

TYRONE: At work where?

MAY: He's doing his regular route.

TYRONE: Neal fired him last week!

MAY: Charlie called the hospital! The doctor told Neal —

TYRONE: Neal told me if he saw Charlie anywhere around he was gonna call the police. But I guess he didn't have to. They came on their own! To talk to me! Because of that crazy muthafucker, I'm in the middle of all of it. *(A beat)* If you see him, tell him I'm looking for him. *(He starts to exit)*

ROSA: Ty! Wait!

TYRONE: Leave me alone, Rosa. Can't you just leave me alone? *(He exits)*

(A beat.)

ROSA: Where do you think he is?

MAY: I don't know.

ROSA: How could that paper have gotten there?

MAY: I don't know.

ROSA: Well, he'll come home, won't he?

MAY: I don't know! I don't know!

(A beat.)

ROSA: I have to ask you, May.

MAY *(A warning)*: Don't.

ROSA: Do you think he could have done it?

MAY: No.

ROSA: I don't believe you.

MAY: Then get out of my house.

ROSA: No! I won't. Tyrone is a suspect! They think it's him!

MAY: They don't know who it is.

ROSA: This isn't a game, May.

MAY: He's sick!

ROSA: He's killing people!

MAY: It's not true.

ROSA: He's killing innocent people!

MAY: He is an innocent person!

ROSA: Not anymore! Don't you see? Not anymore! *(She goes to the door)*

MAY: Rose!

(Rosa stops.)

You're my best friend. I need you to be my best friend.

ROSA *(Gently, but determined)*: We've got to call the police, honey. There's no way around it.

MAY: He can't go to jail. Don't you understand? He's been to jail.

ROSA: And that was wrong, but this is wrong, too.

MAY: You don't understand.

ROSA: Make me! Make me understand!

MAY: We were so young, Rose. We were babies. *(A beat)* We had been out all day trying to get people to come down to the courthouse to register and we didn't get a single one. All day long, trudging up to these little houses, hoping somebody was home. Some of them were so scared when they realized who we were and what we were talking about that they ran in the house and slammed the door. So we were tired and discouraged and we had a long walk back to the Hemphills and it was already getting dark. I knew we needed to hurry, but I wanted to sit down for a minute and catch my breath.

So we walked a little ways off the road and sat down and Charlie put his arm around me but I was so tired and scared and evil, I just sat there. So he started talking about how important it was for us to be in Mississippi and how much he loved me and how he was going to tell our children how brave their mama was and I sort of leaned on him a little bit and he started kissing me and we just forgot everything. Just for a minute. I know it wasn't more than a minute . . .

And then they were shining their flashlights in our faces. They took us to the jail, the sheriff and two deputies, and they locked the front door, and they locked the back door, and they took us down in the basement. At first I thought they were just trying to scare us. They had made a white girl play Russian roulette a couple of days ago until she broke down and started begging them to just let her go home. So I kept demanding the right to call our lawyer until they got mad and told me to shut up and I did.

Then they told Charlie they had a choice for him. They told him he could beat me for having such a smart mouth or he could watch while they finished what he had started by the side of the road. Charlie kept trying to talk to them, telling them if they just let us go, we wouldn't press charges. They laughed at that. Asked him if he'd seen any FBI agents around lately and telling him to choose, but he wouldn't.

Finally, they said, "Okay. This nigger must want us to show him how it's done," and one of the deputies told me to take my clothes off. Then Charlie said, "Stop! Don't touch her. I'll do it." I begged him not to. I didn't care what they did to me, but I was in love with sweet Charles. He was the only man I'd ever had . . . The other deputy took off his belt and gave it to Charlie and I know what he meant to do was just pretend and not really hurt me. I know that! But they knew that too, and they wouldn't let him.

They stood right there and made him hit me harder and harder. I started screaming so they'd let him stop, but they wouldn't. They just laughed and said, "Go on, nigger. We'll tell you when to quit." So they made him beat me half to death and then that one who had told me to take my clothes off pulled my dress over my face and did it anyway. They all did it anyway. Right in front of Charlie.

But see, I knew that already. That's what I kept trying to tell him. I don't care what they do to me, but not you. I can't take it from you.

I had to go home after that. My father came to get me. I was hurt so bad, I couldn't have stayed if I wanted to, which I didn't. My mother, my aunts, my father, all of them went crazy. I thought they would tell me how sorry they were. I thought they would hold my hand and put a cold towel on my head or something, but that wasn't it. That wasn't what they wanted at all. They wanted to fuss. They came to tell me how dumb I was for going in the first place. How next time maybe I'd listen to them and keep my behind at home where it belonged. They were afraid to even look at me. I was living proof of something so terrible nobody wanted to think about it, so they got mad at me instead.

My grandmother was the only one who didn't say anything. She'd just come and sit there by me in the dark. I'd wake up and I could hear her crying. Maybe she could hear me crying, too.

My father was so mad, he couldn't talk to me at all. My mother told me it was killing him to know that somebody had beat his baby worse than you would beat a dog and there was nothing he could do about it. I kept trying to tell her yes there was. What he could do was come and hold me. What he could do was tell me how much he loved me and promise that nobody was ever going to hurt me like that again.

I decided I wasn't going back to school in the fall. I

didn't see the point. Not just in school, but the point of anything. I kept trying to get my mind around what had happened, but I couldn't. It didn't make any sense to me. What they had done, what they were still doing. It was like it had all happened on another planet. Charlie used to call me a lot. I know it was hard for him to get to a phone, but he did it. My mother was afraid he'd talk me into going back so she'd tell him I was asleep, but I'd hear the phone ring and grab it before she could hang up. Neither one of us knew what to say. He'd ask me how I was doing and I'd say better and then I'd ask him how he was doing and he'd lie and tell me he was okay. After that, we'd just sort of hold the phone until one of us started crying and then we'd hang up.

Then one night, one of the other volunteers called to tell me that Charlie had been arrested again, by the same ones who had picked us up before, and this time, they had taken him to Parchman Prison. I just prayed for him. I didn't know what else to do. Two weeks later she called to tell me they had gotten him out, but his leg was broken in three places and he was in the hospital in Jackson. They held him at Parchman for two weeks and did everything they could think of to him, and never even charged him with anything. I left for Mississippi that night.

When I got to the hospital, I walked in and he reached for me like he was drowning so I took his hand and told him I would never let it go. *(A beat)* I thought we would die in that room, but we didn't. When Charlie was well enough, we came here but his family didn't know what to do with him any more than mine knew what to do with me, so we got married and found this place and we just holed up and tried to make sense of it. He used to say we were like desperadoes, drinking bourbon at the border and planning our getaways . . .

But we couldn't figure out a way to talk about what had happened to us in Mississippi and we couldn't find a way to talk around it. We just sort of hoped it would go away, but it didn't. It got bigger and scarier and bigger and scarier until Charlie couldn't touch me anymore without crying.

ROSA: Oh, May . . .

MAY: When we first got back, people broke down. Went crazy. Started doing all kinds of drugs. So many of us were destroyed, Rose. We don't even realize it until something really awful happens and then we say, "Oh, my God! We're not that messed up, are we?" There wasn't anybody to tell. Not just what happened. How it felt. People like to say how brave you are, but they don't want to hear about how scared you were. How you screamed so long you lost your voice and tried to close your mind so you could be someplace else, anyplace else, but there. But what if they don't kill you? What if all the stuff on you heals up except your heart and you can't believe it really happened because if it ever really happened, wouldn't it change the world forever?

ROSA: It did change the world forever.

MAY: Did it?

(A beat.)

ROSA: You always talk about what happened to Charlie. What about what happened to you, May?

MAY: I survived it. He didn't.

ROSA: That doesn't make it right.

MAY: Nothing makes it right.

ROSA: I'm sorry.

MAY *(Suddenly angry)*: You're sorry? Sorry for what? Sorry Charlie's so messed up? Sorry they hurt me so bad I could never have his babies? Sorry they took our whole lives from us in one mean Mississippi summer? *(Purposely cruel)* Or are you just sorry Tyrone probably won't get to be a partner so you can tell him how to do business without getting taken to the cleaners?

ROSA: That's not fair!

MAY: Where were you when it was time to change the world, Rose? Where the fuck were you?

(Rosa, suddenly frightened of May's rage, exits. May sits down and buries her face in her hands as the lights go to black.)

Scene Four

That night. The apartment is dark. The bridge is illuminated outside and provides enough light for us to see Charlie sitting alone. May enters, not realizing he is there and reaches to turn on the light.

CHARLIE: Don't turn on the light, May.

MAY: Charlie! Where were you? I've been all over—!

CHARLIE: Do you remember that story?

MAY: What story?

CHARLIE: The story about the Africans. Don't you remember it?

MAY: Which Africans?

CHARLIE: West Coast Africans. Igbos, I think. From Nigeria.

MAY: Can I turn on the light?

CHARLIE *(Insistent)*: I want you to remember the story.

MAY: And then can I turn on the light?

CHARLIE: Yes.

MAY: Tell me about the Africans.

CHARLIE: They were trying to make them slaves, remember? Rounded 'em up, loaded 'em in, and started back across the ocean with 'em, but when they got here and let 'em out so the people who were going to buy 'em could count their teeth, and figure out which one to mate with which other one, all those Africans just turned around and walked right back into the water. All of 'em. Men, women, children, the whole shipload full of 'em, just walked those chains right on into the ocean. White folks couldn't do nothin' but watch their money wash away to sea. And they all drowned, May. Every single one of 'em. Dead. But they didn't even care, and you know why?

MAY: Why, Charlie?

CHARLIE: Because they believed their spirits would travel home to their ancestors as long as their heads were not separated from their bodies. As long as the head and the heart stayed together, they didn't give a damn about dying.

(May turns on the light. Charlie is wearing a sleeveless undershirt.)

MAY: Where's your shirt?

CHARLIE: I threw it away.

MAY: Why?

CHARLIE: There was blood on it.

MAY: Blood? What happened?

(Throughout this scene, there is about Charlie a strange and growing peace. He is not happy, but he is finally unafraid.)

CHARLIE: They won, May. I thought I had figured it out. I thought I could even things up a little. Reclaim what they took from me down in that hole, but I can't, because I was wrong about what they took. I thought they took my mind, but I was still thinking. Then I thought they took my heart, but I was still feeling, then

I thought they took my soul, but I still had you, May,
and I thought that could be enough. I thought that
could be everything, but I didn't think about one thing.
I didn't consider the one thing I thought nobody could
take, just because, but I was wrong. I was wrong. There's
nothing they can't take if they want it. So they took it,
May. They took the part that can feel something besides
anger all the damn time. The part that knows how to
touch a woman like she's too delicate to bear the weight
of your hands. Can you believe it, May? They took my
head and separated it from my heart, from my memories. They have drugs designed especially to do that. To
make sure what you know doesn't fuck with you to the
point where you might actually have to do something
about it. And you're right, May. Once you start lying, it
changes everything because once you start, you can't
stop. And after a while, you don't even want to.

MAY: Charlie, for God's sake, what happened?

CHARLIE: You remember when I told you about the letter?
About the doctor writing to his woman while he should
have been writing about me? That was the first lie. That
was my letter to you, May. A letter I wrote on my skin
every day. Forgive me, baby. I'm so sorry.

MAY: Sorry for what? What did you do?

CHARLIE: You know those guys they've been finding downtown?

MAY: Yes.

CHARLIE: That was the second lie.

MAY: You're not making any sense!

CHARLIE: I killed them. I killed all three of them.

MAY: Charlie, why?

CHARLIE: All those years, I thought it was fear that was driving
me crazy. I thought that big gray fog inside my head was
a great big ball of being scared. Scared of the power they
had to treat me like an animal or make me act like one.
Scared that if they asked me now, today, I still wouldn't

know enough to look that cracker in the eye and say, "I don't care what you do to me, I'm not going to raise my hand to this woman!" But it wasn't fear I was running from, May. That's what the drugs make you think and the therapy and the doctors—all bullshit! It wasn't fear I was running from. It was the anger, May, because I couldn't protect you. I couldn't forget and you couldn't forgive me for remembering.

MAY: I never blamed you for anything. There was nothing you could do.

CHARLIE: I could have made them kill me.

MAY: But I didn't die.

CHARLIE: I ran for thirty years, May, and then I let it catch me and I picked out three, just like those three in Mississippi picked us out, and I did what a man is supposed to do. And I'm sorry, May. Not for the killing. For all those years I didn't kill anybody. I wasted thirty years. My father wasted seventy. My uncles made eighty and never killed a soul, so I owe, May. I owe for all those other crazy Negroes who didn't understand that all we have to do to get sane is—

MAY: No, Charlie! No. We don't have to do it that way.

CHARLIE: Yeah, May, we do. Because that's the only thing they understand. Not love. Not peace. Not God. Not family. All they know is blood. *(A beat)* And you know the worst part? All that killing? It didn't change a damn thing except me.

MAY: We have to go away, Charlie. They're going to come looking for you here.

CHARLIE *(He leans back, closes his eyes)*: I'm tired, May. I'm just so tired.

MAY: We'll go to Canada. Tonight. You and me. We'll go so deep in the woods they'll never find us and we'll figure it out, Charlie. We'll figure it all out.

CHARLIE: To Canada?

MAY: Just like we talked about.

CHARLIE: Why did we wait so long?

MAY: So you could get well, Charlie. We had to wait until you got well.

CHARLIE: Tell me about the garden.

MAY *(Getting up quickly)*: I need to put some things in a bag for us, Charlie. It's time to go!

(Charlie catches May's hand as she starts toward the bedroom.)

CHARLIE: Better days, May? That's the third lie.

MAY *(Pleading)*: Please, Charlie.

(Charlie pulls May back down beside him gently but firmly.)

CHARLIE: Just tell me about the garden.

(A beat.)

MAY: There's flowers in the front and vegetables in the back. There's carrots and collard greens and corn and sweet potatoes.

CHARLIE: Is there enough sun?

MAY: There's good sun all over. And in the wintertime, we'll have a sleigh and we'll go for rides in the snow and put bells on the horses and chestnuts on the fire like in that song you like. And we'll build a little house like the Hemphills had where you can stand in the front and see clear through to the back and there's nothing inside but love. Just me and you and a whole lot of love.

CHARLIE: Tell me about the tomatoes.

MAY: We grow the best for miles. They're so big and red and juicy that when you eat them the juice runs down your chin and—

(There is a sudden and very loud knocking on the door. This is clearly the police, and the knocking is very loud, intimidating and urgent. May freezes.)

CHARLIE *(As if he hears nothing)*: What kind do we grow, May?

(A beat.)

MAY: We grow all kinds.

(More knocking, even louder, more insistent. It sounds like it will break down the door, and it continues as May recites the names of the tomatoes and the lights fade to black.)

We grow Red Plum. Green Zebra. Big Rainbow. Yellow Pear. Ultra Pink. Sun Gold. Super Sweet 100 . . .

(In the darkness, the insistent knocking continues for several seconds and then stops abruptly.)

END OF PLAY

Chain

Production History

Chain was coproduced by Women's Project & Productions and the New Federal Theatre under the artistic direction of Julia Miles and Woodie King Jr., respectively, at the Judith Anderson Theatre, New York City, from February 28 to March 22, 1992. *Chain* was commissioned and developed by Women's Project & Productions and the Southeast Playwrights Project of Atlanta through a grant from the Multi Arts Production Fund of the Rockefeller Foundation. Imani was the director; the sets were designed by George Xenos, lights by Melody Beal, costumes by Ornyece and sound was by Bill Toles. The cast was:

ROSA   Karen Malina White

Characters

ROSA JENKINS, a sixteen-year-old African-American girl,
addicted to crack

Time

1991

Setting

A one-bedroom apartment in a battered Harlem,
New York, apartment building

Day One

The stage is completely dark. A slide that reads: "Day One" comes up on a screen at the rear of the stage. The slide holds for ten seconds and then disappears, leaving the stage again in complete darkness. Sounds erupt from the darkness suddenly, starting with a loud scream. This is followed by sounds of someone scuffling, struggling, trying to escape and being caught. Only one voice is heard—the voice of Rosa Jenkins, a sixteen-year-old crack addict. Although it is clear that there is a struggle going on, the cause of the struggle is completely unknown, adding to the frightening nature of the sounds.

ROSA *(Screaming, crying, pleading in the darkness)*: What are you doing? No! Stop it! Don't, Daddy! Please don't! Stop it! Stop it! Daddy, don't do that! Please don't do that! Daddy! Daddy! Wait, Daddy! Wait! Don't do it! Please, don't do it! Please, don't do it! Daddy, please! Please!

(The sounds of struggle suddenly stop, but the loud sobbing continues. There is the sound of footsteps and then the sound of a door slamming and a deadbolt lock clicking loudly into place. Then, there is silence, suddenly broken by Rosa's shriek.)

Da-a-a-a-a-deeeeee!

(Lights up full. Rosa is crumpled in a heap in the middle of the floor. She is sobbing loudly. The apartment around her is small and crowded with well-worn furniture, a television set, plastic fruit or flowers, a cheaply framed picture of John F. Kennedy, Martin Luther King, Jr. and Bobby Kennedy, and a framed, dime-store painting of a white Jesus.

Rosa cries bitterly for a few minutes, then she sits up suddenly.)

Mama? *(She listens intently and then speaks tentatively)* Mama? Is that you? *(Listens again and then speaks angrily)* I hear you out there listening. What kind of mother are you? How can you let him do this to me? You don't love me! You never loved me! You hate me! You all hate me! *(She crumples again, sobbing, then stops suddenly and sits up. This time her look is more crafty. She is still listening)* Mama? Mama, are you still there? I didn't mean it, Mama. You know I didn't mean it. I know you love me. It's me. I know it's me. I love you, Mama. *(Listens)* Mama? Can you hear me? I know you can hear me. I can hear you breathing! Talk to me, Mama. Say something. Say anything! *(Angry again)* Well, don't then! I don't care what you do! You can't keep me in here if I don't want to stay! I'll get away just like I always do. You know I can do it, Mama! And you know I will! So you might as well go on to work and stop waiting to see what

276

I'm gonna do. I'm gonna do what I damn well please and there's nothing you can do about it. Not a goddamn thing! Now! How do you like that? *(She listens again. Suddenly frightened)* Mama? Please let me out, Mama? Please let me out! I'm scared to be in here like this! Please let me out, Mama! I won't tell Daddy, I promise. He'll never know the difference. I won't go nowhere, I swear. I was just kiddin'. You can trust me, Mama. Honest! *(No sound at all from outside. She is suddenly enraged)* Open this door and look at me! You scared to see me like this? *(Laughs crazily)* Well, that's just too damn bad because you gotta deal with it. Look at me!

(Rosa lunges for the door, and for the first time we see that she is chained to the radiator with a long, thick chain. The chain is about six feet long and strong enough to hold her. She is shackled by her left foot. The chain is long enough for her to have some range of motion, but not long enough for her to get to the door. As she lunges toward the door, the chain jerks her back, twisting her ankle painfully. She yelps in pain and falls down again. She grabs the chain and tries to pull it off of her leg, but she can't. She goes to the radiator and tries to pull the chain off of the radiator, but she can't. She becomes more and more frantic as she pulls on it futilely. She is like a caged animal, and she growls in her throat in a way that expresses wordless rage and frustration. She paces around the apartment as the reality of what has happened settles on her. She is wild. Almost out of control. She pulls on the chain, shakes it and rattles it. She stands breathlessly looking around at the apartment. Suddenly, she grabs a portrait of her mother and father and herself at a younger age and throws it to the ground. The glass in the frame shatters against the floor, and the noise seems to dissipate her rage. She collapses near the

glass fragments, weeping loudly. After a minute, she sits up and looks at the glass. She picks up a large shard and, still weeping, holds it over her wrist. She slowly tries to bring it down across her arm, but she doesn't have the nerve. She holds it trembling there for a long moment and then throws it away and collapses in a silent heap on the floor.

Blackout.)

Day Two

Slide up: "Day Two." Lights up. Rosa is searching through the house as far as her chain will allow. She is moving awkwardly. She tangles the chain in things and stumbles over it.

ROSA *(Jerking the chain angrily)*: Damn!

(She flops down on the sofa, frustrated and angry. She is facing the audience and seems to see them for the first time. Her face is startled, but almost immediately takes on the craftiness of the dope fiend.)

Got a match? *(She holds up a wrinkled cigarette)* Hey! I'm talking to you! Y'all got a match? *(Disgusted at the lack of response)* It ain't no reefer, okay? It's a Winston or some shit. *(A beat)* Oh, I see. I'm invisible, right? You looking right at me and nobody see me, right? Okay. No problem. *(A beat)* Y'all probably don't smoke no way. Right? Lookin' out for your health and shit. You probably wouldn't give me a damn match if you had it. *(A beat)* My dad told you not to talk to me, right? Not to listen to anything I said 'cause I'm a dope fiend and I might trick you into doin' something bad.

Fuck it.

(She tosses the cigarette aside. Throughout her talking, she moves restlessly around. She touches the chain a lot, because the awkwardness and horror make it impossible for her to keep her hands off of it. She is also a dope fiend and she is already feeling the effects of being deprived of the drug.)

These country-ass niggas think they can keep me chained up in here like some kind of freak. But that's where they wrong. I ain't no dumb-ass dog! I can figure this shit out. Be back on the street before they country asses get home from work tonight.

I wasted a lot of time yesterday 'cause I was in a state of shock or some shit. I couldn't believe this shit was really happening to me. Of all people! Now I know I have been kind of crazy lately, but this shit . . . this is like some movie-of-the-week shit, here. Geraldo and shit. I mean, when I got home, they was actin' so glad to see me and shit and now this?

My dad just gave the guy the money without talking a whole lot of bullshit about what he was gonna do if they didn't leave me alone and shit. Now even I was surprised at that.

He used to go off! Hollerin' and shit. Talkin' about callin' the cops and turnin' everybody in. Next time I'd get loose and come around, nobody wanted to let me in 'cause they were scared my pops was gonna come back and turn out.

He would, too. Every damn time. Them niggas used to crack up behind that shit, too. My dad would start tellin' them how they ought to be ashamed to be sellin' that shit to kids and wadn't nobody in there more than seventeen. Buyin' or sellin'! He didn't do it this time though. I guess he was just tired of the shit.

Or he was tryin' to throw me off. Make me think he

wadn't gonna do nothin' and then, wham! Here come this shit! I slept all day Saturday. I been up for three days. Maybe four. Next morning before they went to work, I came out to tell 'em good-bye and they sittin' at the table talkin' real quiet and they stop real fast when I come in. Then they look at each other and my dad pulls out a chair for me. They was lookin' so serious, I thought they was gettin' ready to send me back to rehab and then my dad goes to the closet and pulls out this big-ass bag and comes over and sits down beside me and hugs me and shit and starts talking about how happy they were when I was first born and shit and how I'll always be their daughter and they love me so much and I'm thinkin', yeah, okay for this *Father Knows Best* crap, but what's in the damn bag? Then I looked at Mama and she's cryin' and shit.

Mama ain't cried when I went to rehab since I was thirteen, so I know this is some serious shit. I know this sounds crazy, but I thought they was gonna kill me. I could tell it was something heavy in the bag and I thought maybe Daddy had, like a sledgehammer, or something and they was gonna beat me to death and then put me in a bag and drop me in the river. *(Laughs)* Crazy shit, right? But you know your mind give you all kinda shit when you get scared.

Then Daddy takes out this big-ass chain and shit and I freaked. I started running around the room and I tried to hold onto Mama and she was holding me and we was both crying. Look like *The Color Purple* and shit. "Save me, Mama! Save me!" But that shit didn't work on Daddy no better than it did that nigga in the movie. He pulled my hands offa her and made her go on to work. She didn't want to go and I was screaming and crying and begging her not do this to me and she was crying, too, but Daddy was holding me so tight I could hardly breathe and he kept talking to Mama in this very calm voice and reminding her that they had talked about this and telling her that this was the only way and it was for my own good. Shit like that. So she looked at me and then she grabbed her purse and ran out the room. Then it was just me and Daddy. *(She picks up the cigarette again)*

I know one of y'all got a damn match. I swear this is a Winston. If it was some reefer I'd eat it, okay? *(A beat)* Fuck it. I hate cigarettes anyway. My junior high school teacher used to catch us smokin' in the bathroom and make us flush them down the toilet. I didn't care. I was just doin' it cause Paula was doin' it and she my girl. A nasty habit, that's what Miss Young would say. "Smoking is a nasty habit!"

Paula say smokin' ain't nothin'. She can tell the bitch about a couple of sho nuff nasty habits if she really interested. *(Laughing)* Paula would do that shit, too. She crazy. She say anything to people and just walk away. Most of the time they too surprised to say anything back or they just start laughing. I can't do that shit. If I say some smart-ass shit to people they wanna fight. That's 'cause she cute. They don't care what she say 'cause they like lookin' at her while she standin' there sayin' it. *(She touches the chain and jumps, having forgotten it for a minute)*

I told Paula she better stop smoking 'cause she pregnant now and that shit make your baby come out real little and be sick all the time. She say she gave up smokin' reefer 'til the nigga born. She ain't givin' up nothin' else. Then she roll her eyes and wink like she know somethin' I don't know. I ask her do she mean her and Darryl still fuckin', big as her stomach done got and she say that is a personal question, which mean yes! Paula a freak anyway, though, so you never can tell. I told her she don't ever need to start smoking no rock 'cause she would be a coke 'ho in about ten seconds. *(Laughs)*

Me and her used to smoke a lot of reefer together when we was in seventh grade. Miss Young's class. She used to read to us at the end of the day right before we went home and I'd be so high, Paula had to keep wakin' me up about every two seconds.

A lotta people like they reefer, but I'm not down wit it. I figure, what's the point? If I'm gonna go to all the trouble to get some money and go buy some shit, I wanna get as high as I can. I don't want to be somewhere sleep with my mouth all open and shit. I want to be awake so I can feel something! *(Looking around, disgusted)*

They didn't even leave the TV in here. One of those tight-ass blond bitches at my last drug rehab told my mom that she thought maybe watching TV was "over-stimulating" me and making me wanna do drugs. And my moms went for it! Made me stop watchin' TV, except for *The Cosby Show* 'cause she think the Cosby kids are role models and shit. Yeah, right. Put my ass in a great big house with a whole lotta money and I'll be a role model, too.

I tried to tell her that TV ain't shit stimulation compared to what's up on the street! It's always somethin' happenin' out there. They just don't see it. Or they see it and they scared of it. I ain't scared of nothin'. I seen more shit in sixteen years than they seen in forty and I know how to handle it. Jesus *(She pronounces it in Spanish— "Hey-suess")* say you either got to get into it or it's gonna get into you. *(A beat)* No. What he says is if it's gonna get into you, you gotta get into . . . no. Wait. *(A beat)* If it gets . . . *(A beat)* Fuck it. It sounds like it makes sense when he say it, but I can't get that shit straight. *(A beat)* I feel like shit. *(A beat, then louder)* I feel like shit! *(A beat)* And don't nobody give a fuck.

They say they do, but they really don't. Otherwise *(This rises to a shriek by the end of the sentence)* they would leave me the fuck alone and bring me some damn rock up in here so I can get high! *(A beat)* Always tellin' me how hard life is. Didn't nobody tell them to be workin' at Harlem Hospital every damn day of the week. *(A beat)*

They never would have found me if Jesus hadn't a told, with his ignorant "I'll be right back" ass. Nobody else knew where I was to be sendin' somebody bustin' up in the place. No reason to. Daddy hadn't offered no reward. "Have you seen this girl? Twenty-five-dollar reward." Goddamn crack addicts will turn your ass in for a quarter so muthafuckas got signs all over the neighborhood. People be turnin' in they friends and shit. Ain't no crack addict gonna keep no secret if there's dope money comin' from tellin' it. If my daddy had offered a reward, I'd a turned myself in! Shit! I figure ain't nobody got more of a right to collect a reward on somebody than that same somebody, right? *(Forgetting the chain, she rises and heads for the kitchen. The chain jerks her back)*

Damn! *(Rising anger)* Damn!

(She sits again, drawing up her knees and rocking back and forth with some agitation. She really wants some crack. She suddenly sees some matches under the couch. She drags the chain over awkwardly and finally reaches them with great effort. She sits on the floor, exhausted, and lights the Winston. She inhales deeply and then explodes into a terrible cough. She cannot get her breath for several seconds. When she regains her composure, she takes a deep breath and looks around. She snubs out the Winston and begins to crumble. She hugs her knees to her chest, bows her head and begins to rock silently back and forth.

Blackout.)

Day Three

Slide: "Day Three." Rosa is trying to sleep on the couch under a child's worn bedspread with colorful cartoon figures on it. She tosses fitfully, but can't figure out a way to sleep comfortably with the chain on her leg. She sits up in frustration.

ROSA: Help! *(She waits. Listens. Then, louder)* Help!! *(Listening)* Help, they're killin' me! *(Listens)* Yeah, right. Niggas run the other way when they hear that shit. *(Thinks for a minute)* Fire! *(Listens. Still nothing)* Shit! I could burn up and nobody would even know I was in this muthafucka. I ought to have them arrested for doing this to me. *(A beat)* I wonder if I really could . . . Daddy would kill me! *(A beat)* He couldn't kill me! His ass would be in jail. That would kill Mama. Shit!

Maybe Jesus will rescue me. That'd be some shit he would do. Come bustin' up in here with the fire department and shit. I'd be out before Mama and Daddy even got home!

Jesus ain't gonna do no shit like that. He probably figurin' I'll get out this time just like I been gettin' out before. He don't know nothin' about no chain. He probably figure they sent me down South again. Naw, he know that ain't happenin'. *(Laughs)* They ain't looking to see Rosa Jackson no time soon in Alabama. Country-ass niggas. Tellin' me how worried my Mama was about me and what a good girl they knew I still was underneath. Yeah, right. I hate when people are so stupid they just make you take their shit. You know, like before you got there, they was on the honor system and shit 'cause they in Alabama. I know they act like I killed somebody when I tried to cash one of grandmama's social security checks. It ain't like the government won't replace that shit! If you tell 'em somebody stole your check, they send you another one. People up here do it all the time. I didn't think that shit was no big deal, but the man at the store knew my grandmother and he called her and told her I'd been there with her check and he had cashed it this time, but could she please send a note the next time. My grandmother just thanked him and said she would, but when I got home she had called my uncle for backup and they both went off on me. Both of them! I had never heard my grandmother talk so much shit. I thought they were goin' to have me arrested and shit, but they didn't. They just sent me back up here.

My grandmother hates to hear me cuss. She heard me on the phone once talking long distance to one of my friends. It might have been Jesus, I don't remember, but I was talking . . . like I talk. My grandmother took that phone and said: "I apologize for my grandaughter's language. She did not learn how to talk like that in this house." And she hung up the phone and took me in the bathroom and washed my mouth out with Ivory Soap. I was almost fifteen years old, but grandmothers don't care about your real age. They got a age they want you to be and that is the age you gonna be when they around you. My grandmother age ain't but ten. That's how old I was the summer we moved up here, and she can't get past it. I was ten then, and to her, I'm gonna be ten. She heard all those "muthafuckas" coming out of my mouth and she just couldn't handle it.

Nobody talks like this in Tuskegee. They cuss and shit, but not like in New York. Everybody in New York cuss all the time. When they happy, when they mad. They just be cussin'. The first day we moved on this block, I was sittin' on the stoop out front while Daddy moved our stuff inside and I was lookin' at this guy staggerin' down the street, bumpin' into people and shit. I had never seen anybody that drunk before, so I was

starin' at him, with my country ass, and he saw me doin'
it. Cussed me out! *(Laughs)* "What the fuck you lookin'
at?" He hollered right in my face. I like to died!

New York is so different from Alabama it might as
well be on another planet or some shit. When we got
here, I was freaked out. I had never even been to
Montgomery, except once on a church bus when I was
three. My parents call themselves movin' to New York so
I could go to good schools and have better opportunities
and shit. Yeah, right. Opportunities to do what?

I ain't complainin' though. It was exciting as hell. I
had never seen kids my age do the shit these New York
niggas were doing. They did everything. I mean eleven-
twelve-year-old kids drinkin' and smokin' and fuckin'
like they was grown already. It was like nobody had control of them or somethin'.

I didn't do none of that shit for a long time. I was real
goody-goody. The kids at my school used to call me
'Bama and shit and make fun of me because I wadn't
down wit the shit they knew from birth or some shit. It
was kind of a drag at first, but then I met Jesus and he
hipped me to a lot of shit about living in New York. Stuff
I really needed to know, right? And plus, he was real
fine and real cool and a Puerto Rican. Wadn't one
Puerto Rican in Tuskegee, Alabama. Period. He thought
I was Puerto Rican before he met me because my name
was Rosa and some nigga told him I had a accent. He
thought they meant a Spanish accent, but they was
talkin' about a Alabama accent. He thought that shit
was real funny, too. Pissed me off 'til I saw he didn't
mean nothin' by it.

See, it wadn't about me. Jesus thought everything
was funny. Not the regular stuff you'd think somebody'd
laugh at. A lot of weird shit. Like he thought it was
funny that my parents had come here so we would have

a better life. "And look at 'em now," he says. "They got shitty-ass jobs and a crackhead kid." He thought that was real funny. Jesus' parents came all the way from Puerto Rico. Well, his mother did. He never said nothin' about his father and I never did ask him. People in Alabama ask you your life story if they sit next to you on the bus, but people in New York don't play that shit.

My parents used to do all that tourist shit when we first got here. They walked my little ass all over New York City lookin' at shit that was supposed to make you go "O-o-o-o-o, shit! New York City! Ain't this a bitch?" It's like that Stevie Wonder oldie where the country-ass guy gets off the bus and says: "New York City! Sky-scrapers and everything!" And then the New York niggas take everything he got! *(She laughs)*

We went to see the Statue of Liberty and shit. Every-body standing around there looking at it like it mean something and this guy with a uniform and shit tell you about how old it is and how they got it and shit and you can tell he say this shit twenty-five times a day 'cause he don't even look at you while he talkin'. He just be talkin'. If you wanna listen, fine. If you don't, that's fine, too. He's gettin' paid to say that shit, not to make you lis-ten. Muthafucka shoulda been a teacher! *(Laughs)*

Jesus' mama was scared to take him a lotta places 'cause she didn't speak English too good yet. So he been here since he was five and he still ain't never seen the Statue of Liberty. I told him we should get high and go down there one day and listen to that guy say his shit. Jesus' mama look like that woman in *West Side Story*. The one with the purple dress and the fine boyfriend? Jesus like to look at the video 'cause it make him think about his mama. Jesus don't look like that, though. He ain't that kinda Puerto Rican. He look just like a nigga, in fact. I always thought Puerto Ricans looked like

Mexicans or some shit, but a lot of them look just like niggas. Maybe there was some country-ass Puerto Ricans in Tuskegee and I just didn't recognize 'em.

Ain't nothin' country about Jesus. He hard about shit. Not that he mean or nothin', not to me, anyway, but don't nothin' fuck with him. He can look at terrible shit and just walk away. He won't even blink. We saw a kid we knew get blown away one time. He owed some people money and he had been talkin' around 'bout how he wasn't payin' shit so they came up to the school and waited for him. When he came out the front door, they jumped out the car, shot his ass and drove the fuck away, cool as shit. Everybody freaked. Runnin' and screamin' and shit. Jesus didn't even jump. He just kept walkin'. It was scary unless you was wit him. Then it made you feel good. Like whatever happen, it ain't gonna be no surprise to this nigga.

I think it was because he had seen such terrible shit already, you know? That's how he started smokin' rock in the first place, behind some really terrible shit. Shit like you would hear about, but not know anybody who been through it personally. Well, Jesus had some of that shit happen to him. *(A beat, then a shrug)* He don't care if I tell it . . . and I don't owe him shit any damn way!

Jesus' mama had a boyfriend, right? And the nigga was a crackhead and she hid his shit from him. Call herself tryin' to help him get off it. Well, she wouldn't tell him where the shit was, so he shot her right there in their apartment, went through all her shit until he found it, and was sittin' there smokin' it when Jesus came home. Jesus' mama layin' right on the floor in the next room, dead as shit, and this nigga so high he don't even give a fuck. Jesus say the nigga didn't even tell him she was dead. He just looked up when he walked in and said, "Your mama in the kitchen." When he came back out, the nigga was gone. *(A beat)* I told you it was some terrible shit.

So after they buried her and shit, Jesus said he started thinkin' about that nigga just sittin' there smokin' while his mama layin' in the next room dead and he said he just thought, well, fuck it. If the shit that damn good let me have it. I told him he was just thinkin' that way 'cause he felt bad about his mom and shit, but he said he wadn't askin' me if he should do it. He was just tellin' me.

He didn't act like no addict either. He don't act like one now, unless he can't get the shit, then he start actin' weird. Talkin' crazy and shit. When Jesus need to get high, he talk about killin' people a lot. He ain't never killed nobody, but he talk about that shit a lot when he can't get high. I know it's because of his mama, so I try to change the subject so he won't go off on it. Paula be scared of Jesus when he talk that shit, but she ain't known him as long as I have. I been knowin' Jesus since I was eleven years old. How he gonna scare me after all that?

I don't think I woulda started smokin' this shit if it wadn't for Jesus. It didn't seem to be doin' nothin' so bad to him and he was sellin' it so he always had some. Plus, he still had the apartment from his mom's insurance, so he didn't have to go to no crack house or nothin' to get high. He could just kick back at his own crib.

But then he told me it made people nervous for me to be around so much if I wadn't gonna be smokin'. They was tellin' him I was fuckin' up their high. People thought I might be a cop or some shit. That's 'cause niggas watch too much TV. Like the cops really gonna hire somebody to live in this neighborhood undercover, right? They gonna train me to spy on a bunch of poor-ass niggas don't nobody care about no way. But niggas are so paranoid, they believe that shit. I actually heard two niggas talkin' about whether or not I was a undercover cop and one of them said no because anybody the cops used undercover had to be fine. It made me mad as hell, and then I said, Rosa! You goin' off on some shit you overheard a crack addict say. What is wrong with you, girl? But I didn't like hearin' that kinda shit just 'cause I wadn't down wit it. So, I said okay, fuck it.

And that shit is good. I am not lying. I mean if you like to get high, it will get you high real fast. Now some people ain't down wit it, and that's cool, but if you wanna get high, that rock is the shit. I mean, it feel so good, you don't care where you are, what you look like, what is happenin' to the other niggas in the room or any of that shit. You just feel good. And like in a real personal way. It ain't like you need nobody else to feel good with you. You feel so good, your own high be keepin' you company. *(A beat)*

The only problem is that shit don't last long. And once you feel that good, you gotta feel that good again, right? I mean, why wouldn't you? You gotta want something. Rock good as anything else you gonna want. And if you careful, you can handle that shit and not let it handle you.

See, my daddy got this old-timey attitude that if he don't like it, I'm not spose to like it. And since he don't smoke no rock, I'm not spose to smoke none either. I wish my dad would get high one time. I'll bet he would be a funny muthafucka. With his country ass. My dad don't even drink nothin' but beer! My mom don't drink shit. So they don't know what the fuck I'm even talkin' about. They brought me all these pamphlets and shit— "Just say no!" What the fuck does that mean?

I used to think my dad knew everything. But you can't know everything about New York City. Not even about Harlem. Not even this one block in Harlem! When I was gone a whole week, I wadn't two buildings down from here. I used to watch my mom and dad out the window. I saw 'em asking who had seen me and shit. Half the niggas they asked had been smokin' with me half the night! They didn't give a fuck.

My dad wanted to kill Jesus when he found out I was smokin' it, but I won't tell him where Jesus live. He act like it's Jesus' fault I'm smokin' it. Say this shit about if Jesus was really my "friend" he wouldn't give me that shit. *(Laughs)* I told you my dad be trippin'! He never did like me to be around Jesus after what happen to Jesus' mom. I told him that wadn't none of Jesus' fault, but my dad didn't wanna hear that shit. Jesus had his own place so my dad thought I'd be over there all the time fuckin' and shit. I don't even think he thought about me gettin' high. He just didn't want me to be fuckin'.

(Laughs) Jesus' place was usually so full of crack-heads wadn't no place to be fuckin' if we wanted to. Jesus didn't care nothin' 'bout that no way. I don't know why. I think all of Jesus' weird shit is because of how that shit went down with his moms. But I know he didn't care nothin' about it 'cause I used to try to get him to do it with me, and he wouldn't. Jesus like to get high. Everything else is take it or leave it. I think that's why he wanted me to start smokin' rock, too. He wanted us to do it together. Romantic and shit, right? *(Laughs)* He always used to tell me he just wadn't down wit no whole lot of fuckin', but that if I wanted to do it with somebody else, he wouldn't be pissed off or nothin'. Well, that wadn't what I wanted, so I kept bringin' it up and bringin' it up and finally he said he would teach me how to do somethin' that he liked to watch. And I said okay . . .

At first I thought I could do it in here to pass the time, right? I mean no TV. No Nintendo. No telephone. Shit! But I can't do it if nobody ain't watching me. I don't know why. I guess I'm as big a freak as Paula, with her pregnant ass.

Sometimes when we needed money, he'd get me to do it in front of some niggas. They thought it was funny that I could get off like that and still be a virgin. It was just Jesus watchin' me, I guess. He'd be lookin' right in my face, too. I'd be goin' off and he just be lookin' at me, thinkin' about gettin' high, calm as shit. He said he used to hear his mother and father fuckin' when he was real little and sometimes he'd pretend his mother was doin' it with him instead of his father. I told him not to tell me none of that freak Puerto Rican shit!

I love to hear Jesus say my name like it was Spanish. "R-r-r-r-r-rosa!" He rolls that "r" around so long I can't stand it. Shit sound like rollin' lemon heads around in your mouth. If I was doin' it and he called my name like that, I'd get off in a second. When it was somebody I didn't want to do it in front of, he would tell me to just listen for my name and it would be easy. He wadn't lyin' either. Worked every time. *(A beat)*

Last night when they got home, my mom was still cryin' and shit. They had both worked double shift, too, so it was late and they was good and worried about how I was gonna be when they got here. I started to lay out like I was dead so when they opened the door they'd see me layin' there with my eyes open and shit. But I knew that would really fuck with them and I didn't want my daddy to go off. So I was just sittin' here when they busted in all hyper and shit. My mom started huggin' me and my dad was lookin' real relieved and shit and it seemed like they were surprised to see me still there, right? They were scared I had figured a way to get out and wouldn't nothin' be here but the goddamn chain. No Rosa! Well, they was wrong this time, but they gonna be right pretty soon.

I shoulda asked them how they figure I could get away, but I know they wouldn't tell me. They did unchain my ass while they were here, but then they followed me around like Dick Tracy. My mom even went in the bathroom with me, which was embarrassing as hell, if you know what I mean, but she didn't care. She started sayin' that shit about how she used to change my dirty diapers and she didn't care nothin' 'bout standin' there until I got through. And she did. She sat in there while I took my shower, too, and then when we all got ready to go to bed, Daddy got this really sad look on his face, and he put this muthafucker right back on me and carried his happy ass to bed like, "This shit is hurting me more than it's hurting you." I hate when people say that shit to their kids. That is bullshit. Muthafuckas be whipping their kids' ass saying some shit like that. The kid should stop cryin' and say, "Just beat me, okay? Don't beat me and bullshit me, too."

(Laughs) Like I'm gonna say some shit like that to my dad. I used to try to scream real loud when he would beat me so he'd feel bad and quit. It usually worked. He didn't wanna be whippin' me in the first place. I didn't even get my first whippin' 'til I was thirteen. I kept runnin' away from rehab and hangin' out and he didn't know what else to do. Me, neither, so we lookin' at each other like, well? And I'm thinkin', do somethin' if you gonna do somethin' or leave me alone so I can go get high! So he took off his belt and hit me a couple of times, but it wadn't bad or nothin'. My dad don't have the heart for that shit.

See, the shit they don't understand is that I like to be high. I like the way it feels. I was in rehab last time and they was goin' around the circle like they always do so you can introduce yourself and confess how sorry you are to be a dope fiend and then everybody cry wit you and tell you some shit about yourself they just thought of since they met you ten minutes ago and you suppose to say, "Oh, shit!" and decide not to smoke no more rock. It's bullshit, so when they got around to me, I said, "My name is Rosa Jackson and I just like to get high!" So everybody laughed and started sayin' shit like, "I know that's right!" and the counselor got mad at me and told me wadn't nothin' funny about bein' a dope fiend and I said, "That's where you wrong. Everything is funny about being a dope fiend!" And that was before my pops had even come up with this chain thing. But I already knew the shit was out. Here lately, I been laughin' at the same shit Jesus find funny, and you know what that mean!

The real bullshit of it is when people talk to you about this shit, the part they always leave off is how good it feel when you doin' it. Ain't nobody robbin' their grandmother for some shit that don't feel good. That don't make no sense.

I gotta pee. I can't close the door all the way with this muthafucker on, so don't look!

(*She crosses awkwardly toward the bathroom door. Blackout.*)

Day Four

Slide: "Day Four." Rosa is smoking a cigarette and pacing as rapidly as she can with the chain. She has mastered walking with it well enough so that her turns now include a practiced flip of the chain that allows her to progress much more efficiently than she did the first few days. The chain is now less a strange imposition and more a constant irritant.

Rosa stubs out her cigarette in an ashtray that is already overflowing. She continues pacing, reaches into her pocket, takes out another cigarette and lights it with a Bic lighter, still pacing. She inhales deeply, coughs, stubs this one out too.

ROSA: My dad says I should try not to start smokin' 'cause it's bad for my health. *(Laughs)* Still trippin'. *(She lights another cigarette, inhales, makes a face)* I hate cigarettes, but I gotta smoke something. I am jonesin' like a muthafucka. My mom keeps tellin' me to just take it one day at a time and shit like they tell you in rehab. That is bullshit. This is like a minute-by-minute trip, right? I want to get high so bad . . . damn! My fingernails wanna get high. My damn toenails wanna get high! "One day at a time." I hate that bullshit.

Jesus shoulda been lookin' for me by now. That muthafucka. He don't give a shit about me. He never did. He just hung around me for the . . . Shit, I don't know why he hung around me. He don't even know I'm here. I know he don't know I'm here or he woulda figured out some way to contact me. He could slide a note under the door or some shit. *(Sudden thought)* Damn! If he could slide a letter under . . .

(She goes to check how wide the space is under the door. She becomes very agitated. She tears a few pages out of a magazine and folds them like a business-size letter. She runs this under the door to see how wide a piece of something could be slipped underneath. There is plenty of room.)

Goddamn! Goddamn! *(She paces excitedly)* He could slip me some shit under there. He could slip me some shit under there every goddamn day. They'd never know it. I'll smoke it in the morning and by the time they get home, they won't even be able to smell nothin'. Shit! Why didn't I think of that before? I gotta get word to Jesus. I gotta let him know what he needs to do.

(Rosa looks around for a piece of paper and a pencil, finds them, and begins to write a letter quickly.

A slide fades in and holds for twenty seconds while she writes:

Dear Jesus,
They got me chained in the house. Bring dope.
                                        —Rosa

Rosa looks critically at the letter and makes an alteration. The slide changes to reflect rewritten letter:

Dear Jesus,
They got me chained in the house. Bring dope.
                              —Forever your girl, Rosa

The slide fades out.
    Rosa folds the letter and then looks around quickly. It dawns on her that she doesn't have any way to get it to him.)

Shit!

(She drags the chain toward the window, but can't reach it. In frustration, she begins to pull and tug at the chain in a rage.)

Goddamn it! I . . . want . . . this . . . shit . . . off . . . of . . . me!

(She tears up the letter to Jesus in a rage and sits down, rocking back and forth rapidly.)

I'm not gonna make it. I'm gonna die up in this mutha-fucka all by myself. I feel like shit and can't do a damn thing about it. I know where the shit at. I know who got it and how to make 'em give it up and I can't get a god-damn thing. They're killin' me. They're killin' me. *(A beat, then trying to calm herself)* But it's gonna be okay.

I just gotta hang in there 'til I'm eighteen, then they got no power over me no more. Jesus say when I get eighteen, I should move in wit him since he got plenty of room. I'm down wit it. I know Jesus dig me and he always got enough rock for us to get high. *(A beat)* Where is that muthafucka? He shoulda come up here and beat on the door and hollered or some shit. He could ride up the hall on a big-ass white horse like they do in the movies. I would love that shit. I love when somethin' weird happens. Somethin' you ain't seen two hundred times a day every day. Sometimes I feel like I seen everything they got to show and ain't none of it shit. Ain't none of it shit. *(A beat, then Rosa yells several times in loud succession in complete frustration)* Jesus ain't shit. I ain't shit. Ain't none of it shit. *(Begins to laugh)* So what the fuck am I cryin' about then, right? If ain't none of it shit, who gives a fuck about it? I just wanna get high, you understand? I don't give a fuck one way or the other, I just need to get high. Goddamn, I need to get high!

When you start smokin' this shit, they don't tell you how bad your ass gonna feel when you ain't got none. They forget to tell you 'bout that shit, right?

You know the funny shit is, I was almost glad to see my daddy when he came to get me. I hadn't seen Jesus in two days and them niggas was acting crazy as shit. He told them he had the hundred he owed them at the crib and he was gonna leave me there with 'em while he went to get it so they would know he wadn't bullshittin'. He ain't said shit to me about that shit, so I said, "Say, what?" He hadn't even told me about owing nobody when we busted up in there or I wouldn't a gone in the first place. Niggas be slitting people's throat for two dollars and here he come owing some niggas I ain't nevah seen before a hundred dollas. He knew I was pissed, 'cause he said, "Don't worry 'bout that shit, baby. I'll be right back and we'll go over to the house and I'll put the rest of the niggas out and we'll get fucked up, just me and you."

Bullshit, right? But I'm so stupid, I believe the muthafucka. "Okay, baby," I say, or some stupid shit like that. I shoulda said, "No, muthafucka. You tell me where the shit is, I'll go get it and they can hold you hostage 'til I get back." But I was tryin' to hang, you know? That's where I fucked up. That muthafucka kissed me good-bye and shit and walked on out the damn door and I ain't seen the nigga since. At first them niggas had a lot of shit to smoke, so we kept getting high and they didn't say too much to me about nothin'. But then when Jesus didn't show for a long time, they started askin' me where he was. Like I knew anything about the shit! I said I didn't know where the nigga was and they said he better bring back a hundred dollars or they gonna fuck me up. I ain't even in the shit, right, but they gonna fuck me up!

So I start figuring what I'm gonna do to get out of the shit and one of 'em asks me how much would I charge him for some pussy and I say a hundred dollars and he say I must think my pussy made outta gold and I tell him I can make him get off good by just watchin' me 'cause I'm that good and he look at the other one and they both laugh and say, maybe the 'ho do got a pussy made a gold. "Show me," say the one who started the shit in the first place and I tell him it gotta be just me and him 'cause I don't want them to jump me or anything. Niggas get brave when they got they boys watchin'. I know I can handle one, but I ain't down wit muthafuckas tryin' to run a train and shit. So we went in the bedroom and he closed the door and told me to hit it.

So I pulled my panties to the side like Jesus showed

me and started rubbin' myself and lookin' at his face
and he grinned at me and started rubbin' hisself
through his jeans. I always watch their faces 'cause
that's how you know if they dig it or not. Then he unzip
his pants so he can hold his dick in his hand and it was
feeling all right to me too, even though Jesus wadn't
there to call my name, and I'm thinkin' maybe this ain't
gonna be so bad after all, but then the nigga reached out
and grabbed my hand and tried to make me sit down on
his lap while he still got his thing out and shit! And I'm
tryin' to tell him I ain't down wit it 'cause a AIDS and
shit and he tellin' me he ain't no faggot and we sorta
wrestlin' around and I'm tryin' not make no noise 'cause
I don't want his boy to come in too. That's when my dad
started beatin' on the door and hollerin' and shit and all
hell broke loose.

They was gettin' ready to shoot through the door at
first, and I said "No, that sound like my dad!" So they
told him if he didn't pay the hundred dollars I owed
them they'd blow my brains out right in front of him. My
daddy just stood there for a minute lookin' at that nigga
holdin' his nine-millimeter against my head and I'm
thinkin', my daddy ain't got that kinda money! I'm dead!
And then he reached in his pocket and took out a roll a
money and handed it to the nigga who had been in the
bedroom with me. The nigga counted it right in front of
my daddy and it was a hundred dollars exactly. That's
how I know Jesus the one told him to come get me. How
else my daddy gonna be walkin' around Harlem with a
pocketful of cash like he the dope man and shit.

Then that nigga told my daddy to get my little crack-
addict ass outta his place and pushed me so hard I fell
against his chest. My daddy didn't even look at me. He
took off his jacket and put it around my shoulders and
we walked the three blocks home with him holdin' my

arm like you do a little kid when they been bad. He wadn't sayin' shit. When we got home, my moms was there and she started cryin' and holdin' my face up so she could look at me and shit. I know I looked like shit. I hadn't eaten in two-three days and my clothes were all twisted around from tusslin' with that nigga in the bedroom. And I know my hair was all over my head 'cause she kept smoothin' it down and I could feel it risin' right back up again and she'd smooth it down again and it would rise on back up. My head was itchin' too, but I couldn't scratch or nothin' because my mom was huggin' me and she had my arms pinned down at my sides and you can't push your mama off you, even if you want to, so I'm standin' there tryin' to get her to calm down and I catch a eyeful of my pops sittin' at the table and tears just runnin' down his face. He ain't cryin' or hollerin' or nothin'. He just sittin' there lookin' at me and mama stumblin' around the room like we drunk.

That hurt me worse than anything. I never seen my daddy cry in my life. Never. I seen him mad plenty of times, but not over me. He be mad about some niggas actin' a fool or some crackers fuckin' over him or somethin' mama said that didn't sit right, but he never cried. He didn't cry when his mama died. Took the phone call, drove down South and buried her, came back and never broke. So I felt real bad when I saw him cryin' over me. I love my daddy . . .

So I got away from mama and I went over and stood in front of him and I said, "Don't worry about me, Daddy. I'm okay." And he just looked at me and tears runnin' all down his chin and he wadn't wipin' shit. Act like he didn't even know he was doin' it. I didn't have no Kleenex or nothin', but I hated to see him like that, so I just wiped him off a little with my sleeve, right? He caught my hand and held it so hard I thought he was gonna crush my damn fingers and he just looked at me and started sayin' my name over and over and over like he wasn't sure it was even me: "Rosa, Rosa, Rosa!" And my mom on the other side of the room runnin' around hollerin' and shit.

It was almost like I was somewhere else watchin' it. It was too weird to be happenin' to me for real. When I went to bed, I could still hear my mom in the other room cryin' and every time I woke up, my dad would be sittin' right by my bed, just lookin' at me like he in a dream or somethin'. Then one time I got up to go to the bathroom and he walked right wit me and stood there outside the door and waited for me and before I got back into bed he hugged me real hard and I could feel him shakin' like he was jonesin' worse than me. Scared the shit outta me. I figured my shit must be even raggedier than I thought if it making my daddy shake.

It's no way for me to tell him how it feels, you know what I mean? They don't understand nothin' about none of it so there's no place to start tellin' them anything. They shoulda kept their country asses in Tuskegee, Alabama.

My daddy used to sing when we lived down there. He can sing, too. He sound like Luther Vandross a little bit. Him and my mama used to sing in the car. Raggedy-ass car they got from somebody. We drove that muthafucka all the way up here, though. Soon as we got to Harlem, the muthafucka broke down. I used to ask my pops if the car had a broke down in Brooklyn, would he a stayed in Brooklyn and he would laugh and say he probably would. *(A beat)*

I think that nigga was gonna rape me if my daddy hadn't busted up in there. And that wadn't gonna be the worst of it. Jesus wadn't comin' back no time soon. That's why he called my pops and told him where I was.

(Laughs) He busted up in there, though. My daddy crazy. They coulda blown him away with his Alabama ass. *(A beat)* I don't think he'd a brought me up here if he'd a known what these niggas up here were like. They treacherous up here in New York. You think you ready for it, but you not ready. These niggas don't care nothin' bout you. Jesus spose to be my friend, and look how he act! *(A beat)* My daddy bad, though. He was beatin' on that door like he was packin' a Uzi and he didn't have shit. Not even no stick or nothin'. He just standin' there talkin' shit about: "Where my baby girl at? Where you got my Rosa?"

And I'm hollerin': "Here I am, Daddy! Here I am!"

(Blackout.)

Day Five

Slide: "Day Five." Rosa is clicking rapidly through the channels on a small TV on the table. It is a tiny, black-and-white model with a very fuzzy picture. She tries in vain to adjust it and find something she likes. She finally snaps it off, frustrated, and begins to pace. The chain is still in place, but by now she handles it casually as if it has always been there.

ROSA: I been tryin' to find somethin' to overstimulate me. My mom said they real proud of me 'cause I'm actin' like my old self so they gonna let me have TV today. How else I'm gonna act, chained to the damn radiator? My old self. Who the hell is that? They mean my Alabama self. My before-I-met-Jesus self. My don't-know-nothin'-'bout-crack-rock self. That's who they lookin' for. *(A beat)* I miss her too, but I think girlfriend is gone, gone, gone. *(She paces, but slowly. She's thinking)*

My daddy say I been doin' so good, he ain't gonna chain me but a couple more days. Just to be sure. I started to tell him, it take longer than that to be sure, but I didn't say nothin'. If I say some shit like that, he'll never take this damn chain offa my leg!

He ask me was I worried about the street takin' me back if he take the chain offa me. He sound so serious when he say shit like that, but to me, he just be trippin'. Like the street some kind of weird, scary shit waitin' for you in the alley instead of a bunch of niggas you know tryin' to get paid and get high.

But how'm I gonna tell him that shit? So I told him no. I wasn't worried about the street takin' me back. And he hug me and shit and tell me there is nothin' out there for me. I say, I know that's right. *(She tries the TV again, then turns it off)*

The thing is, after a couple of days when you don't watch TV seem like when you go back to it, ain't nothin' on there you wanna see. You gotta let it stay on for a little while without payin' no attention, then it start lookin' good to you again, otherwise that shit is too lame.

My pops told me I should pray instead of gettin' high. No bullshit. He really did tell me that. I never been to no religious rehab, but I know some people who did. They tell you shit like that all the time. Let God take the place of the drugs in your life. Give it all to God. Shit like that. It works for some muthafuckas, I guess, but I don't believe all that shit. I used to go to church when I was little 'cause I like to listen to the choir, but I never did get into prayin' a whole lot.

I used to like to sneak and look at people while they be prayin' with their eyes closed. They be looking so serious, frownin' up and shit. I don't know why people think they gotta look all ugly and shit to talk to God. I figure if the muthafucka—scuse me!—if His Highness is really God and a bad muthafucka, he oughta be able to let you talk just sittin' down someplace lookin' like you look when you just bein' regular. I rather have niggas just talk to me that way than be frownin' up and shit, but I ain't God, right? So what the fuck am I talkin' about?

I told my daddy I wish I believe in God, but I don't. "It take time," my dad tell me. "You have to get to know him just like any good friend. You have to put the time in to get the goody out." That's what he said. He talkin' 'bout God and shit and then he come talkin' 'bout the goody! He so country sometime! *(A beat)*

I been thinkin' 'bout if I wanna keep smokin' that shit or not. No, I mean really thinkin' about it for myself. It can make you do shit that is really fucked up. I done some fucked-up shit myself when I was high, or tryin' to get high. I told you I stole my grandmama's check. I stole lots of people checks. Cash and carry. Old people be lookin' all worried 'cause they check ain't come and I know I smoked that shit up two days ago. And you don't care neither! You just say, fuck it.

Like, I keep thinkin' 'bout how Jesus left me with them niggas I didn't even know! He didn't care what they did to me. They coulda thrown me out the window . . . And they do that shit, too! Old crackhead niggas threw a girl out the window right around the corner from here just a week ago. Took her clothes off first so when she hit the ground her titties and shit was all out. People standin' around laughin' and she dead as shit. Nobody even covered her up or nothin'.

My daddy told me only God stronger than crack. I tell him this chain been doin' a pretty good job. I was just kiddin', but I think it made him feel bad 'cause his face got all sad and shit. *(A beat)* I told him I just meant it's hard once you can come and go when you want to not to just go anywhere you can think of goin', right? Even if you not thinkin' about it by yourself, somebody gonna remind me to think about smokin' that rock. They gonna be goin' there, or comin' from there or lookin' for some money to get there or somethin'. It's not like you gotta be lookin' for the shit. *(A beat)*

He told me he knew I was a good girl and he trusted me. I wanted to say, "Hey, man! This is goddamn Harlem! Trust ain't in it!" *(A beat)* I don't trust nobody. *(A beat)* Not about no shit like this. It ain't a goddamn thing out there but a bunch of niggas gonna die and wanna take me wit 'em. Ain't a thing out there. *(She looks around)* At least in here, ain't nobody fuckin' with me. I got food. I got a bathroom. I even got TV and shit, so how bad can it be? *(Suddenly angry)* And what the fuck you lookin' at?

(Blackout.)

Day Six

Slide: "Day Six." Rosa sits on the couch, smoking. She is rubbing her ankle distractedly and thinking. She stubs out the cigarette deliberately, still thinking. She gets up and walks across the room. The chain is no longer on her leg, but she is still limping slightly, and whenever she is not moving, she rubs her ankle as if it were a little sore.

She crosses to the telephone, which is in evidence in the room for the first time, picks it up and dials hesitantly. She hangs up before she finishes the number. Thinks for a minute. Dials again. She waits for it to ring several times.

ROSA: Who is this? . . . Let me speak to Jesus. Rosa.

(Rosa waits for him to come to the phone; when he does, she jumps on him angrily.)

Where you been, muthafucka? Yeah, this is Rosa. Who the fuck you think it was? I know the nigga told you Rosa. You know another Rosa now beside me? Where the fuck you been? . . . No! Don't tell me shit! I don't wanna hear it! You left me, muthafucka! They could have fucked me right up and where the fuck were you? . . . I said don't tell me shit! . . . I don't wanna hear it. They had me chained up because of your triflin' ass! . . . You heard me! Chained up by the foot like a goddamn dog! Right in the living room. If you had brought your ass over here you would have known that shit . . . Don't tell me that shit! You know they be workin' all day just like all the other country-ass niggas in Harlem. You think they boss give them the week off so they can sit home and watch out for their dope-fiend daughter? You know better than that shit, muthafucka. You just didn't give a shit. Got me started smokin' that shit and now you just don't give a damn, do you? Well, fuck you, Jesus! Fuck you! . . . No, I haven't finished. I got a lot more shit to say to your triflin' ass . . .

(Jesus interrupts her now until he breaks her rhythm, and she begins to listen more than fuss. Throughout the following, her demeanor changes from angrily belliger-ent to petulant to needy.)

No. Nobody ain't told me nothin' about where you been. I ain't seen nobody, I told you! I been chained up! . . . Where you been? Why? For real? When? They came to your place? Them two you left me wit? . . . Then why you leave me wit 'em? . . . But if you don't know, you spose to take me wit you and not take a chance, you know? . . . They

coulda killed me, Jesus! You know I'm not lyin'! . . . No
. . . No . . . Nothin' like that happened . . . I can handle
myself, I been tellin' you that . . . I ain't scared of no
crackhead niggas . . . Not even you! . . . What you mean
how long since I been high? I ain't doin' that shit no
more, muthafucka 'cause I ain't no muthafuckin' dope
fiend, all right? I been up here without shit for five days,
right? And I handled it! I am handlin' it! So fuck you,
Jesus! Fuck you! . . . No. My mom be home in a few minutes so don't bring your black ass up here. That's right.
Not tomorrow either. I don't need that shit. I just called
to let you know not to bring your ass around me and
when you see me on the street, don't even act like you
know me, you junkie muthafucka . . . You . . . you . . .
You left me!

(Blackout.)

Day Seven

*Slide: "Day Seven." Rosa is looking out the window, smoking a
cigarette. She smokes it down to the end, stubs it out and lights
another. She keeps her eyes fixed on the street even while she
is getting another cigarette. She is waiting. She goes to the
table, sits. She goes to the couch, sits. She stands near the door
and listens, crosses to the window, scans the street. Nothing.
She sits again, then speaks slowly and fiercely to herself.*

ROSA: Fuck this shit, okay? Just fuck it!

> *(She stubs out another cigarette, turns the TV on, then
> off. She picks up the phone, starts to dial. Stops. Hangs
> up. She is very agitated. She sits and sighs deeply.)*

Okay, look. This is a prayer, okay? *(A beat)* I can't do that shit.

(She starts pacing again. She stops suddenly near the closet and slowly reaches for the knob. She reaches in and gets the bag with the chain in it. She takes the bag out and goes over to the couch with it. She takes the chain out, handling it gingerly. She feels the weight and the chill of it. It is completely familiar and absolutely mysterious: there is both resignation and comfort in her handling of the chain. She places the shackle around her wrist like a bracelet. She is painfully aware of the safety the chain offers by taking away her choices. She suddenly takes it off her wrist and puts it down, but not away. She realizes what she is considering and the thought horrifies her. She sits looking at the chain for a beat and then reaches toward it again.

There is a sudden, furtive knock at the door. She draws her hand back guiltily. She goes quickly and quietly to the door. She listens. Another furtive knock. She speaks quietly.)

Jesus? *(A beat)* Jesus, is that you?

(She begins to quickly unbolt the locks and chains on the door, fumbling in her anxiousness to get the locks open. When she does, she takes a deep breath, closes her eyes for a minute and then opens the door.
Blackout.)

END OF PLAY

Late Bus to Mecca

Late Bus to Mecca was coproduced by Women's Project & Productions and the New Federal Theatre under the artistic direction of Julia Miles and Woodie King, Jr., respectively, at the Judith Anderson Theatre, New York City, from February 28 to March 22, 1992. The play was commissioned and developed by Women's Project & Productions and the Southeast Playwrights Project of Atlanta through a grant from the Multi Arts Production Fund of the Rockefeller Foundation. Imani was the director, the sets were designed by George Xenos, lights by Melody Beal, costumes by Ornyece and sound was by Bill Toles. The cast was as follows:

AVA JOHNSON   Kim Yancey

A BLACK WOMAN (ABW)   Claire Dorsey

Characters

AVA JOHNSON, a twentyish black woman, who has been
earning her living as a prostitute

A BLACK WOMAN (ABW), also a twentyish black woman

Time

October 24, 1970, 10 P.M.

Place

A Greyhound bus station in downtown Detroit, Michigan

Note to the Director

Characterization

Ava represents the possibility of consciously extending the circle of sisterhood to include every black woman specifically, in all her complexity and terribleness. Ava has to be a prostitute, because we have to see the potential for our salvation in every segment of our group. We cannot allow class distinctions, superficial moral judgments and personal prejudices to divide and conquer us. We have to believe that there is enough resilience and residual sisterhood in any and all of us to make it possible for us to redeem ourselves and rescue each other.

It is important that Ava not be painted in broad comedic strokes. Her style and behavior are entirely appropriate to the world she lives in, as are her language and her sexual frankness. Ava must be an admirable and likable character so that the audience's identification with her can help them confront and release their own class prejudices.

It is important that A Black Woman's silence be representative of every physically battered, spirit-bruised black woman whose words have been ignored or used against her so often they seem beside the point. While she represents all of these women, she does not pretend to know all of their pain. She is specific. She is not The Black Woman. She is a black woman.

She must have a strong physical presence on the stage although she never speaks a word. The audience should have concern for her overall well being and for her moment-to-moment ability to maintain balance and consciousness.

A Black Woman's face should often be averted, but it should always be alive. She must make visible on her face and in her body her increasing trust in Ava, but maintain the wariness she has been taught by the harshness of her life.

Blackouts and Slides

The play is arranged in thirteen scenes, separated by blackouts. At each blackout, a slide should immediately be projected on a large, white screen at the back of the stage. The slides will contain the number of the scene coming up and a quote from the dialogue of that scene. All dialogue on the slides should be framed in quotation marks. Each slide should hold for ten seconds and then disappear as the lights come up. The slides are as follows:

1. "Did they just call the bus to Atlanta?"
2. "That's who I'm named after."
3. "Are you on something?"
4. "Blink if you can hear me."
5. "Not as fine as you are."
6. "But animals is different."
7. "Maybe you should fix yourself up a little."
8. "I always have a plan."
9. "What can I say?"
10. "Not after I got to know you."
11. "I told her I wasn't pretending."
12. "I thought a bolt of lightning was gonna strike us dead."
13. "You could have just told me."

Playwright's Note

When Muhammad Ali made his victorious return to the boxing ring after three years of exile because of his consciencious-objector status on the basis of his religious beliefs, it was cause for jubilation in the African-American community. When no other state would issue him a boxing permit, Senator Leroy Johnson was able to secure one through the state of Georgia for a match on the night of October 26, 1970.

Tickets at ringside were going for one hundred dollars each. Hustlers and gamblers from all over the country flocked to Atlanta to bet on the fight, enjoy the parties and show off their ladies. The event became a week-long celebration of the young, black champion who had faced down the American government in the midst of the Vietnam War and emerged victorious. Ali, twenty-eight, defeated Jerry Quarry by technical knockout in the third round.

Act One

Scene One

In the darkness, the sound of bus arrivals and departures is being announced. The last announcement is for the midnight bus to Atlanta with appropriate intermediate stops.

Slide 1: "Did they just call the bus to Atlanta?"

As lights come up, A Black Woman (ABW) is huddled on a bright orange, plastic, bus station chair. Her age is difficult to determine because she is dirty and disheveled. She is dressed in worn bell-bottom jeans, a faded T-shirt with an antiwar slogan on it and battered shoes. She looks very tired. Her face is dirty and smudged. She has a tattered backpack, which is tossed carelessly by the side of her chair.

There are two empty chairs next to her. She shifts uncomfortably, stares at the floor, hugs her arms around her body. She seems to be shivering although the place is warm.

Ava enters in a hurry wearing very high-heeled shoes or boots. She is very agitated. She is carrying a large, shocking pink suitcase, with a matching, shocking pink makeup case.

315

Her clothes are tight and flashy, but she is not a caricature. She is attractive and has tangible physical confidence.

AVA: Did they just call the bus to Atlanta? What time did they say? Midnight, right? There isn't one before that, is there? They told me none after 9:30 until midnight.

(A Black Woman makes no response.)

Did you see a girl come in here? About my size? Leather coat? Real pretty?

(No response.)

Red leather. You couldn't miss her.

(Ava looks around again anxiously, then back to ABW, who has still made no response.)

Hey! Look, if you do see her, tell her I'll be right back. Okay? Hey! Are you asleep or what? Hey!

(No response.)

Shit!

(Ava dashes out. ABW remains motionless. Blackout.)

Scene Two

Slide 2: "That's who I'm named after."
   Slide fades. Lights up. Ava reenters, much calmer. She stacks her things in the chair next to ABW and sits; she looks around with some satisfaction.

AVA: You definately have the best seat in the house. I can see everything from here.

(ABW does not respond.)

I'm Ava.

(Ava sticks out her hand. ABW ignores it.)

You the strong silent type I guess. *(Shrugs)* Suit yourself.

I'm supposed to meet my girlfriend. She's always late. I told her the bus was at ten so she'd be here on time. She probably called to check, knowing I would lie about that shit. Well, the bus ain't 'til midnight, so she's still got plenty of time to make it. I can't miss her from here! You can see the whole damn room. Plus, I got the tickets, so how far is she gonna get, right?

(ABW shifts miserably in her chair.)

Are you okay? Hey! You okay?

(ABW wearily closes her eyes. Ava snaps open her make-up case and looks critically at herself in the mirror. She sighs and searches through the jumble in the case for her makeup. She repairs her makeup while she talks: this routine includes applying lipstick and lip pencil, combing her hair and putting on foundation, powder, blush, eye shadow and mascara. The makeup application should run throughout the scene. Ava looks mostly at herself in the mirror, but checks on ABW every few seconds.)

You don't ride the bus much, do you? *(She puts on lipstick with elaborate unconcern)* I didn't think so. Sitting all by yourself up in this dim-ass corner. You should be glad I sat down 'cause you are asking for trouble. You are a sitting duck for every nigga with his dick in his hand and his eye on what you got. Know what I mean?

You see that guy over there? I saw him looking at me when I first came in. Grinning at me like I got no more class than to be picking up old half-drunk niggas at the bus station! *(Her voice rises with indignation as she speaks in the direction of the man who offended her)* Somebody needs to tell these niggas when they are out of their league. Way out of their league.

Don't worry. He ain't coming over here. They don't mess with you unless you're all by yourself. *(Talking loudly again)* They get real brave then. Can't tell them shit then!

See? He's leaving. I know niggas like the back of my damn hand. I know how they think! *(She looks at ABW with concern)*

I told you I'm Ava, right? Most people have never met anybody with that name other than Ava Gardner and they haven't met her. They just know her name from the movies.

That's who I'm named after. My whole name is Ava Gardner Johnson, but I don't say all that because niggas think everything is so goddamn funny when it ain't none of their business in the first place, you know? *(She begins combing and styling her hair energetically and efficiently)* Did you know she was black? She didn't tell anybody because she wanted to be in the movies, but she was. My mother saw her once and she said you could really tell it close-up.

Her hair and everything. My mother used to say she was related to us, but my mother used to say so much shit you had to take it or leave it.

She said it was almost true because she was pretty sure her and Miss G. had been sisters in another life.

She believed all that stuff about being alive over and over until you get it right? I don't think so though. I mean, how likely you think it is that a big Hollywood movie star like Ava Gardner is gonna have my mother for a sister in any life! *(She puts away hair brush, then ties on a scarf. She looks critically in the mirror, then takes the scarf off)*

I usually look better than this when I'm traveling. But it's nobody but deadbeats on the bus anymore. And this late at night for sure. Present company excepted, of course! *(She tries on several pairs of earrings)*

I hate the bus. I like to fly. First class all the way! First time I was on an airplane, I never wanted it to land. Except I was sitting next to this asshole friend of Tony's who kept trying to get me to do it with him in the bathroom. "Come on baby, don't you wanna join the mile high club?" *(Looks around anxiously for her friend again)* I'll be glad when Sherri gets here though. I know that! She's so flaky sometime. I told her she musta been a white girl in her last life!

I never knew anybody met a nice guy on the bus. Sherri met a nice guy on the train once. Well, he sounded nice when she told me about it anyway. She's taking the train down South to her mother's funeral and this guy asks can he buy her a drink, but since she's going to her mom's funeral, she doesn't feel up for a lot of chat. So she tells the guy straight up and instead of getting an attitude like niggas usually do when you try to tell them something real, he says, he's sorry to hear about her mom and how about if he buys her a drink anyway and they can just sit and contemplate the scenery together for a while. That's what he said: contemplate the scenery.

Sounds like a movie, doesn't it? That's why she believes in so much fantasy shit in the first place. So much of it happens to her, she thinks that's real life.

Niggas always wanna talk to Sherri. She's cool though. She can handle that debonair shit niggas say and never break. If somebody offered to buy me a drink so we could contemplate the scenery, I'd probably think it was a con.

She said he was real suave, all right, but he kept talking suave like that all the way to D.C., which is where he was getting off. She said after a while, she just got tired of hearing it.

Sherri's that way, though. She doesn't like a whole lot of chat. Tony's like that too. They can sit in a room with no TV or nothing and not say a word for an hour! They would love you!

I can't stand that quiet shit. I hafta hear some noise! *(Suddenly agitated again by Sherri's lateness)* I wish she would just come on!

(Blackout.)

Scene Three

Slide 3: "Are you on something?"

Ava is painting her toenails carefully. She has cotton balls in between her toes. She is quiet, concentrating on her work. ABW's eyes are closed. Ava finishes and screws the top back on the bottle, looking at her toes with satisfaction.

AVA: They talking about snow up here next week and it's still Indian summer down South. Sandal weather! *(She blows on her toes)* You going to Atlanta, too?

(Ava sees the sudden panic in ABW's face.)

Relax, honey. I don't care where you're going, okay? You don't have to get paranoid. Is somebody after you?

(ABW looks at Ava.)

Well, more power to you, honey. It's every woman for her-self, I say. When it's time to make a move, make a move. *(She fans her nails with her hands and blows on them)* I've never been any further south than D.C. Sherri hasn't either. She grew up in D.C., but she said as soon as she could, she went North. I hope it's not too country down there. I hate the country. Tony had a friend who lived way out. I thought the nigga was hiding from somebody, but Tony said he just couldn't stand no whole bunch of noise since he got back from Vietnam.

He had these big old bug eyes, too. Always trying to talk up on something and his damn eyes be getting big-ger and bigger . . . But Atlanta's spose to be a big city, so we'll see. *(Ava looks around again for Sherri)* She is really getting on my nerves with this shit. Sometimes I start thinking about all the stuff I don't like about my girl and I say, so what you like about her? And it's there, but it's so much harder to put into words, you know?

Don't get me started thinking about that shit! We got twenty-two hours between here and Atlanta. I do not want to ride that far being evil.

I hate riding the bus by myself. It's okay when you got somebody with you, but when you're by yourself, there's always a nigga with a hard-on grinning up in your face, 'scuse my French.

(ABW closes her eyes again and leans back weakly.)

(Gently) You really look bad, honey. Are you on something?

(Blackout.)

Scene Four

Slide 4: "Blink if you can hear me."
Ava is vigorously chomping and cracking a piece of gum. She is also examining her fingernails critically. She blows a bubble and pops it, then goes back to chomping. She is engrossed in her nails. Another loud pop. ABW is seated with her eyes closed, slumped over her knees. On the third loud pop, she looks at Ava. Ava produces another huge bubble. It bursts loudly.

AVA *(Takes out gum disgustedly)*: I hate gum when you got all the sugar out of it. Wears out your jaws trying to chew it! *(She wraps the gum in paper and tosses it)*

There was a girl in my high school who was the champion gum cracker of all time. She could crack it on every chew. It didn't have to be bubble gum either. She could pop anything! Kathleen DeGracia. They were supposed to be Filipino. That's what they told everybody. Filipino my ass. They were niggas just like the rest of us. They just had that heavy hair, you know? But that don't mean shit. Look at Ava Gardner! *(She sorts through her nail polish to find one that appeals to her)*

Niggas got good hair think they can tell you anything and you gonna believe it just 'cause their hair is so pretty. Tony had that kinda hair. Claimed to be a Mexican, but he didn't have no accent and couldn't speak no Spanish! So who you gonna believe?

When Sherri gets mad she always says: "Niggas ain't shit!" until I remind her that Tony is a spose-to-be Mexican. It ain't just niggas. Ain't none of them shit.

(ABW is still looking at Ava.)

Did somebody beat you up, honey?

(ABW starts to turn away.)

I'm sorry! Look! I'm not trying to get into your business. You just look like . . . you need some help.

Did somebody hurt you? Can you hear me? I know you can hear me. Can't you? Nod if you can hear me! Just nod, okay?

(No response from ABW, but she is still looking at Ava.)

Okay . . . it's okay. You don't have to nod. Just . . . blink. Blink real hard two times, if you can hear me. Or once, just do it once, but do it hard so I'll know it wasn't just a regular blink, you know?

(ABW closes her eyes and turns wearily away.)

(Choosing to interpret this as a blink) Good enough. Good enough. Okay. No problem. Good enough.

(Blackout.)

Scene Five

Slide 5: "Not as fine as you are."
Ava is wiping her hands and cleaning under her fingernails delicately with a Handi-Wipe.

AVA: Are you hungry? I'm starving to death. I'm gonna have to break down and get a sandwich or something. Messing around trying to get out of there before Tony got back. I know how niggas will always show up when you don't need to see 'em.

First time I saw Tony, I made him feed me. I thought he was the finest thing walking. I had a gig dancing at this cheap-ass place downtown and I was late again so I knew I was gonna get some shit anyway and then it started to rain.

I started running and then I said, "Fuck it! I quit! I'm not running in the rain to get to a gig I don't like in the first place." So I just stopped in the middle of the sidewalk to think for a minute. I needed a plan quick!

And then I heard somebody right behind me say, "Baby, you don't ever have to stand out in no rain. Not as fine as you are."

And it was Tony. With a big umbrella.

Niggas make me sick sometime. They always pretending it's anything but what it is. And if they halfway fine, you start pretending too and next thing you know, Fantasyland!

That shit is dangerous too. You step back and forth across that line too many times, you start believing any shit they tell you.

Me, I don't believe one word that comes out of a man's mouth. They all might as well be talking out their ass if you ask me about it.

You want a Handi-Wipe? No offense or anything, but you might want to, you know, wipe your face a little. They gonna pick you up for being a vagrant or something looking like that.

(ABW touches her face with some concern.)

Here you go.

(ABW looks at Ava. Ava places some Handi-Wipes in ABW's hand. ABW just holds them.)

He was having dinner at the twenty-four hour pancake house and he told me I could get anything I wanted. I ate so much food he started laughing his ass off.

Showing all those pretty white teeth. He said, "Girl, you must think this is a Chinese restaurant much stuff as you ordered!"
Go ahead, honey. Wipe your face off a little. You know . . . *(She demonstrates dramatically)*
You in bad shape, honey. You know that? You in real bad shape. *(Sighing, she takes the Handi-Wipes gently. Very gently)* I'm gonna wipe your face, okay? You want me to help you? You want me to help you do it? Huh?

(As Ava talks, she very slowly wipes ABW's cheek. ABW draws back almost imperceptively, but Ava is talking softly and her touch is very gentle.)

It's okay. You just need a little help that's all. And I am the A-number-one girl for helping out, and that's the truth. Sherri will tell you. I've been through a time or two with my girl where nobody thought she was gonna make it but me. But I didn't give up on her. *(She finishes her wiping)* One hundred percent improvement! Look!

(Ava turns the makeup mirror toward ABW, who turns quickly away.
Blackout.)

Scene Six

Slide 6: "But animals is different."
Ava is filing her nails energetically. She looks up periodically, searching for Sherri. ABW watches.

AVA: That girl is gonna be late for her own funeral, I swear.
She always says that's why she can't keep a regular job. Late all the time. I told her that's why she needs to work

with me. I'll cut her a little slack. *(She gets up impatiently and paces. She looks at her watch)*

Shit! *(Still pacing)* Waiting around like this is gonna drive me crazy! How long you been sittin' here? *(She is suddenly irritated at ABW's silence)*

Hey, look! I don't care all right. But we got another hour to sit here before this damn bus comes. Can't you say something? Just to pass the time?

(ABW does not respond.)

Great! I got one on the way who can't tell time and one sittin' here who can't talk. This must be my lucky night! *(She sits and tries to do her nails again, but she's angry)*

Well, I'm going this time even if she doesn't come. I told her that. She can do what she wants, but I'm not fucking no dogs!

And I don't care how much they willing to pay to watch us do it. Them niggas ain't got that much money. And I told both of them that when they first brought it up. No way!

She just sat there and didn't say anything, just rolling her eyes and smiling. I told him, "Look! I can do about anything a regular human being can think up to ask me if they paying cash money, but animals is different."

(ABW looks at Ava with specific curiousity for the first time. Blackout.)

Scene Seven

Slide 7: "Maybe you should fix yourself up a little."
Ava is carefully gluing on some long, curved, fake fingernails.

AVA: Atlanta's gonna be the place to be this weekend. That's where you ought to be trying to get to, honey. People who been there tell me it's live! They said people down there call it "the Black Mecca" 'cause black folks got it so good. I told this Muslim friend of mine about it and he got mad. He just got to be a Muslim since high school, but the way he acts now, you'd think he'd been selling bean pies all his life! He said they all gonna burn because Mecca is about the spirit and them Atlanta niggas ain't about nothing but money.

Well, I know that's what they gonna be about this weekend. Every hustler, and every wanna-be hustler, is gonna be there for that fight. They all want a piece of "Ali! Ali! Ali!" The way these niggas are talking about it, you'd think they were gonna personally go down there an' kick some ass.

Myself, I don't care one way or the other. Boxing is some man shit, even though Ali is fine! But they're gonna be spending big money to celebrate that shit and I am a celebrating something when I put my mind to it.

I told Sherri if we work this week right, we don't ever have to come back to Detroit. For what? We can retire and go to beauty school like we got some sense. I told Sherri I don't wanna be stuck in no gig where the big money comes when you start fucking dogs. We need to make plans. *(Angry again suddenly)* If she ever get here!

Tony had tickets to the fight, 'til he lost them gambling. He was pissed off. His ego couldn't stand going down there and not being able to get in, so he's telling people he decided to just "cool out at the crib." I told Sherri that's why he's pressing that dog shit. Since he ain't goin' to the fight, he's gotta come up with something new to impress the fellas.

Most of them stay so coked up and full of cognac they couldn't do nothing if they wanted to, which they don't. All they wanna do is get high and watch.

Tony was into watching, too. But Sherri wouldn't do nothing when it was just the three of us even though he used to ask her all the time . . . She said she wasn't no freak. She was just trying to make a living. *(Looking at ABW)* I'm not trying to talk you into anything, but there's plenty money to be made in Atlanta this weekend. Maybe you should fix yourself up a little . . . no. I guess not.

(Blackout.)

Scene Eight

Slide 8: "I always have a plan."
Ava enters with sandwiches, chips and Cokes in a flimsy cardboard tray.

AVA: Okay. We got tuna and we got cheese. You can pick.

(ABW looks helplessly at Ava.)

Tuna? No? Okay. Cheese it is.

(Ava unwraps the sandwich, puts it in ABW's hand and sits a can of soda by ABW's feet. Ava unwraps her sandwich and begins to eat.)

You better eat something. It's a long ride on an empty stomach.

(ABW slowly picks up the sandwich. Ava watches her sideways, approvingly.)

Go ahead. It's bad, but it won't kill you.

(ABW slowly raises the sandwich to her mouth, sighs deeply and takes a bite. She chews slowly and swallows with difficulty. Ava smiles at her.)

I know it ain't none of my business, but you gonna get hurt hanging around here by yourself. Do you have a ticket to Atlanta? Do you have a ticket to anywhere?

(ABW eats methodically.)

Your problem is you don't have a plan. You gotta have a plan, honey. Even if you have to adjust it a little every now and then, you gotta have a basic plan that you stick by. I always have a plan.

You're just out here, aren't you? I wish you would say something!

That's okay. I hear you. You don't have to say a damn thing. They took all of it, didn't they? Every little bit they could get their hands on. They just turned you out, didn't they?

(ABW suddenly puts down her sandwich. Her eyes fly open, and she grabs her stomach and her mouth. She is clearly about to throw up.)

What the . . . Quick! The ladies' room! Over there! Hurry up!

(ABW rushes out. Ava watches her to be sure she makes it to the ladies' room.)

Jesus!

(Ava immediately goes over and picks up ABW's back-pack. She goes through it quickly. She finds a tattered

wallet, takes it out and flips through it, looking for information. She removes several dollars and counts them. She takes out a pill bottle and looks at the label. The bottle is empty and topless.

Ava looks toward the ladies' room, registering concern. Then she continues going through the purse, money still in her hand . She does not see ABW return from the ladies' room until she turns to face her. ABW is standing there, watching Ava.

Blackout.)

Scene Nine

Slide 9: "What can I say?"
Ava lights a cigarette and smokes nervously. She jiggles her foot. ABW is holding her bag tightly in her lap. Both women look straight ahead. They should hold this moment until the audience is uncomfortable.

Blackout.

Scene Ten

Slide 10: "Not after I got to know you."

AVA: Look, I'm sorry, okay? It's none of my business what you do or don't do.

But I know they give you those pills and shit at the hospital for a reason. It's so you can take care of yourself out here. A girl Sherri knows was in the crazy house three times and she had these big-ass pills. Horse pills. I told her they look like horse pills. She had to take them every day or she would go off. That's why she kept going back in. She'd stop taking her medicine and then go into the grocery store or something and start cussing people out. When she takes her medicine, she doesn't care how long the lines are or how long the meat's been sitting there. She's in her own world.

It ain't no picnic out here, you know. If they gave you something to take the edges off, go for it.

You throw all of them away?

(ABW looks at Ava.)

Not for you, honey. If you don't want to take them, don't take them. But you can always sell prescription tranqs. It's like money in the bank. People will take anything from a hospital. It's guaranteed to cool you out.

Well, it doesn't matter. But you gonna have to start thinking about stuff like that. You sell people what they want, you gonna always make a living.

You believe me, don't you?

About the money, I mean. I wasn't gonna take your money. I was just being nosy. I probably would have taken it at first, but not after I got to know you. Well, not really know you since you still haven't said shit, but you know what I mean. I got no business stealing from you. All these men out here with pockets full of money. What would that make me to be stealing from you?

But that should be like a warning to you about how dangerous it is out here, honey. Just between us, I think you are way too crazy to be out here walking around on your own. They're gonna eat you alive.

(ABW looks at Ava. Ava gets up and starts pacing again. She looks at her watch.)

I cannot believe this girl is gonna leave me hangin'! *(Angrily turning on ABW all of a sudden)*

331

You not gonna make it! You hear what I'm telling you? They ought to lock you up now and save you and them some trouble. I don't know how they let you out in the first place. I'm tired of being around crazy bitches who don't know how to make a move!

Why don't you fix yourself up!

(Blackout.)

Scene Eleven

Slide 11: "I told her I wasn't pretending."

Ava is tucking in a new blouse on ABW. It is bright and flowery and very much in contrast to ABW's other clothing.

AVA: Much better! Now what about that head? Let's just touch it up a little around the edges, okay? *(She goes and gets a comb and brush. She begins to brush ABW's hair back gently)* Are you tender-headed?

Well, I'll act like you are just to be on the safe side. I always liked to do hair. Even when I was little. Your hair would probably take a press or a perm real good 'cause it's so thick.

My mother said Ava Gardner had to use a hot comb on her hair twice a week just to keep her edges together. *(A beat)*

Anybody ever ask you to do something you just couldn't do? No matter what? That's how I feel about this animal stuff.

When I met Tony, I was practically living on the street. Dancing in those places where they all think they get to fuck you as part of the cover charge. He gave me some place to stay. Some protection . . . from everybody but him, I guess!

I know I owe him, but damn! I don't owe anybody everything!

You gotta have a place where you draw a line you won't cross. Period. Sherri ain't got no line. She zigzags all over the damn map, depending on who's holding the most dope.

Tony and that bug-eyed nigga think because they got some money we just something for them to play with.

(Ava brushes ABW's hair too hard, and ABW winces.)

Sorry! Did I hurt you?

I know she ain't coming. It's almost midnight now. If she was coming, she'd a been here.

She's somewhere with Tony telling her how she is the best 'ho he got and the best one he ever gonna have and how she's special in his life.

When I first met Sherri, she was so pretty. And tiny! Tony wanted to put us together right away 'cause I was a kid and she looked like one.

I didn't know what he was talking about at first but then Sherri started laughing and talking about how low-down Tony was for trying to set us up like that when we had just met a few minutes ago.

And he said, "Yeah, well, okay, that may be the maybe, but what's it gonna be? Can y'all hang? It's big money in it for everybody if y'all can hang."

And she looked at me and I understood what they were talking about. I said, "Hey! I'm a dancer."

So she said, "Well, come on then. Let's dance."

That's the only time she ever let Tony watch us when wasn't nobody else there, but that doesn't really count, I guess, because it was sort of like an audition, you know? He wanted to see how we'd look together.

I was really nervous, too. I had never done anything

like that with a woman. I hadn't done it that many times with no men. She told me to forget about Tony and just think about how beautiful we were. I knew she was beautiful. And I hoped I was . . .

When she asked me about that dog stuff tonight, I said no right off. And she said, "Look, little bit, this ain't nothing new. It's just like when we do each other. We don't really have to enjoy it. We have to pretend that we do."

So I told her she wasn't like no dog to me and I wasn't pretending.

(Blackout.)

Scene Twelve

Slide 12: "I thought a bolt of lightning was gonna strike us dead."
Ava is arranging a scarf unsuccessfully around ABW's hair, neck, shoulders.

AVA: Did you ever kiss a woman in the crazy house? When it wasn't any men around, I mean? It's really not that weird when you think about it. Niggas are who's weird! I used to be at niggas' houses sometimes during the day and their wives' nightgown and stuff would be hanging on the bathroom door and they would ask me to put it on, but I wouldn't do it. I knew it would make me feel bad if my old man was getting off watching somebody parading around in my nightgown while I was out working.

I did it with a minister's son once. He hated his father and he had the keys. He wanted to do it right behind the pulpit. It was funny at first, but when we got up there, it was so quiet, I thought a bolt of lightning was gonna strike us dead. It was kind of exciting, I guess, but I couldn't really believe that God was all of a sudden gonna be so concerned about what I was doing that he'd start throwing lightning bolts at me.

Niggas don't care though. They'll do it anywhere. Sherri knew a coke dealer who had a girl sit in the middle of a poker game and put a snake inside herself. My mother said, "Men will ask you to do anything, but if you fool enough to do it, that's on you!" She had a lot of good advice. She just never took any of it.

It was pretty weird when Tony got me and Sherri together that first time. I thought it would feel nasty, you know, since I had never done anything like that. It didn't. Niggas always try to make you think your stuff smells funky, so you won't ask them to kiss it, but they just lying. We smell sweet.

One night me and Sherri made a bunch of money and she said, "This is what makes all that damn freak shit worth it." It just made me feel funny that she could talk about it that way when she never said that kinda stuff about the other stuff we did. I felt like at least when it was the two of us, we could be two women together. We could help each other out, you know?

One time, I asked her if she was ever with a woman in the crazy house, but she wouldn't talk about anything that happened to her in there. It wasn't like she was ashamed of it or anything. She just wouldn't talk about it. The most she would do is laugh sometime when I'd get on her about taking that shit and tell me she'd done a lot worse drugs than some nigga-cut cocaine.

I think they scared her real bad in there. Made her think she might be crazy for real . . .

They didn't make you think that, did they?

(Ava looks directly at ABW, who returns her gaze and then turns away.)

Why do you bitches believe that shit? Of course that's what they're gonna say. What else are they gonna tell you? "It's niggas driving you crazy. Cut them loose. Close your legs and open your eyes and make a move!" They not gonna tell you no helpful shit like that. They'd be out of a job in a minute!

(Ava catches ABW gently by the chin and turns her face back around.)

I'm sorry, honey. You don't need for me to be fussing at you. You're doing real good. At least you got nerve enough to be out here trying, right? The only time it's really over is when you stop trying, right? *(Softly)* Isn't that right?

(Ava looks at ABW, leans over and kisses her very gently on the mouth.
  Blackout.)

Scene Thirteen

Slide 13: "You could have just told me."
  Audio announcement: "Late bus for Atlanta, Georgia, with intermediate stops in Toledo, Ohio; Lexington, Kentucky and Chattanooga, Tennessee." Lights up. Ava is gathering up her makeup bag, looking at the final effect of a much more presentable ABW.

AVA: You can see why I'm going to beauty school, right? I told Sherri we could open a shop together and call it, "Shop Sherava." "Ah-vah" not "AAA-va." I think it sounds classier if you say it that way. Sherri says there's only two sure ways for a colored woman to make any kind of independent living: slinging pussy or frying hair. I told her that the first option was working my last nerve and seemed to be driving her crazy, so what have we got to lose? She said she didn't know whether or not she'd like it. I said, "Fuck it! If we don't like it, we'll do something else!"

I might keep that name anyway, even though, you know, it technically won't be her place. I still like the way it sounds: "Shop Sherava." I'll do all the hair stuff and maybe some manicures and makeup. But no pedicures! I ain't messing with nobody's Negro feet!

I did okay with you, though. You might make it out of the bus station anyway. *(She looks at ABW)*

They're gonna start boarding for Atlanta in a minute or so . . . You can keep that stuff if you want. The scarf and stuff, I mean. Maybe you'll make it down to Atlanta after all and this way at least you'll be ready. Well, at least you'll have a fighting chance.

Here's ten bucks, honey. *(She puts it in ABW's pocket)* I wish I had more, you know, but I spent all my damn money on these tickets. I guess I'll leave Sherri's at the counter so if she comes late they can, you know, give it to her and she can just meet me down there.

You gonna be okay?

Sure you are. You got this far, didn't you? Right?

You just gotta work on your plan a little. You know, starting from now. From now on. You remember I was telling you about makin' a plan.

Well, if you do get down there, look me up, okay? I'll be listed under "Ava" 'cause a lot of people that wanna call me don't know my last name is Johnson.

I gotta drop Sherri's ticket off. If you see her, tell her, you know, that I left it for her, okay? Maybe I should write her a note and you just hand it to her, okay? Never mind. You be careful. *(She exits to the ticket counter)*

(Audio announcement: "Final boarding call for the late bus to Atlanta."

ABW reaches up and pulls off the scarf that Ava has draped on her and sits slowly, dropping the scarf to the floor. Ava reenters with the tickets still in her hand. She sees the scarf fall. ABW is looking away and doesn't notice Ava's return.)

The line is too long. I'll miss the damn bus myself worrying about her maybe getting on it. I could use some company, you know?

(ABW looks at Ava. Ava reaches down to pick up the scarf where ABW has dropped it.)

If you didn't like the damn thing you could have just told me.

(Ava smiles and puts the scarf back around ABW's neck. Ava holds out a ticket to ABW, who stands slowly and looks at her.)

At least it's warm in Atlanta.

(ABW reaches out slowly and takes the ticket. She smiles at Ava tentatively.)

Come on then, we gonna miss the damn bus. *(Talking as they walk toward the bus)* First thing we gotta do is names. I'll write down some names and you point when I get to yours. Or point to one you like. You can pick a new one! I won't know the difference.

(Ava and ABW exit.

The following slides come up in a quick sequence. "Remember Me," sung by Diana Ross, a popular song during this period, plays.

Slide 1: "The lessons:"

Slide 2: "1. Take care of your sisters."

Slide 3: "2. Be resourceful."

Slide 4: "3. Make a plan."

Slide 5: "4. Make a move."

Slide 6: "5. Don't do animals."

Slide 7: Contains all of the six previous slides, and remains as the stage goes to black. The song continues playing.)

END OF PLAY

Pearl Cleage is an Atlanta-based writer whose works include a novel, *What Looks Like Crazy on an Ordinary Day* (Avon Books, 1997; an Oprah Book Club Selection and *New York Times'* bestseller); plays, including *Flyin' West* and *Blues for an Alabama Sky*; essays, including "Mad at Miles" and "Good Brother Blues"; and articles that have appeared in *Essence* magazine, *Ms.*, *Vibe*, *Rap Pages* and many other publications.

Barry Forbus

Her recent theatrical works include *Bourbon at the Border*, a full-length drama commissioned and premiered at The Alliance Theatre Company in 1997 under the direction of frequent Cleage collaborator and Alliance Artistic Director, Kenny Leon. Their previous collaborations include *Blues for an Alabama Sky* (1995) and *Flyin' West* (1992).

Blues returned to Atlanta as part of the 1996 Cultural Olympiad in conjunction with the 1996 Olympic Games. Since opening at The Alliance under Leon's direction, *Flyin' West* has received more than a dozen productions across the country, including The Kennedy Center in Washington, D.C.

Cleage's collection of essays, *Deals with the Devil and Other Reasons to Riot*, was published by Ballantine/One World in 1993. *Mad at Miles: A Blackwoman's Guide to Truth* was published by The Cleage Group in 1991. She is a former columnist for *The Atlanta Tribune*, and her work has appeared in numerous anthologies, including *Double Stitch, Black Drama in America, New Plays from The Women's Project* and *Contemporary Plays by Women of Color*.

Ms. Cleage is the mother of one daughter, Deignan, and the wife of Zaron W. Burnett, Jr.

17071